THE
UNITED STATES
SKI TEAM

ISBN 0-913927-01-5
Library of Congress Catalog Card Number: 83-82974
Printed in U.S.A.

CINDY NELSON, U.S. NATIONAL, DOWNHILL—1983

COOPER, McKINNEY,
NELSON — NEW ZEALAND

PLASTIC JUMP
MADISON, WISCONSIN

PUBLISHER International Sport Publications
Michael J. Bray, President

U.S.S.T. ADMINISTRATION Inez Aimee, Executive Director
Kristi Scott, Executive Assistant
John Dakin, Information Director

U.S.S.T. EDITORIAL STAFF John Dakin
Kristi Scott

PHOTOGRAPHIC EDITORS Ed Bowers
John Dakin

DESIGNER Ray Morales

PRODUCTION ARTISTS Brian Milne
Karen S. Morales

PROJECT MANAGER Colleen Kreher

WRITERS Sandy Caligiore
John Dakin
Nicholas Howe
Paul Robbins

PHOTOGRAPHERS Lori Adamski
A.B.C., Inc.
John Atkins
Audrey Stevens
Nathan Bilow
Bruce Fritz
Steve Gaskill
Andy Hanson
Jim Hills
Tim Hinterzarten
Nicholas Howe
Tom Kelley
John Kelley
Jerry LeBlond
Clarkson Lindley
Jury Novak
Steve Powell
Powers Photos
Neil G. Rossmiller
John Russell
Doug Smith

SEPARATIONS Paragon Press

PRINTING Paragon Press

TYPESETTING Twin Typographers

BINDERY Hiller Industries

INTERNATIONAL SPORT PUBLICATION ADMINISTRATIVE COMMITTEE Reed Peterson
Keith Christensen
William Weyher
D. Gary Christian

PREFACE 16 *Inez Amee*
Executive Director, USST

INTRODUCTION 17 *Michael J. Bray*
President, International Sport Publications

HISTORY OF THE 18 *John Dakin*
UNITED STATES
SKI TEAM

PREVIEW 1984:
FOCUS ON
AMERICA'S BEST

PHIL MAHRE 36 *Sandy Caligiore*

STEVE MAHRE 40 *Sandy Caligiore*

TAMARA McKINNEY 44 *Nicholas Howe*

CINDY NELSON 48 *Nicholas Howe*

CHRISTIN COOPER 52 *Nicholas Howe*

BILL KOCH 56 *Paul Robbins*

JUDY ENDESTAD 60 *Paul Robbins*

JEFF HASTINGS 64 *Paul Robbins*

KERRY LYNCH 68 *Paul Robbins*

HISTORY OF THE 72 *John Dakin*
WORLD CUP

ALPINE TRAINING 98 *Nicholas Howe*

NORDIC TRAINING 106 *Paul Robbins*

THE PRICE 114 *John Dakin*
OF GOLD

THE UNITED STATES 124
SKI TEAM MEMBERS
AND STATISTICS

It takes a lifetime of dedication and sacrifice just to be able to step into the Olympic starting gate. It then takes a special breed of athlete to take on the rest of the world and climb to the top of the victory stand.

This book concerns itself with a special breed of athletes, the young men and women who comprise the U.S. Alpine and Nordic Ski Teams. It is a group that has taken the world of international ski racing by storm, walked away with its top honors, and left the Europeans shaking their heads in disbelief.

But, as in all success stories, the historic accomplishments of the U.S. Ski Team did not come overnight or without an enormous amount of hard work on the part of these athletes as well as the staffs who guide them.

Consider the fact that World Cup skiers dedicate eleven months of every year to training and competition. In addition, 90 percent of that competition takes place on foreign soil. For the U.S. Ski Team, each winter is one continuous away game.

However . . .

The present list of U.S. Ski Team members reads like a Who's Who of international ski competition — Phil and Steve Mahre, Tamara McKinney, Christin Cooper, Cindy Nelson, Bill Koch, Jeff Hastings, and Kerry Lynch. But there are many additional people, who made up the teams and staffs of years past when fortunes were not always as good, who have laid the groundwork for what we know today.

This book then is a look at both the present and the past of the U.S. Ski Team. It is an indepth look at how the Team came to be one of the true powerhouses of international athletics as well as a glimpse into the future as we prepare for the XIVth Winter Olympic Games in Sarajevo, Yugoslavia.

As we move forward into this Olympic year, there is a tendency to look back to the last Winter Games in Lake Placid, New York and take stock of just how far the U.S. Ski Team has come. Since the Olympic flame was extinguished, Americans have claimed five overall World Cup titles and nine discipline crowns. Prior to the 1981 season, the U.S. had won a lone discipline title in 1969.

We at the U.S. Ski Team are extremely excited about the coming World Cup season and the prospects that the 1984 Winter Olympic Games hold for this country. We are equally excited about this book as we now have a vehicle to tell the U.S. Ski Team story and chronicle the historic accomplishments of athletes who have dedicated their lives to represent the United States throughout the world.

For twelve days in February, the eyes of the world will be focused on the tiny community of Sarajevo. When this Olympic flame is extinguished, the rest of the world may well have yet another reminder that the athletes and coaches who comprise the U.S. Ski Team are not only the best this country has to offer, but the best in the world as well.

Inez Aimee
Executive Director

This coming 1984 year will be one of the most exciting years in Olympic history. This is especially true for the United States Ski Team.

The US Ski Team is the team to watch in international competition. They expect greater success than has ever been known. They are going for the GOLD.

International Sport Publications is honored to be a part of the Ski Team's spirited race. We are proud to be working on this book with the United States Ski Team in celebration of the coming Olympic year.

We would like to thank Inez Aimee, the Executive Director of the United States Ski Team, for her support in this project. Additionally, we would like to express our appreciation of both Kristi Scott and John Dakin of the USST, for without their assistance, this book would not have been possible.

We would also like to thank Raymond Morales for his hours of work devoted to this project.

We hope you enjoy reading and rereading the ''United States Ski Team'' book. It will be a festive season for the Ski Team, and this book shall guide far past this celebration.

Michael J. Bray
President

THE HISTORY OF THE U.S. SKI TEAM 1904-1984

Nearly half a century after the sport of skiing was introduced to the United States, the National Ski Association was founded with 17 charter members on February 21, 1904, the same day as the first national ski tournament in Ishpeming, Michigan, and twenty years before the first Winter Olympics.

At first, concerned exclusively with Nordic skiing events, the NSA (renamed the United States Ski Association in 1961) expanded to incorporate the phenomenal growth of Alpine skiing. Comprised of eight divisions (nine today with the addition of Alaska), the NSA gave impetus to the growth of recreational skiing, ski area development, historical programs, and developmental programs of Alpine and Nordic competition in each division from which athletes were drawn to comprise the United States Ski Team.

International Ski Congress meetings were held beginning in 1910, but with interruptions for war years and political problems, it was not until 1924 that the FIS (Federation Internationale de Ski) was formally founded as the international governing body of ski competition. Although the NSA of the United States

**WHITEFACE MOUNTAIN
LAKE PLACID, NEW YORK — 1980**

was appraised of activities and in communication with Congress members as early as 1910, it was 1924 when the U.S. became its first non-European member.

That same year, the U.S. entered the first Winter Olympics in Chamonix, France, although competing only in Nordic events. At the conclusion of the 1924 Games, the official results showed the U.S. shut out of the medals chase with Norway's Thorlief Haug as the third place finisher in the 70 meter jumping and American Anders Haugen in fourth position.

It was not until decades later, during a reunion of the Norwegian team, that Thoralf Stromstad, himself a double silver medal winner, discovered an improper computation of award points had been made. In September of 1974, 50 years later, the error was corrected and Haugen honored as the first American Olympic medalist with his bronze medal.

Alpine skiing did not gain national

attention until 1933 when the first national downhill championship was held. In 1935, the first national slalom was conducted and 1934 marked the installation of the first uphill ski lift in America. Women joined the ranks of sanctioned competition with their first national alpine meet taking place in 1938. It should be noted that although the United States Olympic Committee has been operating since 1921, it was only incorporated by an act of Congress in 1950.

It was the U.S. women, however, who claimed the first alpine Olympic medals for the United States as Gretchen Fraser mined both gold in the slalom and silver in the combined during the 1948 Games in St. Moritz, Switzerland. Four years later in Oslo, Norway, Andrea Mead Lawrence recorded twin victories in slalom and giant slalom to mark the first and only time that American skiers have ever claimed a pair of Olympic gold skiing medals.

During the 1950 season, the National

**BOB TREADWELL
CROSS-COUNTRY—1977**

Ski Association faced the question of whether to leap into a nationalistic battle for Olympic gold or to place emphasis on domestic competition and the development of skiing as a growing part of the American athletic and educational systems. If the former was to take priority, a program providing for European training was necessary in order to meet the competition on their own ground in this European dominated sport.

To fully understand the situation, it

must be remembered that prior to 1965, there was no full-time national team. International teams were selected to represent the U.S. only at Olympic Games and World Championships and these teams were only named for a maximum of two months.

During the 1950's, U.S. teams were budgeted in the vicinity of $20,000-$30,000 for competition abroad, with a low point in 1958 when the manager personally had to advance funds for return transportation to the U.S. All the then-used methods of funding were essentially low-key, with a night tax on lodging and a nickel-a-ticket tax on lifts rarely raising more than $9,000, except when subsidized by the USOC in an Olympic year.

The major handicap during the 50's was the fact that there was no real continuity of programs directed by coaches who had an opportunity to make long range plans. The need for a year-round program of development backed by a solid and dependable cash flow became increasingly apparent.

So it was that the initial step toward gaining impetus in fund raising was taken with the creation in 1960 of the U.S. Ski Educational Foundation, the non-profit funding arm of the Team,

JOHN BROMAN
SKI JUMPING — 1976

which was incorporated and given its tax-exempt charitable status in 1964. Centralization was undertaken the following year with the hiring of the first full-time Alpine Director.

By 1965, the Europeans had established full-time racer development programs and the rise of the French team in the 1960's under Honore Bonnet symbolized the first international racing program on a national level. With this as an example, the USSA began a full-time athletic program for alpine racing in June of 1965. They began systematic ski training and the first national teams were named with organized fund raising efforts to support the team.

FISHER, PATTERSON
AND NELSON — 1978

The year before, the American men broke into the medals on the next to the last day of the 1964 Winter Games in Innsbruck, Austria when Billy Kidd and Jimmie Heuga earned silver and bronze slalom medals to cap what head coach Bob Beattie called ''the greatest day for Olympic skiing.''

A change in USSA leadership in 1972 combined with severe fund raising limitations that year initiated the period of greatest turmoil in the Team's young history. Coaches and team members were charged at random and by early 1973, the Team was well over $250,000 in debt. By spring of 1973, the Team was on the verge of extinction as an athletic organization.

The eventual reorganization of U.S. Ski Team activities occurred at the USSA convention in June of 1973 with the creation of the U.S. Ski Team, Inc. and the establishment of national headquarters of this entity and Ski Team programs under the USSEF in Park City, Utah. The USSEF became a separate organization with its own officers and trustees, comprised mainly of those interested in funding the Team's activities. For the first time in its history, the U.S. Ski Team was structured similarly to the administration of a professional sports franchise.

Due to the efforts of many people, the funding was stabilized, the debts were paid off, professional coaching staffs were hired and given the funding and organizational support to create sound athletic programs, and specific athletic goals of international success were outlined.

The Winter Olympics shifted to Asia for the first time in 1972 as the Games were held in Sapporo, Japan and again, it was the American women who carried the colors as Barbara Cochran won the slalom and Susie Corrock snatched a bronze in the downhill. Cochran, whose sister and brother were also members of the Ski Team, claimed the slalom gold by two-hundredths of a second over French teenager Daniele Debernard, the narrowest winning margin in Olympic alpine history.

The U.S. stunned the international nordic community four years later in Innsbruck, Austria as a quiet Vermonter by the name of Bill Koch claimed the first nordic Olympic medal since Haugen's belated bronze in the initial Winter Games with his silver medal performance in the 30 kilometer event. Cindy Nelson kept the American women's medal streak alive with her bronze in downhill.

**ALISON OWEN-SPENCER
CROSS-COUNTRY — 1979**

One of only two full-time national teams in the United States that train and compete year-round every year (the other is the Equestrian Team), the U.S. Ski Team was beginning to make its presence felt on the World Cup circuit on an annual basis. Marilyn Cochran broke the European dominance of World Cup titles in 1969 with her giant slalom crown, but it was to be a 12-year wait for another World Cup crown.

The U.S. Ski Team entered the 80's with a wealth of talent and the prospects of having the Winter Olympic Games on home turf in Lake Placid, New York. The previous winter, America's best medal hope, Phil Mahre, had shattered his ankle during the pre-Olympic giant slalom competition at Lake Placid and there was some doubt that he would ever ski again. But on the same hill nearly a year to the day later, Phil Mahre captured a silver medal in slalom to begin one of the greatest ski racing legacies of all time.

The remainder of the story is literally history. In 1981, Phil Mahre became the first American to ever win the coveted World Cup crystal globe that signifies annual ski racing supremacy while Tamara McKinney swept to the women's World Cup giant slalom title. Mahre was to add a second overall title in 1982, winning the championship with two months still remaining in the season. In addition to his overall crown, Phil also claimed the slalom, giant slalom, and combined World Cup titles, making him the first man since the legendary Frenchman, Jean Claude Killy, to win four World Cup titles in the same season, that season being 1967, the initial year of the World Cup.

Joining Mahre in the winners' circle in 1982 was Bill Koch, who staged a dramatic final race victory to claim the first ever Nordic World Cup crown for the United States. Koch's victory along with Mahre's marked the first time in World Cup history that skiers from the same nation had collected both the alpine and nordic overall championships.

Add to these accomplishments the fact that during that same 1982 season, Phil's twin brother Steve ended America's 51-year search for a men's World Championship individual gold medal as he sped to victory in giant slalom at the World Championships in Schladming, Austria. Steve was joined in the medals chase by veteran Cindy Nelson, who claimed a silver medal in downhill to equal the best previous World Championship downhill effort by an American woman, while Christin Cooper collected a bronze in the combined and silvers in both slalom and giant slalom to become the first American racer to ever win a trio of World Championship medals. In addition, the U.S. women claimed the top spot in the chase for the Nation's Cup to rank as the best women's alpine ski team in the world.

The 1983 season had more "firsts" in store as Tamara McKinney skied her way into the history books as the first American woman to ever win the World Cup overall title, racking up a record seven individual World Cup victories en route to the crown. Phil Mahre also claimed his third consecutive overall title to become only the third man in World Cup history to have ever won three in a row while both Phil and Tamara added World Cup giant slalom titles, Phil also picking up his third consecutive combined title.

The U.S. Ski Team has come a long way from the rag-tag group of skiers that were never quite sure if they were going to be able to come up with enough money to even get to Europe to compete, much less have enough for the return fare. For much of its existence, the story of the Team was one of "wait until next year." Well, "next year" came in 1981 and the story of the U.S. Ski Team has continued to grow. Thanks to the likes of Phil and Steve Mahre, Tamara McKinney, Christin Cooper, Cindy Nelson, Bill Koch, Tim Caldwell, Jeff Hastings, Kerry Lynch, and all the ski racers who paved the way for the 80's to become a reality, "next year" is now a part of the European vocabulary.

TOP ROW—CINDY NELSON, KERRY LYNCH,
TAMARA McKINNEY, STEVE MAHRE

PREVIEW 1984
FOCUS ON
AMERICA'S BEST

Unlike the last Winter Olympics, Phil Mahre enters the upcoming season sound in body and mind.

Specifically, one recalls the shattered ankle Mahre suffered in March of 1979. It not only eliminated him from World Cup contention that year, but placed an ominous cloud over his future. Although "no one told me I might never even walk normally again," Mahre rehabilitated himself. With the aid of screws which held the ankle together, he showed resilience and determination in racing back to world-class form.

In February 1980, Mahre put all that aside. He lead the first run of the Olympic slalom, but lost the gold medal to Sweden's Ingemar Stenmark when Phil came to a virtual stop to avoid skiing off the course well into the second run. The silver was his nevertheless, equaling, the best Olympic performance by an American male.

Since then, the amiable Mahre has raised his ski racing level to new plateaus. Witness three consecutive World Cup overall titles, a total of 27 World Cup race victories, improvement in giant slalom, and a marriage which has produced a baby girl with a second child on the way.

The sum total of these factors has given Phil the confidence, independence, and peace of mind to continue training his way. Even though 1983-84 is an Olympic season, the preparatory process remains unchanged. There is no on-snow training from season's end until November save a week of equipment testing in the spring and two weeks of gate-skiing in the fall. The reason for this approach is ''burn-out'', that aspect of competition which leaves the athlete physically and emotionally drained prior to the end of the season. This PHILosophy and subsequent skiing regimen has not always met the approval of the US Ski Team staff, but those three World Cup crystals are trump cards that Mahre utilizes for more than what meets the eye. For Phil Mahre, you see, is the supreme homebody . . . the epitome of the family man.

''The World Cup is no place to raise a family,'' he has stated. ''There are more important things.''

One of which is the completion of a house in Yakima, Washington. Phil, wife Holly, and 1-year-old daughter

PHIL MAHRE
WORLD CUP GIANT SLALOM

Lindsey moved into their new home in early August, 1983.

Another is the significance of being close to his family — something which would be impossible if he were to attend all the off-season training camps.

This is not to say however, that the three-time champion lounges around all summer. Mahre remains active by participating in football, water skiing, and basketball; the latter activity is now almost legendary in American skiing.

His nickname of "Pearl" (taken from Earl Monroe of NBA fame) attests to that. The US Ski Team finally persuaded him and brother Steve to relinquish their affinity for moto-cross action, although the duo still enjoys bouncing around on their cycles.

Whatever the activity, Phil's attitude is one of all-out exertion. His pre-season gate-training can leave one breathless. But don't expect him to bear down even more just because this happens to be an Olympic year.

"It's just another race, yet it's one that everyone is viewing," said Mahre in his typically nonchalant manner. "There's more emphasis placed on the Olympics than any other races there are. I'm out to win regardless of what it is."

Unfortunately, Phil's performance in World Championships and Olympic competition has not matched his season-long triumphs along the World Cup trail. The 1980 slalom silver is the lone accomplishment on those so-called special days. But for those searching for a harbinger of his Sarajevo results, we take you back to the final technical race of the 1980-81 campaign.

"I can say that Laax, Switzerland in 1981 was as much of an Olympic race as the Olympics were," reflected Phil. It was a reference to the fact that he needed a top result and had to ski better than archrival Stenmark to annex his first World Cup title. Mahre withstood the acid test that is international ski racing that sunny day in the Swiss Alps and has continued to improve his technique and strengthen his mental outlook.

Certainly he will require the forces of both particularly if Stenmark is in the Sarajevo field. Currently, Stenmark who has earned literally millions of dollars by securing a B-license after copping a pair of gold medals at the Lake Placid Games, is awaiting judgement from the International Olympic Committee as to his 1984 eligibility. If allowed participation, Stenmark's case would be a

watershed since the B-license stipulates that a skier may overtly endorse products, receive payment, ski the World Cup, but is prohibited from entering the Olympic Games.

"Now he wants to have his cake and eat it too," said Mahre at an August gathering of the US Ski Team.

"He seems to want to make all the money that he can."

Yet the American realizes the value of defeating a Stenmark in the Olympics.

"If he's not there and I win, people will say, 'Well, he won but Stenmark is the best in the world and he was not there!' I can't worry about that."

And in brief, that "what, me worry?" demeanor is the definition of this great racer. He takes victory in stride, challenges himself, and while sometimes showing anger and disgust at a poor performance, is adept at putting those aside and starting anew. What makes his achievements even more remarkable is the fact that they have occurred essentially on foreign soil. Mahre has met the Europeans at their game, in their ballpark, and taken the glory which those skiers cherish from childhood.

Consequently, an Olympics in Yugoslavia, as different as that nation is, will pose no concern to a 10-year veteran of the suitcase existence. If a problem arises, perhaps it will concern attitude as it did the first half of last season when inclement and inconsistent weather hampered training and racing conditions. Mahre, however, corrected that by himself by first rallying to claim another overall championship and then apologizing to his coaching staff for any irritability he may have shown.

"I think attitude has a lot to do with how you ski," Phil theorized. "If you have a good attitude you usually concentrate better. And if you concentrate better, you ski better. Attitude is a mental aspect of the sport, and if you don't have it you are not competitive."

"I was born four minutes behind Phil and have been trying to catch up ever since."

The statement, vintage Steve Mahre, is mostly humorous with a dash of truth. But one should not feel that Steve is always the one in pursuit. His nine World Cup victories testify to the fact that he can and does defeat his twin brother, the Stenmarks, the Wenzels, et al. And while Phil is perhaps skiing into the sport's history books with his streak of overall accomplishments, it is the slightly younger Mahre who became the USA's very first gold medalist in Olympic or World Championship competition when he won the 1982 Giant Slalom race at the World Championships. Steve was the first and only American to achieve this. In addition, he placed third in the World Cup standings two years ago behind Phil and Sweden's Ingemar

Stenmark. Perhaps if he were not susceptible to a trick knee, Steve would be more of an overall threat to Phil, for it is those past injuries which preclude him from skiing in the downhill thus rendering him impossible to win the overall World Cup.

Mahre captured a pair of slaloms in 1982-83, but had his season tainted, ironically, by a shoulder mishap suffered in an innocuous exhibition race the evening of his first triumph. It was a painful rotator cuff injury, the kind of shoulder problem which can end a baseball pitcher's career. It never healed completely, and even into late summer was bothersome.

"It's really not 100%, but I'd say it's improved a lot in the last 2-3 weeks," commented Steve at the end of August. "All summer long there were periods where it didn't seem to be doing anything. Then all of a sudden there was an improvement. The last few weeks, I've been hardly getting any pain. Hopefully by November I'll be strong — no problem!"

Hopefully he is right! If the US Ski Team is to grab headlines at the 14th Winter Olympics — this is the most talented group of alpine and nordic skiers in Team history — Steve Mahre is expected to be a main contributor.

But as is the case with Phil, he will not let the hype nor the expectations affect him.

"I won't really gear for just the Olympics. I'll gear for the World Cup," Mahre said recently. "If you win on the World Cup, your chances of winning in the Olympics are there too. Hopefully things will work that way — we'll be able to be strong not only in the World Cup but in the Olympics as well."

By their comments, one sees how the twins are mirror images not only in appearance but in thought. Neither skier gets too excited in victory nor too despondent in defeat. As a result they do not ride the roller coaster of emotions that other athletes experience. It is that mental stability, in a sport which is head-oriented at this level, that has been the key to their success. They also seem not to take a world-calibre ski event seriously despite all the victories. In discussing the sport, the word "fun" surfaces while the duo at times bristle when they see the sport overrun with TV cameras, reporters, crowds and the like changing the activity from fun to business. However they have come to understand the metamorphosis even if not in total agreement. And when you segue from the World Cup into an Olympics, that transformation is more dramatic. Nevertheless, there is a

perspective that an Olympic athlete attempts to maintain. He cannot let the build-up affect him. Each has his own way.

"The big thing at the Olympics is going through the opening ceremonies where you see not only ski racers like we do on the rest of the circuit, but you see all the other athletes in winter sports," theorized Steve. "It's very exciting to see all those athletes coming to represent their country. I think that's more of a thrill than actually saying, 'OK, I'm here, and these are the Olympics and I have to do something! You just do your best and that's it. They're no different than any other races. You're always trying to do your best and I don't understand why you should say the Olympics are more important than that race. To win a race is what I'm out there to do whether it's the Olympics, a World Cup, or the National Championships."

The technical races (slalom and giant slalom) of the World Cup and the Olympics may turn out to be unpredictable battles. Stenmark, the defending slalom and GS gold medal winner and Phil Mahre are expected to be the protagonists that will provide world-wide journalists with reams of copy. That is, if the Silent Swede is granted an exemption. Others cannot be overlooked. Rising Swiss stars Pirmin Zurbriggen and Max Julen, and Austrian Hans Enn himself a 1980 Olympic medalist all should challenge in the GS.

Meanwhile, the slalom medals could go to any of a cadre of racers. No less than seven skiers won the 10 World Cup slaloms last year. Steve Mahre emerged victorious twice, but as the 1982 World Champion in Giant Slalom he had no results. Thus he was dropped from first-seed status.

"Last year was funny. I skied way too much slalom, especially early on when our season was that way. I just never got away from it," Mahre analyzed. "I didn't train enough GS. I think you should train 2/3 GS and 1/3 slalom. If you can ski GS you can ski good slalom. Right now, I think it's just a matter of going back and skiing more giant slalom again this year and hopefully we can get that turned around . . . and be doing what I did at the end of the 1982 season."

If Steve can rebound to that level (when he copped three giant slalom triumphs) and maintain his slalom excellence, Mt. Bjelasnica just might provide the scenario for two twin brothers to re-write American Olympic ski racing history.

STEVE MAHRE SLALOM

One of the prevailing realities of World Cup life is roads. Some are very long and straight, some very long and curvy, some turn out to be the wrong ones but they all must be negotiated.

The road to the 1983 women's overall World Cup championship began in Val d'Isere, France as the clouds closed in on the Haute Savoie and the rains came to the Criterium of the First Snow.

First on the ladies agenda was the downhill and veterans like Cindy Nelson labored with the rain that accumulated on their goggles during the lower half of the course.

Goggles played another kind of part in Tamara McKinney's race. The rivet in the strap broke while she was standing in the start and she was still winding on a small piece of friction tape as the clock sounded the five second count-down. As the start signal sounded,

McKinney blasted out onto the course while everyone in the start area began to wager how much of the run she would be able to negotiate.

"I'm glad no one told me it was raining down below," she said later following a 19th place finish, the best downhill placing of her career. "I sort of realized that the rain was a problem about half way down, but by that time, I didn't care."

The ability to negotiate these sort of curves is not the least of the skills a top racer needs. These agilities had an early start. She's the youngest of seven children, all of whom were educated in the Ponderosa Day School, K-12, whose staff and entire enrollment were all McKinney's — the result of her mother's characteristically enterprising approach to the Governor of Nevada.

Everyone went to school in the morning and went skiing at Mt. Rose in the afternoon, where the nearly infant Tamara was introduced to the joy of skiing by Sven Coomer, a former coach on the international circuit. Anderl Molterer, veteran of the Austrian juggernaut team of the 1950s, succeeded Coomer at Mt. Rose with Team McKinney, four of whom eventually reached the national level of competition. "An inspiration," says Tamara now. "He had so much energy and it was so positive and honest. He'd tell somebody they were skiing like a mother goose if it looked like they weren't trying hard, but when he said a compliment you knew he meant it. And the energy! We'd get on the lift and he'd hike up and beat us to the top." Molterer was succeeded by Phillipe Mallard: "So quiet and calm. We'd go up to the ridges at Squaw Valley and ski down those very steep things — he'd have a trail of ten kids that were scared to death and he'd just cruise along and act like it was no big thing."

Those days were the source of Tamara's two most admired assets today — her subtle instinct for terrain and her feathery touch on the snow. Those qualities might even have been present in her first recognized race at the age of four, though documentation is scanty.

Tamara was a serious, observant little girl, without any of the bratty nature that has marked the early years of some other great competitors. But everyone did notice one thing: Tamara's father is a Hall of Fame steeplechase jockey and

the family has always been heavily involved in breeding and showing horses at their home base in Lexington, Kentucky. "When she was showing she never made mistakes in judgement," says her mother, "she could always adjust the horse's stride to the distance of the fence. I don't think it was because she was fiercely competitive — she just liked to do things well."

She also showed a certain flair for skiing. One day Molterer had the older children up on "Northwest Passage" to practice schussing. Tamara had followed them up and Molterer planned to take her down making turns behind him. But before he could start, the fifty pound child slipped past and went straight down her older brothers' tracks. She made it quite a long way, then disappeared in an explosion of snow — it hadn't occurred to her that she couldn't do what the big people did.

Competition did get more serious, though: "I saw a movie when I was fourteen showing Gustavo (Thoeni) and all the best girls and I can remember thinking: 'Gee, I think I can do that — I bet I can keep up.'" Her first World Cup race did come that year, but she finished 26th, with a 7th in the slalom at the Nationals. "That was the first inkling that there was something hiding inside that was waiting to get out. When I started doing well I knew that it was in there but I wasn't sure how to bottle it — how to control and depend on its presence at all times. I think when you're first awakened to something you're always afraid it's going to desert you in your time of need."

Tamara's first years on the World Cup tour did prove to be erratic, twenty brilliant turns and a fall, an astonishing 3rd place in the first slalom of the '79 season, a 13th six weeks later, and 14th in the last two races of the year. She was only 16, "but we were already worried," says one of the Austrian coaches now. "It always takes three years to learn to ski World Cup — in her first race Annemarie Moser fell three times and finished last."

It took Tamara two years. On January 23, 1981, she won the giant slalom at Haute Nendaz, Switzerland. "I remember lying in bed the next morning and I'm thinking 'Wow!' and wondering which way it was going to go. Before I used to think I had to have two FANTASTIC runs, but I realized that I

could just ski well — I didn't have to ski DESPERATELY, not like it was the last race of my life." Tamara needn't have worried which way it was going to go: two days later she ran away with the GS in Les Gets, France winning by over two and a half seconds, won again in the Aspen GS, and took the World Cup GS title for the year. It was just the second title for an American woman, after Marilyn Cochran in 1969. And, as a finale, she won every run in the parallel slalom that closed the season.

Then in 1982, Tamara broke her hand and arm while training for the first downhill of the season and raced most of the year with her ski pole taped to the palm of her cast.

1983 looked for a while like a runaway. Tamara won the first run of the opening GS, and still finished 2nd despite taking the second run with her skis on the wrong feet. She won the first slalom of the year, placed 3rd and 4th in the first two Super G races in history, won the Davos, Switzerland slalom on the steepest hill anyone had every seen, and won the St. Gervais, France, GS. But it was a year of chaotic weather and endless schedule changes, and the next slalom was her tenth race in three weeks, run in a torrential rainstorm. Tamara's long-time best friend Abbi Fisher had left the team in December, her first-seed running-mate Christin Cooper had broken her leg and gone home that morning, leaving Tamara alone in the first seed. She finished in 6th place, a little disappointing, but she seemed to be her old self. It was Pam Fletcher's 20th birthday and that night at supper the sponsors brought her champagne and a snowman trophy. Rising instantly to the occasion, Tamara offered a toast: "May all men melt in your arms." But she was wearing thin.

Tamara fell in the next race, a slalom in Maribor, Yugoslavia. Two days later she fell again in the slalom at Vysoke Tatry, Czech. Then the teams went home for the mid-season rest: Hanni Wenzel had passed her in the Overall standings, and Erika Hess was almost even. "Whenever I was having trouble and I didn't know what to do about it, my family was always so helpful. They made me realize that I was still an okay person even if I didn't ski right — that's always been the most important part of it for me." But the World Cup reconvened in Canada and Tamara, still trying too hard, fell in the giant slalom. It looked as if America's first solid hope for the Overall title had gone aglimmering.

After the '81 season Tamara had said "A lot of coaches are good to have around when you're skiing well because what bad advice can they give you when you're doing well? But if you're doing badly and you don't know why, it's hard to find a coach that'll pull you through that." John Atkins and John McMurtry of the American staff found a moment to talk to Tamara just as she faced three races in three days at Waterville, N.H. "Look," they said, "If the season ended right now we'd be happy, so just don't worry about the rest. If it happens it happens, and if it doesn't we're still happy and proud — it's still been a great year.

That morning Tamara placed 2nd in the slalom. She won the GS the next day, won again the next day, and won again two days later in Vail, Colorado. The teams left for the finals in Japan, where Tamara fell in the GS but still placed 11th, then she won the slalom that ended the season. The World Cup GS title was hers again, and she brought the women's Overall World Cup title home to America for the first time in its history.

There had been another trophy, earlier in the winter. In December, five team people had stopped for lunch at a tiny family restaurant in Italy. Tamara had won a race the day before and her picture was in all the papers. Now a brown-eyed girl of perhaps eight peeks around the corner from the kitchen, then disappears and reappears with her brother and a paper to confirm their astounding fortune. Tamara smiles them over and signs by her picture in their paper, then poses for the parents' camera. Soon more neighborhood children come in to see the celebrated visitor, and U.S. Team pins and stickers are handed around, but there aren't quite enough. Sadly, the first child is shier than the rest and, hanging back, she has nothing. Then Tamara remembers something the hotelkeeper had given her after the win yesterday, so she goes out to the car and brings the little girl a rose.

TAMARA McKINNEY
NATIONAL SLALOM

CINDY NELSON
FIS MEDALIST

When Cindy Nelson was a little girl, she decided that she could probably fly if she tried hard enough. Lots of children have this idea at one time or another, but they give it up soon enough. Cindy's approach, though, was characteristic. Close study of the airborn superheroes in the comic books taught her the correct position of the leading arm and how to steamline the trailing members, and she had her cape ready. So Cindy climbed to the sill of a second story window and took off. Her form was perfect, but it lacked lift—she landed flat on her tummy far below. Then, in a state of considerably reduced air-worthiness, she spent a long time wheezing for breath on the living room sofa.

Skiing worked better. The Nelsons live in Lutsen, Minnesota far up the long north shore of Lake Superior, and there's a small

ski area a mile or so back from the family's home on the ancient beach. Here the five little Nelsons went skiing every winter day with the Bensons from next door — the only other children within miles in that remote forest — and Cindy showed the same forthright qualities. The elder Benson doubled as ski patrolman: "One day I saw Cindy fall down and I went over and said 'Oh, it's probably nothing.' But she looked up at me and said 'No, I heard it break.'" That was about the only setback, and the Nelsons and the Bensons piled into the family station wagons each weekend for Central Division races, their mothers staying up till one in the morning to file edges on all the skis. Cindy went furthest afield. Hank Tauber (former U.S. Ski Team Alpine Director) remembers seeing her when she was eleven: "She had a unique identity even then, a real presence as an athlete. She ran faster and listened better and skied harder — you always see that in the ones who are going to get better later on." Tauber saw her again in the Junior Nationals when she was fifteen. She fell halfway through the first run of GS, but he was so impressed by what he saw that he invited her to train with the national team that summer, and by November Cindy was in Europe getting ready for the World Cup circuit.

The first downhill was at St. Moritz, Switzerland. Cindy's start number was in the 70s, she finished 12th. Next, at Val d'Isere, France she started 69th and finished 13th. Tauber was still with her: As she's shown throughout her career, she was able to rise up on race day to a level way above where she'd been training." Others noticed other things: "She was technically far from being perfect," says a European coach from that era, "but I remember that she skied fantastically gutsy and we were all talking about that, and she paid the price." At the Grindewald, Switzerland downhill that January, her interval time showed a chance for a top-five finish, but she missed a prejump, fell through thirty five feet of vertical to the flat, and dislocated her hip. It cost her a place on the Olympic downhill team, at the age of sixteen.

"It was such a weird situation," Cindy says now, "Central Division hot-shot to the World Cup in one year. My only release was to ski, so I'd go up there and just go all out. When you're that young you just go like crazy — you don't have the experience to do something if you get in trouble. You just have instinct, and sometimes that can't help you." In another age, the Greeks plotted the course of the hero: the youngest was Jason, flinging himself against a world he hardly knew.

Cindy came back the next year, and

was met by the first of the confusions and crossed-purposes that marked the years ahead. The team had a Christmas training camp at Stratton, Vt., and the coaches told Cindy to go to New York and fly to Yugoslavia for the first World Cup races of the new year. When she got to the airport, her ticket had been cancelled by the headquarters staff in Denver — they were using different criteria for team assignments. So she paid her own way, joined the team in Yugoslavia, then was told to go home the next day. In eight years Cindy was to have ten head coaches, with two or three assistants. And if that wasn't enough to contend with, there was always Annemarie Moser-Proell.

Moser is the most overwhelming skier of the World Cup era, with sixty-two victories in all three alpine disciplines. She won all eight downhills in 1973, and she won four of the five in '74, but Cindy won the other one. In '78 Moser won five of seven as well as the World Championship downhill, but Cindy finished the season just behind her. In 1979 Cindy was the only downhiller to beat Moser — they spent 47:55.79 minutes racing against each other and Moser finished the year with a net average margin of 1.83 seconds. The Austrian racer retired for the '76 season, but Cindy didn't like it: "I'd rather be second to Moser than win without her," she says now. "She's the greatest female ski racer I've ever seen, and to be competitive with Moser, to know it was going to be her or me — I'll never forget that. Not ever."

Cindy went back to Grindelwald, her downhill nemesis, and she beat Moser there in '74; she won at Saalbach, Austria and Pfronten, W. Germany and she won a giant slalom in Garibaldi, Canada; she won the combined at Meiringen, Switzerland and she gained first seed ranking in all three events. But there was bad luck, too: she hit a frozen hay bale in the short finish area at Garmisch, W. Germany in 1977 and broke her foot; she developed a susceptibility to bronchitis and was sick for most of three seasons, unable to sleep, unable to take any medication because of the chemical checks. There were severe equipment problems, and she couldn't get downhill skis that suited her: "At the pre-Olympics at Lake Placid in '79 I was eight-tenths ahead of Moser at halfway and two and a half seconds behind her at the bottom. That really took my whole spirit out — I wouldn't talk to anyone related to skiing. I couldn't believe how much it affected me."

1980 was one of the years Cindy was sick, and Pat Nelson went to meet her daughter when the team came home for the Games. "Cindy had dark circles under her eyes and she was so gaunt and haggard I hardly recognized her. I remember thinking 'My God — look at her! And these are HER Olympics — everyone's talking about a gold medal.'" The sense of national duty was almost palpable at Lake Placid. The talk was of gold, but Cindy finished 7th in the downhill.

Michel Rudigoz had taken over as women's downhill coach in 1979: "Cindy often appeared solemn and thoughtful — she certainly must have had many questions about whether the team was doing the right things for her during the bad years." Sometimes victorious, sometimes moody and withdrawn, Achilles was the second stage of the Greek hero.

Then, in the spring of 1980, Rudigoz was promoted to Head coach for the women and, with assistants Ernst Hager, John McMurtry, Chip Woods, and trainer John Atkins, a four year commitment was made. "Suddenly everything was so simple," says Cindy, "just a strong positive sense of what was best for each one of us on the team." The women moved up to second place among the nations the next year, into first place in 1982, and Cindy moved

into the broad sunny uplands of her career.

"She was not afraid of anyone," says Hager, "she was helping the younger ones too much, almost, at the expense of her own needs. But she doesn't try to make them ski like her. She knows they won't think the same way about the course or the speed or their equipment, so she helps them in ways that are right for THEM." At the same time, though, she had the race of her life at the 1982 World Championships. The women's downhill at Schladming is a real racer's course: very fast, with a long flat, big bumps, steep fallaways, and high speed turns. Cindy took the silver medal behind Canada's Gerry Sorensen. "I didn't make any mistakes," she said afterwards, "but Gerry was perfect, and that's what it takes to win a gold medal. So I'm happy with my silver."

Cindy also had the disappointment of her life at Schladming. There was an authentic combined event at Schladming, the first since 1950. Cindy has always taken pride in her determination to compete in all three alpine events, even though it might have cost her a title as a specialist. Now, in the combined races, she placed second in the downhill and had the third best slalom race of her career to place sixth in that event. Everyone at the World Championships knew that a 2/6 placing meant she was the best combined skier on the mountain, but an absurdly complex and irrational scoring system gave the gold medal to a downhill/slalom combination of 21/1. Fourth place, and no medal, went to Cindy. The tough old campaigner, veteran of a thousand finishes, went away by herself and wept.

Cindy isn't the raucus, noisy type of leader, but in good times and bad she's always there at the head of her team and she was at the core of their drive to first place among the nations in 1982. But at the same time she had been overtaken by a curious irony. International race courses tend to reflect the strengths of the best racers: Gustavo Thoeni and Bernard Russi skied well on courses that were set fairly straight, so habits among course setters moved in that direction; Stenmark doesn't like straight courses, so men's slalom and giant slalom have become turnier since Thoeni and Russi retired. Similarly, the effect of great technical racers like Moser, Nadig, and Cindy herself was to keep women's downhills tough, with big bumps and turns. But since Moser and Nadig retired, Doris deAgostini led a

new generation of gliders into the ascendency in women's downhill and course selection and setting moved quickly to the smooth straight venues that suit their technique.

The effect of all this is that Cindy has outlived the very strengths that brought her to the top of the league. "The first time I saw her race," says a coach from 1974, "I realized that she was unusually quiet in her upper body. That's good: it takes too long to move the mass of the upper body, and it also changes your optical perspective." By mid-career, she was recognized as one of the best technical skiers in the world, one of the best at analysis, edge control, bumps and compressions, one of the most secure on ice. Now, only Irene Epple can challenge her for technical mastery. But those skills no longer count for much — indeed, she tends to over ski most courses of the '80s, and her skills actually cost her time. "If she didn't ski so well," the course-side wisdom goes, "she'd race a lot better."

So Cindy went back to work, and returned to the top step of the victory stand with a Super G win in 1983, then went on to place second in the giant slalom standings for the year, matching her career-best downhill ranking from 1978.

But there was a bad moment in 1983, also. Schruns, Austria was the only real downhiller's downhill on the circuit last year and Cindy, hoping for the win, landed in soft snow after a bump and had a heavy crash — so rare an occasion that there are coaches who can't remember the last time it happened. There was another downhill on the same course the next day, but the conditions were appalling — a swirling blizzard with warm, soft snow. Riding up to the mountain that morning with Christin Cooper, Cindy had that fall to think about, the promise of another in sub-marginal conditions, and all the other private thoughts that can glaze the eyes of a downhiller. Suddenly she turned to Christin: "What fun for the children," she said. "You wake up in the morning and there's all this new snow and you put on your four-buckle galoshes and go out after breakfast and it's just right for snowball fights and a snowman and there's no school all day. What a neat feeling!"

Those who wonder how Cindy Nelson has kept going for thirteen years may find part of their answer in that blizzard-wracked morning in Schruns. And in another age, Nestor was the oldest and wisest of the Greek heroes, the one who came to terms with who he was and what he did.

Music floated up through the motionless air to the downhill course at Megeve, France, the kind of introspective sound that often accompanied the New Wave cinema of the 1960s. It came from the speakers outside a restaurant far below, and as the early morning shadows shrank up through the valleys the women of the World Cup gathered above a slope with fluffy new snow and rolling bumps big as cottages, then pushed off into the kind of warm-up runs known only to World Cup racers—part fury and part joy as they brought the engines up to racing speed.

Christin Cooper was up there too, the only gate racing specialist among seventy-nine downhillers. She'd been leading the first run of slalom five days earlier when she and most of the other first seed racers went out just before the finish, and she'd been 4th in

the Davos slalom five days before that. So, to the amazement of a lot of the Europeans, Christin trained downhill for three days at Megeve, then entered the two downhills there. "Yeah!" she said that day. "I don't think Nadig used to worry when she saw me in a training number, but I really love it — a real breath of fresh air with another whole mentality and you can try different strategies with another group of people. A course like this makes me loosen up and ski kind of free and easy — running slalom all the time can get you pretty cramped in the way you think."

Her skiing was not cramped that week. Some of the competitors seemed to be overcoming the terrain, the good ones seemed to be cooperating with it — but Christin seemed to be part of that mountain in Megeve, the way water is part of a stream bed. She beat two-thirds of the field in those two downhills, and on the third day she went to St. Gervais with the gate racers and placed second behind Tamara McKinney's win in the giant slalom for the first American double in slalom or GS since 1969.

That kind of self-direction has always been Christin's way. She and her four brothers and sisters were the children of daring parents, of the waves and wind of the California beaches where they were young. Mrs. Cooper brought her children to live near Sun Valley, Idaho,

when Christin was in grade school, "an independent little girl" says one of her teachers, "with an inward, thoughtful kind of life." She came to competitive skiing ten years later than some of her team-mates, but her marvelous athletic instincts carried her quickly to the top: she won the Can-Am championship at 15, she won the 1977 National slalom title the next year and had three top-10 World Cup finishes. Still, though Christin was a born racer, she was not a great natural technician when it came to skiing. She had to work hard for her technique, and she had to come to terms with the inevitable strictures of team life: "I'd always gotten in shape as a natural thing — hiking up to the top of some peak and run around in the mountains like a goat and with my dancing, and I used to ice skate a lot. Then there was someone telling me what to do and when to do it and how intense to be and how competitive to be and it was really hard for the coaches, I think, because I just wasn't happy being there." Those were the tough years. "Then I finally realized how I really loved the sport and I wanted to see what I could do with it."

She did well. Christin was the top scoring American in both slalom and GS at the 1980 Olympics, she was ranked 2nd in the world in slalom in 1981, and in 1982 she won two World Cup

races and she won two silver medals and a bronze at the World Championships. And, loyal as ever to all the parts of her life, she kept going with her studies in dance and finally put the finishing touches on her high-school education.

Christin is still not a faultless technician, and form-book overachievers will point to a dozen small mistakes in a race. But they'll miss the real Christin. The morning of the World Championship slalom, someone got close enough to her to ask who she thought was going to be tough in the race that day, expecting perhaps the name of some celebrated European titlist. Christin shot back a quick look: "I think *I'm* going to be tough!" She was standing third after the first run. Then, just above the most critical section of the second run, she got whipped in the face by a pole and lost her goggles — and went on to the silver medal, 0.2 seconds behind Erika Hess.

Those are the eye-blink days, and it's a delicate balance: "Sometimes the harder you try the worse it gets and it's — phew, phew — such a fine line you have to tune that makes the difference between fantastic results and not doing it at all." Not all days are like that, though. A year later, for instance, there was a day off after the races in Megeve and St. Gervais. Christin and the well loved "Chamonix Mafia" — three boy-

hood chums who take care of skis with the French and American teams — went skiing on their home slopes around Mt. Blanc. "It was so beautiful," said Christin the next day. "Like you'd imagine springtime in Nepal. We went down glaciers and woods and ravines and it was so huge we only made five runs all day — just the last run took two hours. I'll never forget that — not ever."

Four days later Christin had a freak training accident and broke her leg right at the knee. So she said good-bye to the World Cup and told her team-mates to punch it once for her, then just before the plane left she called Tamara McKinney to wish her luck in the race that morning. They'd had another pre-race talk, at Davos. It was the third race in three days, the teams had gotten there late in the evening, and were on the mountain before dawn: "Tamara and I were riding up the lift and thinking about it. It was dark and everyone was running into each other on the ice and it was just crazy. But it seems that when things are really tough like this it makes everyone bring out the best in themselves."

Back home in America, Dr. Steadman operated on Christin to repair the damage in her leg, and that afternoon she went to work on her rehabilitation program. She was skiing again in the spring, getting ready for the '84 season.

Bill Koch is, quite simply, the finest cross-country skier the United States has ever produced.

Olympic medalist. World Championship medalist. World Cup champion. National championship titlist. You name it, he's done it.

And this winter, as he heads into his third Olympics, his season comes down to just a few days in February, i.e., The Games in Sarajevo.

"This is an Olympic year and that's the most important thing. That's where I'll concentrate," he says. "Everything is geared toward being ready and peaking in Sarajevo. "That's what I'm concentrating on."

And if there's one thing Bill Koch does well, it's concentrate.

"That's what sets him apart," says Mike Gallagher, U.S. head coach. "He has developed strong physical skills, no question, but what really sets him apart is his mental strength. He can concentrate so that he brings out the very best in himself in races.''

''Kochie has such mental strength,'' says teammate Jim Galanes, ''that he can tune-in on a race right way, even if he's been away for a week or two. Some of us need to maintain contact and have to race more frequently to keep a racing edge — I like to race every week, for instance — but Kochie can go away, train by himself and then when he shows up, wherever it is, he's ready to go just like he never broke contact.''

Dr. Rainer Martens, who heads the psychological skills program for the U.S. cross-country squad, is quick to add, ''he's done it himself. I couldn't claim any credit for Bill's success — I've only met him once. He has done his own reading, then trained himself to develop that concentration and focus on his *performance* — not the *outcome* of any race because he doesn't control that, but concentrate on his *performance*, enabling him to ski as well as he does.''

However, lest anyone think Koch's mental skills are some sort of black magic or hypnotic wizardry, he says, ''I haven't done a lot of reading but I have done some. It's all basic stuff and easily available. I think it's a good idea for anyone who's really serious about racing to at least look at it. It's just as important as anything else and should be practiced by everyone.''

The almost ironic part about Koch's cross-country success is that it almost didn't happen. He had been a four-event skier (X-C, jumping, slalom and giant slalom) at The Putney School in Vermont, where he credits former Olympian Bob Gray with fanning his competitive fires. Koch, 28, tried out as a 16-year-old for the 1972 nordic combined Olympic team but was the fifth man on a four-man team. He didn't go to Sapporo; instead, he went to cross-country. He concedes he was miffed about not making the team and decided a short time later to zero-in on X-C.

Four years later, he electrified the sports world by capturing a silver medal in the 30-kilometer race at the 1976 Olympics. In one race, he became the legitimate hero for the sport . . . and torpedoed all the reasons which were being given about why Americans didn't do better in international racing.

BILL KOCH, WORLD CUP CROSS-COUNTRY

Again, though, more irony: the last thing Bill Koch wants to be is anyone's hero. For him, the central factor in all of this is a deep love of skiing; he is cross-country's reluctant hero.

Time and again he had said. ''There is more, much more to skiing than racing. It's such a beautiful sport. Why limit it to just racing?'' After he had won the World Cup championship in 1982, he re-emphasized his feeling: ''now that I've won it, I still say it — all this racing is overrated. It's not the most important thing. It's only one small part of a terrific sport.

And as much as he cares for skiing, even that doesn't take first place in his life. ''Nothing is more important to me than my family,'' he says. ''My girls,'' as he calls them, include wife Katie, a former national team skier, and daughters Leah, 6, who started kindergarten this fall, and Elisabeth, who turns three in January.

Koch's impact on X-C skiing has not been limited to the United States where he elevated the sport from near obscurity. On the international level, it was his ''marathon skate'' technique which has revolutionized the sport . . . and led to its biggest controversy in recent years.

Always looking for something that can help his skiing, Koch watched in amazement a few years ago, after the Cup season had concluded, as Ole Hassis won a race down a frozen river in Sweden using a technique in which he pushed off to the side with one ski, double-poling while the other ski continued to point straight ahead. ''He skated the whole way; that's all he did,'' Koch recalls. ''I struck me that he had an excellent technique for the flats. TC (teammate Tim Caldwell) and I had fiddled around with that for a couple

of years, playing 'cat and mouse' before races and just fooling around with it, but here was someone who had used the skate for an entire race — and won."

Result: Koch went back to fine-tuning the skate. When he won his first World Cup race in LeBrassus, Switzerland, in January 1982, observers were dazzled by what they felt was some new style. Other racers tried to adopt it although Scandinavian coaches just as quickly tried to ban it, claiming it wasn't "traditional" (and, of course, we all know how "traditional" fiberglass skis and ski poles using Space Age metals are) and destroyed the tracks. The controversy flared into last season and finally was settled last spring when the FIS, conceding there was no way to stop skating out on the course, outlawed skating at the start of mass start races and near the finish in all races.

"I don't claim to have developed skating — I got that from the Scandinavians, in fact — but I did popularize it," Koch says. "So what have they proven by banning it? That they can make a law? If it's wrong or bad, as they say, then it should be banned outright." Still, he shrugs and notes most top skiers have come to his conclusion about its value, and then he kicks into a sort of mental hyper-space and dismisses any potential distraction from the lingering skating flap so he can re-focus on his training.

Koch's deep love of skiing was spawned in the southeastern Vermont town of Guilford where he grew up. He and younger brother Fritz, a former national team racer, used to sprint through the woods and across meadowlands on skis, racing a school bus in winter when they were younger. He still enjoys breaking loose for some alpine skiing and maybe even an occasional jump, practicing what he preaches about enjoying all aspects of the sport.

Koch — his ancestors are Dutch, not German, he says — spent a year in Switzerland when he was in high school and learned to speak French. A favorite of the Europeans since he was a top junior skier a decade ago (he was third in the '74 World Junior Championships and was well-known on the Continent before his Olympic medal made him an instant American celebrity), he nonetheless amazed and pleased foreign journalists by fielding questions in French after that first Cup win at LeBrassus, which is on the French border. "That makes him even more a champion — that he is not limited only to English," said one admiring reporter.

In the last few years, Koch has taken up flying, piloting a rented plane to several training sites in addition to pleasure flying, and has laid some of the groundwork for a post-racing career by designing trail systems. He did one at Telemark resort in Wisconsin and another at Labrador City, Newfoundland. "When you talk with Bill," says one resort planning executive, "you can tell very quickly that he has a real feel for how a course should go, the flow of the terrain, the various factors which would go into making a first-rate trail and a quality trails system."

He also was introduced to boardsailing this past summer and plans to try his hand at it more.

Still, though, his biggest consideration is being with his family. Given his choice, Koch obviously would prefer to train on his own with his family nearby, show up for races and then retreat back to the family setting. "They're No. 1," he says.

He isn't thinking past the Olympics. Such long-range visions would be distracting, might break his concentration on the Games. This is his 13th year on the national team and although the World Championships will be held in 1985, he remains non-commital about anything past February 19, 1984, the last day of the Olympics. "I'm not making any plans, pro or con, for after the Olympics. I'm totally open about all of that. Right now I'm just going to concentrate on Sarajevo."

One pleasant thought: Koch won the World Cup 30-km last February on the Olympic course.

JUDY ENDESTAD
NATIONAL CHAMPION

Judy Endestad is the classic case of an overnight success. "Overnight," of course, meaning five years.

In 1978, she took a leave of absence after her sophomore year at Harvard and decided to see if she could earn a spot on the U.S. women's cross-country ski team. She not only gained a place on the team, she was named to the A Team during the Subaru USSA Nationals that season at Waterville Valley. A year later she was picked for the Olympic team at Lake Placid although she did not get to compete.

And last season, after nibbling at the edges of success for a couple of years, she emerged on the international scene, producing the finest performance by an American woman in three seasons. (Alison Owen was second in the Holmenkollen 10-kilometer and third in a 10-km at Reit-im-Winkl in 1980.)

Endestad had six Top-20 finishes last winter and, overall, ranked 20th in the final World Cup standings. Truly, an ''overnight success''...which had been evolving since 1978.

She also picked up her first two national championships last spring, winning the 10-km and 5-km crowns in Anchorage, succeeding fellow Alaskan Lynn Spencer-Galanes of Anchorage who had won both titles in 1982 (similarly succeeding ex-Alaskan Alison Owen who won both events in 1979-81).

One difference, she says, is that she feels more comfortable on the international circuit. She enjoys being in Europe, which helps defuse some anxieties, and she feels her fine performance last season was as much a case of feeling at home oversees as any physical training which she may have completed. (For the record, she will have about 625 hours of training time this year, the same as it's been since 1981-82.)

''I think last year was a combination of things, although it obviously had something to do with my training. I skied a lot more during the summer and fall, and maybe I just needed that extra skiing. I was in Norway this summer during July and there's the Dachstein Glacier (in Austria in September). On-snow skiing always helps,'' she says.

''Last year I also was fortunate to ski most of November in West Yellowstone (Montana)...and you can do a lot of things when you get to train enough on snow. The spring races (1982) after the World Cup was finished, also were a big help. These skiers we'd been racing against all year became more human, more lifelike...no longer some super skier, someone you couldn't get to know. And I think one of the most important learning phases for me was to have Kveta Jeriova (the 1980 Olympic and 1982 World Championships bronze medalist from Czechoslovakia) pass me during a race and I hung on for three or four kilometers,'' she goes on. ''You learn to ski faster, you learn you can do it. You get that exposure to such good skiers and it's all so important.''

However, she repeats, ski racing isn't just a case of having a lot of preseason training under your belt.

''That's one thing about this sport. You've still got to be a good technician, too. Your summer training only relates so much; you still have to be able to ski.

''And you have to know how to race. You can learn only so much in the United States but (on the international tour) there's a real visual impact from just seeing someone skiing so fast. It has a real uplifting effect,'' Endestad says.

She can identify with that uplifting effect, thinking back to her first contact with the high-flying, fast-moving European scene. She's a late-comer to cross-country skiing, a former swimmer and runner who was asked to try out for her high school X-C team in Fairbanks, Alaska; she was 17 when she competed in her first race.

When she entered Harvard, she was left to train on her own. Blessed with the deep-snow winters of 1977 and '78 in the East, she skied quite a bit ''but it was hard with no coach and no one to give some help, so I decided I had to leave school and really try for the (national) team if I were going to be serious about racing.''

Fighting a lack of technical experience, her determination helped overcome what might have been insurmountable obstacles. ''Judy's a scrapper, a real fighter,'' says U.S. women's coach Ruff Patterson. ''She keeps working away at everything, just keeps going at it. She won't give up.''

Still, it hasn't been all expenses — paid trips to glamorous spots in Europe and two visits to the Soviet Union, although that's been part of it. The travel can be glamorous and enjoyable but living out of a suitcase can wear thin after a few weeks, too.

Last winter, for example, the lack of snow in Europe created nightmarish conditions for every team as they bounced from one mountain site to another in quest of enough snow for training and a race. And when Alaska is home, it's not likely you'll be bouncing home during the season unless there's a gaping hole in the schedule...and there never is. And last winter there were the grim trips behind the Iron Curtain — January in East Germany and Czechoslovakia, February to (politically non-aligned) Yugoslavia and then Russia — before three weeks in Scandinavia. Undeniably glamorous but also undeniably wearing.

Endestad, however, looks to the positive side of such travel. ''I enjoy being in Europe. We had over a month in Eastern Bloc countries, so now I've got a better idea of what it's like. We're not in there as tourists, of course, seeing all the cathedrals and museums and historic places, but it still can be fascinating.''

So, international skiing becomes an intriguing mix of physical and mental skills. It's not only picking the right wax and scrambling as fast as you can go on race day; there are other considerations.

For one thing, she says, society has the perception that ski racing is frivolous and not "productive" in the traditional sense. For another, there are so many other career opportunities tugging at skiers, which can be distracting. There also is the training and the competing — competing with the travel and competing against other well-conditioned athletes.

"That first trip can be a trying time but learning to get settled is an important development step," Endestad says, "and I think the Ski Team's development trips (for younger skiers) are crucial in helping expose our skiers to

what it's like in Europe. It is different, definitely different, and it does take some time to get used to."

"Now, I enjoy being in Europe . . . but it took a while."

She resists any temptation to set a specific numerical goal for the '84 season, such as moving up from 20th to Top-15 this winter.

"The point is to always do your best," says the 25-year-old daughter of an Alaska Supreme Court judge. "I'm not in Kochie's (Bill Koch) position (where there's pressure to win). The U.S. women are trying to ski well at the international level. We want to ski well

consistently, but we know we're not up there with him, so we're focusing on doing our best.

"I also think it's important for the women to keep our own identity, have our coaches keep focused on us so we'll improve. We're part of the (national) team with the men, sure, but we're also ourselves. I'm really excited about this year, the Olympics and everything, but I'm being careful with my goals and want to keep reminding myself to do my best every time . . . and let the results take care of themselves."

JEFF HASTINGS
NATIONAL CHAMPION

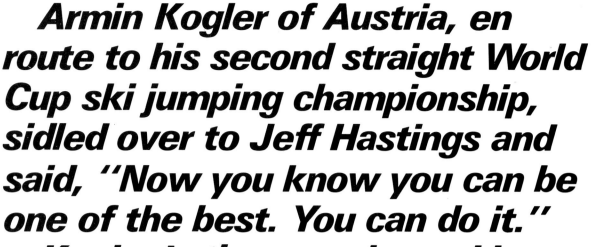

Armin Kogler of Austria, en route to his second straight World Cup ski jumping championship, sidled over to Jeff Hastings and said, "Now you know you can be one of the best. You can do it."

Kogler is the experienced international jumping king, and Hastings is the new kid on the block—in only his second season on the U.S. national team and halfway through his first real winter on the World Cup circuit. They were awaiting the start of the 90-meter jumping competition which would conclude the 1982 World Championships in Oslo, Norway. Despite pea soup fog that cut visibility to inches, Hastings had soared 110 meters to lead the trial round.

Okay, so it's practice and they don't give medals for practice. But, for Hastings, recovering—mentally and physically— from a savage spill a couple of weeks earlier in which he mashed his face and his confidence, that may have been the spark he needed to become a top-flight ski jumper. "Jeff has incredible talent, a really beautiful style, but he needs to be more consistent," says U.S. coach Greg Windsperger. "As he gets more jumps — in practice and in competition, he'll get even better."

Hastings went on to finish 15th in that 90-meter event, perhaps disappointing to some, based on the trial ride, but he apparently felt he was making his way back through the mental cobwebs and he caught fire over the second half of the '82 season. He finished in the Top-10 five times, including a third place at Strebske Pleso, Czechoslovakia, and finished seventh during the second half of the schedule, 20th overall for the season. Not too shabby for a kid who was one step away from being human hamburger when he crashed at Iron Mountain, Mich., in January.

A year ago, Hastings once again started slowly but then flashed to a third place finish on the Olympic 90-meter hill at Lake Placid in January, was fourth a week later at Thunder Bay, Ont., and topped all of that with an eye-opening second place performance off the 90-meter jump at Engelberg to close Swiss Ski Week in late January. On the season, he finished 11th in the World Cup standings. He also won his second straight U.S. national 90-meter jumping championship.

This season, Hastings, 24, knows he has to work more on his consistency. Getting married in August to high school sweetheart Kathy Emery has redirected his focus. "Marriage has renewed me," he says, beaming.

One of three Hastings boys who ski jump (younger brother Chris, a junior, is also a member of the U.S. team), he has been skiing since he was two and his father Paul would lug him up on a rope tow serving a small knoll on a golf course in Hanover, N.H.

JEFF HASTINGS
SKI JUMPING

"He was like a teddy bear. Paul would take him up tucked under his arm and they'd ski down," says his mother, Suzy Hastings. "When he was three or four, he started making ski jumps in the back yard. We didn't have any kind of a slope, it was practically flat, but that didn't bother Jeff; he just kept making ski jumps . . . and he started jumping in the Ford Sayre Program when he was eight. I don't know where he got that idea about the ski jumps but he was determined and he kept building them when he was just a kid, long before he started jumping. I guess he just knew he was going to be a jumper . . . somehow."

Hastings jumped through high school, although off-season training was non-existent. He was too busy being a topflight club golfer, picking up a junior

bounced back to eighth place on the final day. At Lake Placid last winter, after he finished third, he booted everything the next day.

Hastings sees two reasons for such a rollercoaster record: that bad spill, which continued to ''spook'' him and the simple lack of a big training base, i.e., a lot of jumps. However, he feels merely being a year older, with another year's experience, is one partial solution and although he was bothered by flashbacks of the Iron Mountain spill for more than a year, ''I think of it less and less now, and I think everything's okay.''

He explains, ''I started skiing when I was young but I didn't do a lot of jumping during the summer. In fact, I think that's probably a reason for our whole team being inconsistent, the fact that none of us has a real base the way the Europeans do, although we're getting more and more jumps every year.

''I didn't jump in summer until I was 18 or 19 while the Europeans would have a couple of hundred practice jumps before each season. I took jumping seriously but this kind of seriousness now is at a completely different level. I'll have about 300 practice jumps going into the season and I'm really just beginning to find out more about me and jumping. My base is getting up there and I think I'll be more consistent.''

And will the Olympics present any special pressure? ''Oh, there are going to be some anxieties but the pressure is really based on expectations and I don't think there will be any great expectations for me, so there shouldn't be too much pressure. I just want to be skiing well going into the Olympics. The better you ski, the more confidence you get.''

Four years ago, Jeff Hastings was one of the kids on the sideline, wearing bib No. 1, the first kid down the chute in practice before each event. This year, he'll be up with the ''big kids'' of the sport. More than one observer believes he can be one of the biggest.

title or two. These days, Hastings, a lefty swinger, seldom plays; his summers are devoted to working as a management trainee for Sheraton Hotels.

At Williams College, he continued to improve, just missing the 1980 Olympic team although he was picked to be one of the fore-jumpers for each event. His fore-jumpers bib hangs with his other memory-joggers in the souvenir- and photo-clogged bedroom at his parents'

home in Norwich, VT.

He concedes consistency has been a problem although he has shown signs of brilliance in the last couple of seasons. At the 1982 World Ski Flying Championships in Bad Mitterndorf, Austria, for example, he was 10th the first day — the first time he had jumped on a 120-meter hill, plummeted to 40th (last) on the second day and then

KERRY LYNCH
NATIONAL CHAMPION

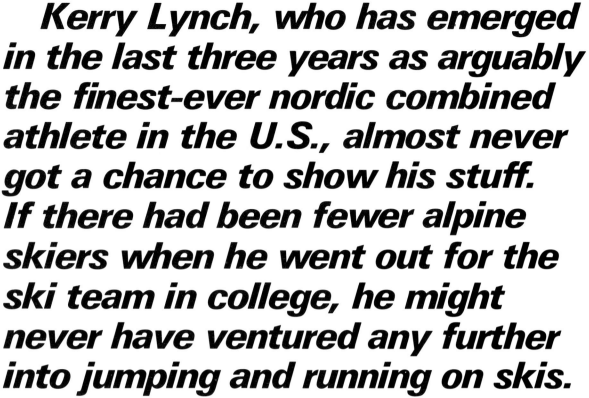

Kerry Lynch, who has emerged in the last three years as arguably the finest-ever nordic combined athlete in the U.S., almost never got a chance to show his stuff. If there had been fewer alpine skiers when he went out for the ski team in college, he might never have ventured any further into jumping and running on skis.

But he did, and that decision has helped produce one of the world's premier nordic combined skiers.

The combined event is so named because it blends 15-kilometer skiing and 70-meter jumping. Lynch, 26, realized the potential many had envisioned for him during the 1982-83 season when he won the unofficial World Cup for combined.

However, he had his pocket picked in the last race of the season—when after all the leading athletes had conceded in Oslo

Lynch had won the championship (based on an individual's three best finishes during the season) and they would all skip the last meet and cut short the season by a week — the East Germans changed their minds and decided to compete, even though the field was obviously sub-par. Although there was virtually no competition, the East Germans claimed they had "won" the nordic combined title with Uwe Dotzauer and Gunther Schmieder, in that order, slipping past Lynch, who had been dropped to third overall.

All that has done is heighten Lynch's resolve for this Olympic season.

"I don't have to say anything. The East Germans may try to get some propaganda at home about their 'championship,' but they know how they 'won' it, I certainly know and, most important, they know everyone else knows, too, so what's the 'victory'?

"Last year is over and done," he says. "I don't think I've got anything to prove. I just want to be in good shape this season. I don't feel any tremendous pressure because of the Olympics. I'm anxious and psyched-up but I don't think I'm nervous about them."

Being in tip-top shape is Consideration No. 1 for Lynch this season. Last spring he underwent surgery on his right knee to repair a calcified tendon. Dr. Richard Steadman, the U.S. Ski Team surgeon, made several incisions to give the tendon some flex; Lynch probably will have major surgery next spring but he expects to be slugging it out with the top combined athletes this season. Again.

"I haven't been able to jump as much as usual during the summer because the knee wouldn't take a lot of pressure and strain, as it would in a jump landing, until August, so I've had to completely change my training program. I've put in the most intensive technique workouts and I've done a lot of biking to help keep the snap and quickness in my legs for the takeoff in jumping."

Lynch, who began skiing at 3½, added jumping to his skills at 14. He was a four-event skier (slalom and giant slalom, jumping and running) in high school, a skier so strong and talented that even though he was unable to compete in the Colorado high school cross-country and jumping championships as a senior because of a broken shoulder, he strapped his arm to his side and still captured the state slalom championship.

KERRY LYNCH
NORDIC COMBINED

"My elbow was pinned to my side. I couldn't jump and I couldn't extend it for cross-country striding, but I still could plant my poles, so I raced in the slalom," he says.

When he entered Western State College in Gunnison, Colo., Lynch was undecided about whether to concentrate on alpine or nordic skiing.

"There were 50 or 60 skiers for alpine and maybe 10 or 12 trying out for the nordic ski team. I won the jumping and was second in cross-country, so I stayed with nordic," he recalls. And didn't bother trying out for alpine. "Oh, I tried that, too. I was third in the slalom tryout race but I figured I'd still go nordic."

In 1976, he won the junior national nordic combined championship and was named to the U.S. Ski Team. He's been with the team ever since.

"I hadn't thought much about competing up until then, but that's when I really started to train. I went back to college for my sophomore year, skied in some more races — some alpine races, too, as a matter of fact — and was second as a senior in the 1977 national combined championships. (Nordic Program Director John) Bower talked to

me, said combined was hard and required plenty of work, and he said it looked like I'd be doing a lot of traveling with the team. I thought that sounded pretty worthwhile so I started to train fulltime with the team," Lynch says.

He dropped out of college and began

to hone his skills. Lynch credits Steve Gaskill, now head of the U.S. Nordic Coaches Association but then assistant nordic combined coach, with developing those talents, designing a training program which has boosted him to the front ranks of the world's combined skiers.

He won the Olympic tryouts in 1980 and finished 18th in the two-day event

at Lake Placid; good but not good enough, he felt.

In 1981, Lynch began to blossom. He won a meet at Reit-Im-Winkl, West Germany, and helped carry the Americans to a second place team finish in

Nesselwang, West Germany. He also earned his first U.S. national combined championship. The 1982 season was one of the most frustrating for the Americans — as a team and for Lynch in particular.

The team trained at home, passing up vital international meets at the start of the '81-82 season to focus on individual training with an eye toward the first-ever championship and the World Championships later that season. The strategy backfired disastrously, though, and the season is seldom spoken of in more than hushed terms. Lynch provided perhaps the lone highlight, finishing second in the running portion at the Worlds in Oslo but poor jumping the previous day sabotaged him and he finished only 14th overall.

Last year showed he has bounced back from the psychological dip of '82. He finished second in a meet in Sapporo, Japan, in the first part of the schedule and then won consecutive meets in Lahti, Finland, and Oslo at the tail end of the year to apparently win the unofficial world title . . . until the East Germans began playing their games. But title or no, Lynch knows he's where he felt he could be — at the front of the pack.

Although the operation curtailed his preseason training, Lynch still focused on jumping, hoping to further buttress the weaker phase of his event.

"I know I can run," he said after taking a break in his summer workouts at several sites in Switzerland, "and that's why I've concentrated so much on jumping during the summer. Jumping is a real skill and although I might not have the strength in my leg, I'm working to have the best technique possible. The top combined guys are better jumpers than I've been, so I've stressed improving my takeoff and my form as well as my mental approach as much as I can under the circumstances. The running doesn't concern me that much, and maybe it's a gamble focusing so much on jumping but that's where I need the work, so . . ."

THE HISTORY
OF THE WORLD CUP

The Federation Inernationale de Ski (FIS) World Cup was created in 1967 to reward the world's best ski racers— ideally, the skiers who performed well in all three disciplines of the sport; downhill, slalom, and giant slalom. The idea was to give a points system and better identity to the ramshackle circuit of FIS races run independently by resorts and European ski clubs.

In the years prior to the inception of the World Cup, there were the traditional classics such as the Arlberg- Kandahar, rotating among the fashionable resorts of St. Anton, Chamonix, and Garmisch; the Hahnenkamm at Kitzbuhel; and the Lauberhorn at Wengen. In addition to these classic events were the FIS World Championships and Olympic Winter Games.

These races, however, only measured a skier's ability in a single race. There was no way to assess the top performers in international ski racing in any given year until the birth of the World Cup circuit.

Borrowing from the Grand Prix of auto racing, French journalist Serge Lang, U.S. Ski Team coach Bob Beattie, and French National Team coach Honore Bonnet set out to construct a season-long series of races where competitors would be able to earn points in each race. At the conclusion of the season, the man and woman who had accumulated the greatest number of points would win the World Cup and be acknowledged as the top racers in the world that year.

Initial sponsorship for the idea came from Evian, the French mineral water firm, who was eventually succeeded by Seven-Up. That same year, Ski Magazine's Editorial Director John Fry, proposed the creation of the Nation's Cup which would be awarded to the country whose racers had accumulated the greatest number of World Cup individual points during the course of the winter. The illusion of a traveling winter sports circuit was growing rather than fading and the "La Cirque Blanche" (The White Circus) had arrived.

The FIS, who serves as the international governing body for ski racing, at times seemed a bit bemused by it all. A largely self-elected body centered in Bern, Switzerland, it was largely controlled then as now by its president, Marc Hodler of Switzerland.

Hodler, under his other hat, Treasurer of the International Olympic Committee, shared the idea of keeping skiing as a member of the Olympic family. But as the years went by, Olympism moved nearer the World Cup rather than vice-versa.

The early World Cups were an excellent indication of what was to come in the Winter Games as French legend Jean Claude Killy captured the first two men's overall titles in 1967 and 1968 en route to his triple medal performance at the Winter Games in Grenoble, France while two-time women's overall World Cup titlist Nancy Greene of Canada claimed a giant slalom gold medal while 1967 overall runnerup

Marielle Gotschel of France mined gold in slalom. Other World Cup champions who have gone on to Olympic fame include Italy's Gustavo Thoeni and Piero Gros along with Austria's Annemarie Moser-Proell and Swiss star Marie-Theres Nadig.

There have been numerous changes in the original idea since its inception in 1967. Hardly a year has gone by since that first winter in which some major or minor adjustment has not been made in the scoring system. In the 70's, it was designed to encourage the all-around skier but, specifically, it was to stop an

individual—first Gustavo Thoeni, then Ingemar Stenmark—from winning year after year because they were annually the best slalom and giant slalom skiers.

The World Cup Committee tried going back to the original formula of all races counting toward the overall but Stenmark still emerged victorious because there were so many more races. They tried limiting scoring to only the best four races in each discipline and giving points down to the 25th finisher in each race rather than just the first ten. In

1979, Peter Luescher of Switzerland was possibly the most embarrassed winner in World Cup history. A good slalom and giant slalom skier, he won only one race and never made the top 25 to score a point in downhill, although scoring enough points in combined events to capture the title.

The current system allows a skier to count the best five results in each discipline (four for women) and the best three of five combined results with the top 15 finishers receiving World Cup points in an individual race.

Other changes have included the reduction of the number of giant slalom gates to increase the speed, making giant slalom a two-run event for women, and installing the ''bibbo'' system whereby the second run start order in slalom and giant slalom is determined by results of the first run rather than simply reversing the starting order of the first ''seed'' of 15 racers.

BILL KOCH, WORLD CUP CROSS-COUNTRY

The newest addition to the World Cup was introduced during the 1983 season as the Super Giant Slalom or Giant Slalom In One Run became an official part of the calendar. A cross between downhill and giant slalom, the Super G was designed to give the down-hillers an additional opportunity to score world cup points as the race is a one-run event as in downhill with gates spaced farther apart to increase the overall speed. Critics of the event believe that it should be a separate event rather than included in the regular giant slalom race quota but the Super G remains a part of three men's combineds.

Nordic World Cups have existed, first unofficially, then in odd years only since 1975 in Cross-Country and since 1981 in Ski Jumping. The 1982 season saw the first complete schedules for World Cup nordic events in Olympic or World Championship years while the 1984 season will mark the first year for Nordic Combined to be run with World Cup status.

There has never been an overwhelming enthusiasm for the concept among many Scandinavian and Eastern ski nations, but nonetheless, support has grown gradually and the final agreement, reached in the spring of 1981, to support annual official World Cups in both cross-country and jumping indicates that the World Cup concept is here to stay in nordic skiing.

Nordic World Cup champions have also experienced success during Winter Olympic competition as 1977 cross-country champion Thomas Wassberg of Sweden collected a gold medal in the 15 kilometer event in Lake Placid while Soviets Galina Kulakova and Raisa Smetanina have both produced gold medal efforts, Kulakova earning a pair of top finishes in 1972 in Sapporo, Japan and Smetanina skiing to gold in both 1976 in Innsbruck, Austria and 1980 in Lake Placid.

THE FIRST LADIES AND PRESIDENT REAGAN

CINDY NELSON, HOLLY FLANDERS

The World Cup season for both alpine and nordic begins in early December and runs through the end of March, culminating with the World Cup Finals in all disciplines except downhill. A dual slalom format was added to the alpine Finals in 1975 for the purpose of accumulating final Nation's Cup points although the parallel is not used for individual World Cup scoring. The top 32 finishers in the final individual list are eligible for the parallel.

During the course of a single season, skiers may race in as many as 11 different countries during the four-month season, competing in one country one day and driving all night to a race in another country the following day. Some U.S. skiers may make as many as three trips to Europe during the course of the winter. It is a grueling circuit that takes its toll both physically and mentally of all involved.

Traditionally, the World Cup circuits for both alpine and nordic have been dominated by the Europeans and Scandinavians. With 90 percent of all the events being held in Europe, it was one continual ''road game'' for the American contingents who traveled across the Atlantic to do battle.

Americans had had limited success prior to the dawning of the 80's. Marilyn Cochran had captured the World Cup giant slalom crown in 1969 to become the first U.S. skier to ever claim a World Cup title of any sort and Phil Mahre had placed third in the final overall standings in 1979 despite shattering an ankle during the pre-Olympic giant slalom in Lake Placid and missing the remainder of the season. However, no one among long-time World Cup watchers was prepared for what was to come.

The 80's dawned with the dynamic duo from Liechtenstein, Andreas and Hanni Wenzel, taking top honors in the final World Cup alpine ratings. Phil Mahre again found himself in third position following a silver medal slalom performance in the Winter Games. In second position sat the silent Swede, Ingemar Stenmark.

Mahre and Stenmark waged an epic battle the following year for the overall title and 1981 marked the coming of age of the U.S. Ski Team. For the first time in the 14-year history of World Cup alpine competition, the coveted crystal globe that signifies annual skiing supremacy made its way across the Atlantic to Yakima, Washington as Phil Mahre became the first American to ever win a World Cup overall title.

The race went right down to the wire, however. The next to the last race of the season came in the form of a slalom in Borovetz, Bulgaria. A win or a second place showing for Mahre would wrap up the historic title. The win went to

Soviet Alexander Zhirov but the result sheet showed a Mahre in second position—Steve Mahre, Phil's twin. Despite a third place effort by Phil, the chase for the overall title went down to the final race of the season, the 31st stop on the tour and the Europeans were astounded that Steve had kept his brother from winning the crown.

Laax, Switzerland, March 29, 1981 —the final giant slalom of the 1981 season. Again, the win goes to Zhirov and again, there is a Mahre in second place. This time, it is Phil and a 14-year dream comes true. The United States could claim the best alpine skier in the world.

Also on the horizon was another up-and-coming star for the U.S. from a rather unlikely place—Lexington, Kentucky. Tamara McKinney, all of 18 years old, won the first World Cup race of her career, a giant slalom in Huate Nendaz, Switzerland, to set the ball rolling on what was to become one of American skiing's greatest success stories. She rolled to two more giant slalom wins during the course of the winter to claim the World Cup giant slalom title, the first American woman since Marilyn Cochran in 1969 to win a World Cup crown. It was merely a preview of what was to come.

**DEBBIE ARMSTRONG
NATIONAL DOWNHILL**

As the 1982 season rolled around, the talk turns to whether Phil can repeat as overall champion. The answer to that question comes rather quickly as he sprinted to a 76-point lead over Stenmark at the Christmas break and wrapped up his second consecutive World Cup title on Super Bowl Sunday, January 24, with a slalom win in Wengen, Switzerland, two months still remaining in the season.

It now came down to the discipline titles. Stenmark had run off a total of eight consecutive World Cup slalom titles and had skied his way to four straight giant slalom crowns prior to the 1982 season. It was not to be in 1982, however, as Phil Mahre walked off with both slalom and giant slalom championships as well as his third consecutive combined crown. In 18 World Cup slalom or giant slalom races during the course of the winter, Phil failed to finish in the top three only once, racking up five individual wins and nine second place finishes. All five of the possible men's World Cup titles now resided in North America, Canada's Steve Podborski having won the downhill crown.

Brother Steve literally made the men's 1982 World Cup season a family affair as he posted four individual World Cup wins to finish third in the final overall standings to complete the "Swedish Sandwich." Two of those wins came in the form of one-two slalom finishes with Phil to mark the first time in World Cup history that American men have ever swept the top two places. But the highlight of Steve's winter was to come in the form of his first ever international giant slalom win. It was not just any race, however. It came on February 3 in Schaldming, Austria at the World Championships and marked the first time in history that an American male had won an individual World Championship gold medal, the win coming just two weeks after surgery to both knees. Between the brothers Mahre, they won seven of the final nine technical events of the 1982 World Cup season.

The U.S. women have always kept pace with their male counterparts and 1982 was no exception as the American ladies, sparked by the experience of Cindy Nelson, the talents of Christin Cooper, and the determination of Tamara McKinney, ended the winter ranked as the best women's alpine team in the world and the recipient of the women's Nations Cup.

The charge to the top was led by Cooper, who not only scored the highest World Cup overall finish for an American woman with her third place ranking, but collected a trio of medals from the World Championships, the most ever for a U.S. ski racer, male or female. Nelson skied off with a silver medal in downhill at the World Championships and finished the season ranked fifth in the World Cup standings while McKinney, hampered for the majority of the season with a broken hand, placed ninth in the final point standings. In addition, Holly Flanders came within one race of capturing the World Cup downhill title.

On the nordic side of the coin, the plot was astonishingly familiar to that of Phil Mahre in 1981. At the outset of the season, Bill Koch had become the first American to ever win a World Cup cross-country race in Europe and he had teamed with Dan Simoneau for the first ever one-two nordic sweep for U.S. skiers as well as earning a bronze medal at the Nordic World Championships to set the stage for another final race drama.

Going into the final race of the World Cup season in Castelrotto, Italy, Koch's destiny was in his own hands—win the race and win the first ever nordic World Cup for the United States over another Swede, Olympic gold medalist Thomas Wassberg. Koch started in the middle of the pack and by the midway point of the 15 kilometer competition, it was all over. Picking up close to one minute over the last portion of the course on runnerup Milos Becvar of Czechoslovakia, Koch captured one of the most important individual victories in the history of the U.S. Ski Team to become the first American Nordic World Cup champion.

As for the traditional nordic ski powers, their worst fears had become reality. The final blow came the following day when the U.S. relay team comprised of Koch, Simoneau, Tim Caldwell, and Jim Galanes captured the first ever World Cup relay victory for the United States. American nordic skiers were no longer cause for a good laugh among the Europeans and Scandinavians, but rather a serious threat to their traditional dominance of the sport.

With the dawning of the 1983 World season, the questions centered around whether the U.S. Ski Team could possibly come up with a year that could top 1982. It was that awkward season that comes between a World Championship year and the Winter Olympic Games and rumor has it that it is tougher to stay on top than to get there in the first place.

If such is the case, you could not have proved it by the U.S. Ski Team as Phil Mahre collected his third consecutive overall World Cup title, despite a much slower start than the previous winter. Mahre now ranks as one of only three men in World Cup history to have won a trio of consecutive overall crowns along with Italy's Gustavo Thoeni and Sweden's Stenmark. Now only Thoeni has more career championships with four.

The lack of good early snow in Europe and a large amount of early season downhills meant that Mahre was a little slow getting untracked in 1983, his first individual victory coming in the form of a giant slalom win in Aspen, Colorado on March 7. Interestingly enough, however, this was the race which gave him his third title as Stenmark came up short. Combined points and downhill results such as a fifth place showing in St. Anton, Austria helped Phil to regain his crown after sitting in 19th position in the overall standings as late in the season as January 22.

In addition to his overall championship, Mahre also claimed his second consecutive World Cup giant slalom title by virtue of victories in the final three giant slaloms of the season. The final win in Furano, Japan, which assured him of the title, came by a mere one hundredth of a second over Max Julen of Switzerland.

However, for the first time in the history of World Cup competition, the young lady that stood next to Phil on the final victory platform in Furano also came from this side of the Atlantic. Tamara McKinney, coming off a frustrating season the year before that saw her pole taped to the cast that encased her right hand for a good part of the season, had stood the women's alpine circuit on its collective ear by becoming the first American woman to ever win an overall World Cup crown. Mahre and McKinney's wins also marked only the third time in World Cup history that skiers from the same nation have won both the men's and women's alpine titles in the same season.

For McKinney, the season got off to a fast start as she posted the first World Cup slalom win of her career in the initial slalom of the winter, the third stop on the tour in Limone, Italy. She followed that up with a second slalom win in Davos, Switzerland and then capped off January by posting a one-two giant slalom finish with teammate Christin Cooper in St. Gervais, France which gave her the overall lead for the first time since mid-December.

The season then took a downward turn for McKinney as teammates Cooper and Maria Maricich were injured the week following the St. Gervais win and were sidelined for the remainder of the season. She returned to Copper Mountain, Colorado for the U.S. National Championships in mid-February on the heels of two non-finishing World Cup slaloms.

Being home seemed to revitalize McKinney, however, as she rolled to victories in both the slalom and giant slalom at the Nationals. She was ready when the World Cup circuit moved to the U.S. and in the space of five days in March, McKinney scored three giant slalom wins in Waterville Valley, New Hampshire and Vail, Colorado to put her back on top of the standings, a spot she was not to relinquish. The race that eventually meant the title came in Furano, Japan and although McKinney fell during the second run and only managed to finish 12th, the only skier who could catch her, Switzerland's 1982 overall World Cup champion Erika Hess, could only come up with a tenth place showing. The dream was reality.

The stage is now set for the 1984 World Cup season and the XIVth Winter Olympic Games in Sarajevo, Yugoslavia. For quite a few years, U.S. alpine and nordic skiers had stood at the base of victory stands around the world and looked up at Europeans and Scandinavians accepting the accolades of the crowds, hoping to someday witness the view from the top. Now the roles have been reversed. The U.S. Ski Team is Number One and still climbing.

TAMARA McKINNEY
1983 CHAMPION

PHIL MAHRE
1981-83 CHAMPION

KERRY LYNCH
NORDIC COMBINED

COOPER & OAK
HAWAII CAMP

ALPINE
TRAINING

In June of 1979 a young woman looked thoughtfully at a set of hand-grips mounted at about the level of her shoulders. Then she hiked herself up onto them and did a dozen or so vertical push-ups, an exercise that was interrupted when she fainted. It took her a minute or so to recover, then she finished the workout. Across the room, another person about her age was pumping a sort of horizontal bicycle. The drag is set so high that she can hardly move the pedals, but she cranked out ten repetitions before she got off, sagged against the equipment for a moment, then got back on for two more sets of ten. All around the room there are other teenagers working at the fourteen pieces of equipment on the Universal Gym: ten more pounds on the weight rack, five more repetitions on the next set.

Actually, they're the veterans and hopefuls of the U.S. Women's Ski Team, out in Bend, Oregon, for the first training camp of the 1980 racing season. The dew was still frozen on the lawn of the hotel when they went to breakfast, then there was race training up on the summer snows of Mt. Bachelor until early in the afternoon, lunch, a crunching one-hour soccer game with no time-outs, and then this. There'll be video sessions of the day's on-snow workout before supper, and probably a swim or something to burn off the extra energy.

One of the veterans wasn't at the Bend training camp. Abbi Fisher had torn up both her knees in a fall at the Lake Placid pre-Olympic downhill in March, and she's at Dr. Steadman's clinic in South Lake Tahoe, California.

Steadman found that she'd torn one of the ligaments completely off the bone, two other ligaments had internal tears, and a piece of cartilage had also been torn loose from the bone. He sewed down the cartilage, fastened the loose end of ligament in place with a screw and a washer, and put on a protective cast. Later that afternoon, he came back to Abbi's room and they started on her rehabilitation workouts, then a week later Dr. Steadman repaired her other knee.

Before long, Abbi was running the two miles from Steadman's house to the therapy clinic, using the crutches and double hip cast running technique pioneered by Peter Patterson of the men's team. Once she'd gotten the hang of it she went out to the local track and started running successive quarter miles. "I'd do three or four of them," she said later, "and get my pulse up to about 220. I didn't really need to count it—I can tell pretty accurately by the way it feels. Your body sort of hums."

Abbi was done with the casts on the first of May, and in June she entered the eight mile run that climbs 4,688 feet up Mt. Washington, near her home in New Hampshire. She placed fourth among the women, but by the middle of August she'd improved her record: she won both the slalom and giant slalom titles in the Australian national championships. A coach was thinking over that summer: "You have someone down on the floor doing push-ups and she gets to fifty and she says she can't do any more. I say 'Yes you can. Try to do ten more.' And she DOES ten more, then five more. That's the way you get to know an athlete, and the ONLY way she can get to know herself from a competitive point of view—to know where the limits are."

There are several kinds of limits for World Cup racers. Some are set by character, and others are governed by the laws of physics. Christin Cooper was one of those women in the Universal Gym room at Bend, and in January of 1982 she pushed a little too hard against the latter kind. The downhill at Bad Gastein, Austria, ends with a long and very fast sidehill schuss into a sharp left turn with a compression and a bump right at its apex. Christin got thrown by the bump and into a crash that stilled the crowd at the finish; she was flung through the air, through the boundary fence, and into the moorings of a utility pole, shedding skis, poles, goggles, even her crash helmet as she went. But it was the flight of a rag doll and she walked away from it, placed second in the slalom two days later, and scored her first World Cup slalom win three days after that.

"You really take it to the limit now," Christin said once, "you've just got a shoestring that's holding you to the course and that's when you have the best runs—but it's also when you're most vulnerable."

The best ski racers have always been at those limits, though over the years equipment, technique, and course preparation has raised the ante of vulnerability to an astonishing degree. But at the same time, training methods and sports medicine have pushed the limits of the possible higher than the pioneers could ever have dreamed. Dick Durrance left his Florida home when he was eleven years old and spent six years at school in the fledgling ski town of Garmisch-Partenkirchen, Germany. When he returned to America in 1933 he was far and away the best racer in the country, and he was hardly challenged as the decade turned.

Durrance went back to Garmisch to prepare for the 1936 Olympics, the first to include alpine skiing. "I'd work myself to exhaustion as much as I could that summer," he recalls. "I'd haul bricks up to a cliff place an build little houses up there. I'd always keep in mind that it was to get in shape—a constant effort to build your body. There were no trainers to speak of then; we had Otto Schneibs at Dartmouth, but there were none in international competition. The team hired Toni Seelos for a day or two just before the Games, but other than that there was no trainer or coach for the American team—no training camps. We were mostly just college students."

"Training was a hell of an honor system," says Gretchen Fraser. "We got a letter in the fall suggesting some exercises and telling us not to wear high heels so our Achilles tendons wouldn't shorten. None of the boots we were given fit so we just ran round and round the deck of the liner on the way over. That broke in the boots and it also gave us some roadwork." Undaunted, Gretchen went on to win the slalom gold medal and place second in the combined in those 1948 Olympics.

Four years later, Walter Prager's Dartmouth skiers led the U.S. Olympic team, but training was still essentially an honor system: "We did a little running and

bicycling," Bill Beck recalled later. "Everyone trained on their own until they left for Europe in January—a self-inflicted training program." Nevertheless, Beck placed fifth in the Olympic downhilll, still unsurpassed by an American man, and Andrea Mead Lawrence took the gold medal in both slalom and giant slalom. Andrea was on the team from '48 through '56: "We got in shape by climbing the courses and skiing —it would take two or three weeks of really hard work to get in shape," she says now. "Looking back at it, I think of it as a good holistic approach—you got in shape by doing it."

Safety bindings were still years away in the future then but the skis were made of wood and they tended to break before bones did. "Still," says Andrea's team-mate George Macomber, "it seems we were always skiing with sprained ankles." (Some of the Americans anticipated the safety-binding era by shaving thin spots in their long-thong bindings for training—the leather would break in a bad fall. The Austrians couldn't believe it.) Beyond such all-American enterprise, sports medicine of the era was heavily indebted to the accumulated folk-wisdom of the ages. Some top-rank racers believed, for instance, that hot water softened their muscles and they stayed away from baths and showers during race weeks. Others, on firmer ground, made sure they always had a pair of dirty socks for race day: clean socks were too slippery and their feet slipped a little inside their all-leather boots. Ralph Miller, a U.S. team skier of the '50s, went even further—he raced with no socks at all. "You didn't have to tighten your boots so much to get a good fit," he says now, "that meant you had better circulation, your feet stayed warmer, you had better control, and you ran less risk of injury."

Ralph went on to become a leading neuro-endrocrinologist. "Looking back, I realize that we were always tired. We didn't understand about the rest needs of the body—we'd just train harder and harder before the big races. We'd see twenty Austrians skiing slalom better than we'd ever seen anybody in the States, so we'd start training FIERCELY, even though we'd been working hard for several months already. What we should have been doing was light touch-up drills to stay sharp. I'd say that, from a clinical point of view, I was suffering from Neurasthenia—a lowered nerve capacity, the fibers are no longer able to function at full capacity. Overtraining is a vague term, but it's an identifiable physical syndrome.

Full year-round training for ski teams began when the Austrian men's team brought Dr. Fred Rossner over from track and field in the 1950's and that team dominated the decade. Bob Beattie brought it to the Americans when he took over the alpine program in 1962, and now it's the Americans that are setting the pace—so much so, in fact, that several leading European racers, and even a whole national team, has asked to get in on the American training program.

Just a few years ago a crash like Abbi Fisher's might well have ended a career, and Christin Cooper might have been out of action for weeks after she went through the fence. Now, though, the

recoveries of those two, and many others on the team, has been at the heart of the American success in the past several years. This has been largely the work of Dr. Richard Steadman, who took over the medical program for the U.S. team in 1976, and John Atkins who came to the team as trainer in 1978 and was given responsibility for the year-round training program in the spring of 1980.

The racing season ends in April, and training for the next year begins on May 1st. There are certain differences of calendar, location, and emphasis between the men and women, but the pattern is established. The 12-month program is built around a "two peak" year: spring rest, a low intensity summer

DR. STEADMAN AND TRIS COCHRANE

building to an August peak, tapering again to a low intensity in the fall, building again to a mid-winter peak.

"Rest" and "low intensity" have to be understood in context. A veteran once described her resting time this way: "I've seen enough of the Cybex and Universal gym for awhile, so I just mainly keep up my stretching and strength program, and I like to run in the water for my legs and take a bike ride whenever I can—usually about fifty miles. And I like to go climbing." (One of the climbs she meant was a hike to 22,000 feet in the Andes with her skis, then the long ride down.)

The younger team skiers usually have a more well-defined program from Atkins, with carefully planned sequences and progressions of weight routines, flexibility regimens, and a variety of speed and endurance running for cardiovascular strength. Then, early in the summer, everyone will gather at a dry-

land camp for more intensive work-outs and a testing program to see how each of the athletes is coming along in terms of physical goals John has established. The easiest these standards ever get is considerably beyond anything the average fitness buff can imagine. There's the bench jump, for instance: find a knee-high bench, then, feet together, jump back and forth over it sideways for sixty seconds. At one June camp, Christin Cooper had been working hard since breakfast just after dawn. Now, late in the afternoon, she's at the bench jump. Christin finishes the punishing routine, then goes over to Atkins. "John," she says, "I can do better than that. I'd like to do it again."

The pace begins to quicken at the on-snow camp that's scheduled early in summer, usually at Mt. Hood, Oregon. This is a five day sprint, "thousands and thousands of gates," as one team skier put it: start off cold-turkey with 850 gates of slalom the first day, then keep going in blistering sun or drenching rain to the end of the week. Then, for the last three years, the women have repaired to balmier climates. Ed Fair was a college friend of John Atkins', and now he's manager of the Huehue Ranch in Hawaii and a friend of the team. He invites the women over to the Islands each summer and donates the facilities of the ranch, a jeep, and miles of running trails and beach for a midsummer dry-land conditioning camp.

These dry-land camps are an intensified version of the athletes' home programs. When they're on their own, Atkins' program calls for three days a week of work: one hour of weight training with Nautilus, Universal Gym, or free weight equipment, whichever is available; at least an hour and a half of hard bike riding; including 60 second sprints; and 45 minutes to an hour of running. And, both at home and at camp, there's the sports menu. The emphasis is on quickness: soccer, racquetball, tennis, volleyball, with 40 yard sprints, backwards running, and football-type agility routines; running around rubber cones, trees, or whatever is available.

The home routines in the training camps are more standardized. It starts with knee and ankle ''partner'' strength routines—three sets of ten repetitions apiece (3x10). Then there's a 3x10

series of deep pushups done between chairs, 3x15-20 dips—vertical pushups between chairs, 3x15-20 stomach wheel roll-outs, and 3x15-20 on a stretch cord strength routine to simulate racing starts. Following this it's a fifteen minute program on the stationary bike: a five minute warm-up, five minutes of hard peddling against stiff resistance, and five 60 second sprints with 60 seconds of rest between each one. The series ends on the rowing machine: 3x25 pulling and 3x10 pushing. And, now that they're warmed up, there's almost always a knock-down drag-out soccer game—one hour with no time outs is preferred. The women refer to John Atkins' program, affectionately, as ''The Fun Club.'' Proudly, too.

The summer training schedule peaks with the Southern Hemisphere on-snow camp. It's usually in New Zealand, where it's winter, and it's a full-scale

three-week racing program building to sanctioned Europa Cup races and, often, the New Zealand or Australian national championships. After the on-snow camp the athletes return to the comparatively easy life of their home routines for a few weeks, then there's often another five-day snow camp at Mt. Hood as a sort of tune-up to prepare for the next major snow camp—usually a three-week stint on the glacier at Solden, Austria, but moved back to New Zealand in '83 due to poor conditions in Europe.

And, every two or three years, there's the wind tunnel camp. Dr. Mike Holden is one of the world's leading authorities in space vehicle re-entry dynamics, and his laboratories are at the Calspan Atmospheric Testing Facility in Buffalo, New York. He's also a certified ski-instructor, high-level hobbyist, and friend of the Ski Team. Nothing if not enthusiastic, Mike has invented a wind tunnel module in which the racer, in full racing kit, stands on a measuring force-plate that has a two-aspect video monitor mounted between their skis along with a digital meter reading to hundredths of a pound of air drag.

The downhillers of the women's team stopped in Buffalo on their way to the Solden glacier camp in October of '81. Mike Holden was donating the tunnel and his expertise, and Kevin Yelmgren had come east from California for the occasion. Kevin is a major in the Air Force at the Norton Air Base, a Ph.D. in aerodynamics, a specialist in flow visualization, an amateur ski racer, and another friend of the team. Everyone

gathers in the vast echoing steel building that holds the wind tunnel, and the women take forty-five minute turns in the test module as the engineers, Ernst Hager, the women's downhill coach, and (usually) Cindy Nelson sit at the control panel with the computer printouts, video monitors, helmet communicator microphones, and a drag meter reading to eight decimal places. Standing up on their skis, the women usually pull about 35 pounds of drag, and their accustomed racing tuck usually brings this down to the twelve to fifteen pound range. Then they begin to work—trimming their elbows, adjusting their hands, rounding their shoulders first this way, then that way, they wear away the drag by tenths and hundredths of a pound until the best of them get their readings below nine pounds. They work from mid morning till long after midnight, then again the next day until the plane leaves for Austria. Holden had developed a computer-simulated downhill race, and Holly Flanders learns to save .3 second on a 15 second schuss; Cindy Nelson trims .14 to .18 second on a 1,200 foot run—no small achievement for a downhiller whose event can be decided by hundredths of a second in a two minute race.

The next week the men come in on their way back from the Solden glacier, a place that's usually thick with European teams in their fall training. ''We spent two weeks skiing in the rain and fog,'' says one of the men. ''We were the only team up there. Eight in the morning 'til three-thirty in the afternoon—we're soaking wet and cold, and we keep skiing—snowing and blowing, and we're getting in the training runs. Even the Canadians went home early, but we're out there putting in the miles.'' Now the men settle in at Buffalo for five more days of high speed wind.

Mike Holden and Kevin Yelmgren are typical of the widening circle of people who pitch in to help the Ski Team. Steve Folsom is another: he's a tight end in professional football who comes to the training camps to help the skiers with their running and weight programs. And, in a different league, there's Bob Wort, who runs the training program for the Dallas Cowboys. Bob and John Atkins get together whenever they can to trade insights and techniques in weight training, accupressure, agility drills, and other interests that 115 pound skiers and 300 pound linemen have in common—extrapolating the curve, the women are right with the Cowboys in power lifting.

Weights and running isn't all that

Steve Folsom brings to the training camps; he's also one of John Atkins's karate sparring partners. Atkins is a Third Degree Black Belt instructor, and he added karate to the program several years ago. The physical and mental disciplines of this ancient practice help the racers keep track of their body in the midst of violent motion and sudden changes of loading and direction. And it pays off in the start enclosure, too: when the Americans throw a few kicks and chops into their warm-up routine, it's sure to annex a little extra space around them, not to mention a few hundredths worth of intimidation on the time clock when the race begins.

And there's one more unsuspected element in the U.S. Team training program, guided by Dr. Jerry May, of the University of Nevada at Reno. "Cognitive restructuring" and "autogenics" are up-to-date names for another ancient discipline: the human ability to change one's physical capacities by thinking about them. At one level, this is used to promote deep muscle relaxation in active rest. In a more aggressive mode, the racers practice "visual motor rehearsal" to help them come back from injuries and to get double value from summer training. Pete Patterson spent most of his marvelous career virtually as an out-patient, and he recalls the summer he was coming back from a fractured femur: "When I was doing my tuck exercises that summer I'd think about all the little roads and turns and the fallaways and the different forces you have against you on the different courses—I'd RUN THE RACES in my mind, and the next winter it really helped me. And I had a coach who'd give me things to think about during the summer—major technical problems that used to get me into a lot of trouble. Then when I got on snow again in the fall they'd be gone."

In a more familiar vein of practice, there's the pool of about fifty orthopedic doctors who contribute their services to the team during the racing season. The policy is to have an American doctor with the team at least during race weeks that include a downhill and, paying their own way, they're often on hand for a two week stay with the team. John Atkins is far above average as team trainers go—he did a tour of duty as a front line combat medic in Vietnam and worked for several years as an operating room technician in Salt Lake City. Out on the World Cup he directs the therapy and workouts for racers who are coming back from injuries and advises them on training strategies that will protect

them during on-snow workouts, and he works closely with Dr. Steadman in diagnosing injuries and planning rehabilitation programs when the racers are at home. The doctors in the medical pool always hope they won't have any work to do, but on race days they're out there on the course in radio contact with all the coaches in case of need.

The U.S. men's team has not been far behind their female counterparts in the field of sports medicine and training. Gene "Topper" Hagerman enters his second season as head men's trainer with the 1984 campaign, charged with the responsibility of keeping the alpine men in top-condition. A former co-head of the U.S. Olympic Committee's Sports Physiology Lab at the Olympic Training Center in Colorado Springs, Topper found himself with a downhill team that had only two of its original ten members healthy enough to compete in the final event of the season the previous year.

Through a series of weight training and fitness maintenance during the course of the winter, there were no serious injuries in 1983 and the results mirrored the success as Bill Johnson became the first American male to ever win the Europa Cup overall title, winning three of the four downhills and placing second in the final one.

A graduate of the University of Wisconsin-La Crosse with both a master's and Ph.D. from Ohio State University, Hagerman has also conducted physiological evaluations on athletes who have represented the U.S. in both Summer and Winter Olympic Games as well as the Pan American Games during his six-year stint with the Olympic Committee.

The American competitors on the World Cup circuit face almost an entire season of "away games"—the '83 schedule started late in November and ended late in March, and the Ski Team raced on home ground for just eight days. Now the purpose of the training is three-fold: to stay healthy, to stay happy, and to ski fast. The odds against the first goal are extremely heavy. It's a continuous diet of strange food, stress, fatigue, rainsoaked clothes, endless drives packed into crowded vehicles, the sneezes of strangers in lift trams—no bacillus could ask for more. Yet the American team has a level of vitality that could bring a gasp from the most optimistic school nurse that ever lived: in the five thousand person-days of the past three racing seasons, the Team has not missed a single day of work.

Those days begin at dawn with a run, then everyone is up on the mountain by the time the lifts open and down again for a late lunch. This is the "high peak" time and there's none of the

fierce training that Dr. Miller had cautioned about: whereas the off-season training days would have three hours of slalom or giant slalom drills, now there's maybe a half hour of light slalom to stay sharp, then miles of free-skiing to keep the joy going. There's almost always a high-spirited volley-ball game in the afternoon—race day rivalries hardly compare to the passion of the season-long matches in out-of-the-way European gyms and town halls. Even the lobby of a Yugoslav airport was pressed into service during a long wait last winter.

Those fourteen-hour days in the summer training camps come home to roost as the season wears on, and the evidence shows best in the finish area on race day. The racers on most of the other teams come to a stop and hang on their poles for breath, but the Americans slide right on over to the fence and reach for the radio to call a course report up to their teammates still waiting to make their run. In fact, it's a double evidence of the American spirit—our racers are almost the only ones who call back up to help the others on their team. Later in the afternoon, the team is back in the hotel for the inevitable exercises of the home-routines, with the rowing machine and exercise bike set up in a lobby or hallway. For the women, these are peaceful moments in the life of the Fun Club: there's the grind of the machines and there's sweat and some panting, but someone usually brings out their tape deck for some music, or Pam Fletcher gets done early and brings out her guitar to sing, while Karen Lancaster and Debbie Armstrong find a way to make the harmonies while they work. But the fires are always there. The British bob-sled team was staying in the women's hotel at one stop, and in the afternoon they came up to the hall landing to enjoy the common language and the pleasant company. One massive bobsledder sat down on the rowing machine, confident that even though the British Empire isn't what it used to be, the British bobsledder is still the match of any man. He pulled through a dozen or so repetitions and then, tiring visibly, he rested on the oars. An American woman half his size turned to him and asked, in accents straight out of a nineteenth century novel: "How many sets are you going to do?"

Finn Gunderson was a coach with the women's team for three years: "Later on I looked back and tried to think what it was about those gals that made them separate from so many others you see in the world. It's that whole characteristic—they make more out of life than just what is given to them."

MATT DAVIDSON
BERG UND THAL

If alpine skiers are the sprinters of skiing, zipping down a hillside in seconds —less than a minute for the slalom and GS, under two minutes for the downhill —then nordic skiers are the middle distance and marathon runners of the sport. And their training reflects that difference.

In cross-country, the women compete at five kilometers, 10 and 20-km distances while the men battle at 15, 30 and 50 kilometers. Nordic combined has the 15-km run and 70-meter ski jumping. Biathlon, which is a discipline with its own organization apart from the U.S. Ski Team, blends 10- and 20-km racing with rifle shooting. Only ski jumping doesn't have distance running in it but dryland, i.e., off the jumping hill, training is still designed to build an athlete's endurance. (How would you like to walk up all those steps to the top of the jump six, eight, maybe 10 times a day in practice.)

On top of the physical training, members of the USST's nordic teams also undergo psychological skills exercises. The training, which is an outgrowth of the team's sports medicine program, is designed in line with the ''sound mind in a sound body'' concept of the ancient Greeks.

Or, as U.S. cross-country coach Mike Gallagher points out, ''American athletes are right up there with the best skiers in the world when it comes to physical training. We've done our homework and we're up there—physically. What we need work on, though, is at the psychological level. It's reached the point where once an athlete spends a number of years training and competing in this sport, he or she simply can't train any more physically—but there's no question they can do more psychologically. I think you'll find psychological strength is going to be one of the things which helps determine champions in the next few years; they're all pretty much equal from a physical training standpoint but their mental strength is what will separate the champions from the rest. That's certainly what helps set Bill Koch apart from everyone; physically, he's no great specimen—he's not even the best physical specimen on our team—but his mental strength sets him apart.''

''We may not get to Koch's level with our psychological skills training,'' adds Jim Page, U.S. nordic program director, ''but making ourselves tougher mentally is one more way of improving our athletes' potential.''

The underlying principle for all this training, be it with running or jumping, biathlon or nordic combined, is all the same, according to Page: ''You have to put in your time to get your reward.

''There's a delayed gratification to all of this training, eight or nine months of training—from late spring through summer and fall—so you can get a reward in a very short period in winter. But you have to put in your time. There are no shortcuts,'' he says.

Another underlying principle is that every athlete is different. Training is not like one giant stretch sock; one training program does not fit everyone. There are modifications and fine-tuning which each athlete makes to tailor training to his or her likes and capabilities. Koch is different from Dan Simoneau who's not the same as Jim Galanes or a junior like George Welk; Judy Endestad trains differently from Chrissy Lewis or talent pool skier Karen Henry; Jeff Hastings works out a little differently from his brother Chris or maybe Dennis McGrane.

Early in their careers, athletes need strong guidance from their coach(es) to insure they get into good training habits as they build their training base. As they grow and develop, coaches usually backoff and take more of a monitoring role, perhaps helping setup a training schedule to emphasize certain things such as tempo workouts. However, as they develop, athletes take more responsibility for running their own show.

There is no formula for guaranteed success other than hard work. However, there are a few guidelines.

Perhaps the most basic principle in training is that it's always best to train on snow, whether you're jumping or running. Living in the United States, that's not always possible to do near home and it explains why many athletes break away in summer to find snow.

The nordic combined and jumping teams returned to Europe during the summer for training in Switzerland and Scandinavia; the cross-country squad trained on snow at Bend, Oregon, in May and Kirkwood, California—near Lake Tahoe—in summer, followed by a two-week visit to the Dachstein Glacier in Austria in September. In addition, Kerry Lynch of the nordic combined team has spent the past two summers working out in Switzerland and Germany, as has Chrissy Lewis of the X-C team; Judy and Audun Endestad have skied in Norway; Tim Caldwell went to Australia this past summer while Koch spent some time on a glacier in British Columbia; and Lynn and Jim Galanes spent

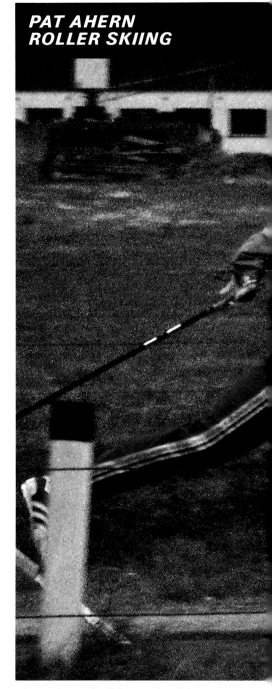

PAT AHERN ROLLER SKIING

about six weeks living and training on a glacier not far from Anchorage, Alaska. The team has paid part of those expenses for the individuals and the athletes have paid for the rest as they sought the improved results from on-snow training.

''Dryland training, whether roller-skiing, running, biking or anything else—is only a poor substitute for actual skiing,'' Page says. ''It's all better than nothing but it doesn't approach 'the real thing' of being on snow. The new plastic jumps at Lake Placid ($135,000 spent this past summer to carpet the 15-, 40- and 70-meter jumps for year-round training) are infinitely better than what we've had but even that isn't the same as the experience of on-snow jumping.''

He says American nordic athletes follow a "naturalistic" training regimen, doing *strength* training but not *weight* training. The strength training is designed to give an athlete endurance and stamina as opposed to the power of weight training.

And, just as there is a fine line between straining and training, there is a razor-thin margin between the right training and the wrong, between the proper amount and over-training. Athletes have to mix quality with quantity in their workouts, having the right amount of training with the ability to put it to use when they need it. Being able to ski five kilometers or 50 is of little value if an athlete can't blend speed with the ability to go the distance.

There is also a need, which the teams have pushed since Page became program chief after the 1980 Olympics, for athletes to "get tough" about their training, not to make excuses about missing training because it's raining or for some other lame reason.

"You only wind up cheating yourself if you try to skip workouts," he says. "We're trying to get our athletes up to the level of European athletes and you can be sure those kids are out running, jumping, working out every day . . . and that's something we've stressed with our athletes.

"For the cross-country kids, for instance, it's a case of 'out that door every day, rain or shine.' They've learned to make training more a part of their life, to do it every day just like eating or sleeping; they run, hike, bike, rollerski, ski-walk (hiking with ski poles), maybe kayak or canoe strenuously. The jumpers have different drills, getting in as many jumps as possible but also working out on their own, as do the combined athletes . . . but it's something every day, not just the last six weeks before the season, not just on weekends or when it's not too hot. Our kids know they have to put in the time and they're doing it."

In general, athletes' training starts in springtime, picks up through the summer, and intensifies in November with a concerted effort to maximize the last month before the season. A year ago, to point out the value of that final preseason month, Bill Koch missed much of November because of so-so snow in the Laborador City training camp and a nagging cold which eventually forced him to go home. He was able to

compete through most of the season at a top level, thanks to his training base which had been developed through 'the years and his mental toughness; however, when he needed some snap at the end of the season, he just didn't have it—20th in Lahti, Finland, a week off to rest and train on his own at home, third place in Anchorage but then that final sag (ninth in the last race at Lab City) and a second consecutive World Cup title slipped from his grasp. (He finished third behind 1981 Cup champion Alexander Zavjalov of the Soviet Union, who won his second title.)

Cross-country. World class athletes are training up to 750 hours a year— 650-800 hours for the top men, 600-750 for the best women, according to Gallagher. That works out to about two hours a day of training, every day, rain or shine, day in and day out, all year. He says subtract about 10 percent per year to determine what level an athlete should be at; if a 20-year-old should be at, say, 600 hours, a 19-year-old should be training 540-550 hours a year, an 18-year-old around 500 hours, and so on. Any skier who is 16 or 17 with

perhaps 300 hours knows he or she is going to have to make quantum leaps in his or her training in the next couple of years to get up to the proper level, if he or she hopes to compete on the international circuit. Such a massive jump in training means an athlete might sacrifice the next couple of years while building that base, but once the base exists, the results should start to show.

As an example, Gallagher points to Dan Simoneau, who dramatically increased his training volume after Gallagher was named coach by Page in 1980. Simmy slugged it out for two years and exploded on the World Cup

scene in 1982, finishing an impressive seventh overall as he produced the finest season any American skier has had except for Koch's fabled exploits. He was second (to Koch) at Falun, Sweden, and had five other Top-15 results.

Last winter, his body adjusted to such significant training jumps and he wound up struggling; he tied for 54th on the World Cup. However, his coach is quick to point out, "That's to be expected a little. Dan had made big jumps for a couple of summers, he cer-

tainly got the results but then his body stabilized last year. I expect him back up with the leaders this winter. There is too much talent there, for one thing, and now that Simmy has the training base, he's ready to go again. It was a tough lesson but last winter taught all of us a lot about that kind of training."

Cross-country is more than simply running, more than just having strong legs and lungs. Undeniably, that's an important ingredient in any X-C success, but upper body strength is vital. The diagonal stride and double-poling count on upper body strength.

Again, though, while an athlete wants upper body strength, it's a very delicate balance. The athlete wants endurance strength but there also is a power component . . . but not brute force power.

Or, as Page says, "You need that power when you're double-poling but it's really only a power component. After all, you don't get any points for bending your poles."

Upper body training has to be tailored to the athlete. Not every athlete has the same strengths and weaknesses, so each training program varies. One runner might do nothing but rollerskiing while another rollerskis but also works out on arm exercisers such as the Gym-in-a-bag or Exergenie, among others. When ski-walking, athletes get some real benefit when they push off on their poles with each stride, sometimes running and sometimes walking. The idea is to use the poles to simulate a race, not just as a hiking staff.

Ski jumping. This training varies greatly from X-C. While a jumper may not need strength in the obvious way a cross-country runner does, he (there are no women at the international jumping level although some jump locally and in regional meets in the U.S.) nonetheless needs strength to make the climb to the top of each jump and to let loose that explosive power at just the right moment on takeoff.

"Ski jumping is very much like golf," Page says. "It's a technical move that starts from a static position and in which you hope to hit a certain groove. There's a very small margin of error and the only difference is that golfers can't affect the ball once it leaves the tee and is in the air. Jumpers can maneuver themselves in the air to take advantage of the air conditions.

"The key to ski jumping, other than strength to walk up the hill," he goes on, "is the muscle memory in making a jump. The liftoff must be the same every time. The liftoff is the same and then the jumper makes adjustments in mid-air depending on conditions."

Ski jumping takes place at a very high rate of speed—they can hit the takeoff at about 60 miles an hour—and is over in just a couple of seconds, so a skier must be able to maintain concentration and execute precisely in a split-second.

U.S. coach Greg Windsperger, another ex-Olympian who was brought in by Page in the spring of '80, says, "The speed of everything telescopes the need for precision. It compresses everything about the sport. It's not a case of how much you explode on that takeoff, though, as much as being the right technical position each time."

"You want to make sure you're in the right position, down at the right angle as you come down the in-run and then carry that correct position through your liftoff and your ride. The great jumpers are great because they've practice for years and have the ability to stay at the right angle, keep that proper position throughout their jump," Windsperger says.

The exact angle. Not too far forward, not too far back as a skier hunkers down over his skis. Precision. But when you're doing something that last perhaps only five seconds, you have to be precise.

Jumpers also do some running but it isn't in the same way as the X-C team

Page says the U.S. jumpers also have more structure to their training with the coaches taking a more active role than is found with the cross-country squad. "The two teams are at different points. The cross-country team, especially the men, are more mature in terms of training and they don't need Mike or Ruff (U.S. women's coach Ruff Patterson) to play as active a role. The jumpers, though, are a younger team, so we feel they still need a little stronger role from the coach," he says.

Nordic combined. Athletes who compete in combined often are maligned as "not good enough to be cross-country and not good enough to be a

members. While cross-country is trying to build stamina and endurance, jumpers will train in 10- or 15-minute segments, working on speed and agility. They also can be found kicking a soccer ball to fine tune eye-foot coordination, another subtle ingredient in a sport which banks so much on the ability of an athlete to hit the takeoff just right, come off his feet at the right moment of takeoff.

umper" but that's not necessarily true. The simple fact is that Kerry Lynch, for instance, probably could make either the cross-country or the jumping squad if he put his mind to it. "He's not super human," Page says, "but he's a fine athlete and he's shown he could do well if he chose to concentrate in either special field."

Combined skiers make compromises to both jumping and X-C programs but train under both regimens. Since the event is made up of the 15-km run and 70-meter jumping, they can't focus on just one specialty. Lynch, for example, is a superb runner; Walter Malmquist, on the other hand, was an excellent jumper who never could run (he was second in the jumping phase at Lake Placid in 1980 but blew apart the next day in the race, finishing 27th (of 29) and winding up 12th overall.)

The nordic combined squad added a cross-country coach this season, two-time Olympian Doug Peterson, and head coach Joe Lamb also can pick the brains of jumping coaches Windsperger and Erling Rimeslatten. "If I've got a question, I go to whoever can help," Lamb says. Lynch credits Rimeslatten with smoothing out his jumping style last season in time to win crucial meets in Lahti, Finland, and at Holmenkollen, the

about something. The nordic teams have, for the most part, done their research and are pushing on to apply what they've learned in biomechanical tests and physiological experiments and tests.

Details of the various programs within this extensive—and expensive—program are too numerous to mention, but the top concepts involve nutritional assistance during training and at the Olympics, psychological skills exercises during the preseason and throughout the season—not just a one-shot, three-day burst of sitdown sessions timing studies for X-C, and wind tunnel testing for the jumpers.

The wind at Calspan Corporation helps skiers simulate jumping conditions and deal with some of the stresses in the sport.

But, as Gallagher indicated earlier, the psychological skills training probably will have the longest, most far-reaching impact. Dr. Rainer Martens of the University of Illinois (Urbana campus) conducts the sessions with athletes during the summer, late pre-season, and in Sarajevo.

The psychological training deals with stress management, goal-setting and, among other things, helping an athlete better concentrate. Imagery is used in some of the exercises to help a skier recall a situation, analyze it and then learn from it, perhaps how to cope with poor conditions or a pesty reporter.

"These kids have technical coaches who sharpen their physical skills," says Martens, "and I'm a mental coach. I work with them so they can control anxiety, improve their concentration and self control, how they can better deal with any number of circumstances. I try to point out, for instance, that their *performance* is what counts, not the *outcome* of a race; sure, we'd all like to see somebody win but as long as that person does the best he or she can do, that's really all we have a right to ask—to do your best."

He adds, "Each race, each jumping meet has just one winner. That doesn't mean, though, that everyone else is a loser . . . and I work with these athletes with a program which sharpens their mental approach."

NORDIC COMBINED DISTANCE RUNNING

next weekend, in Olso, Norway.

Sports medicine. This covers a lot of territory, from the strictly medical aspect to nutritional, from physiological to biomechanical and psychological. The nordic teams have different applications from alpine, too, but in general seem to be moving beyond what Gallagher calls "paralysis by analysis," i.e., over-analyzing, sometimes over-reacting to what a computer printout might say

The timing studies were taken at a couple of times during the World Cup season and revolve around each racer being timed at various points over a course. It entails clocking *every* skier in a race, not just the Americans, so that coaches can get an idea of where a U.S. runner might be gaining or losing in comparison to everyone else. That data is then converted into modifications on a training schedule, depending on what weakness are pinpointed.

That pretty well completes the circle for nordic training. Gallagher, Windsperger, Lamb and their assistant coaches work on physical skills and upgrading various techniques while Martens adds mental strength to those physical talents. And all it takes to work is a training program, for mind and body, that covers 365 days a year.

CELEBRITY CLASSIC PARADE

The Osmonds Present
United States Ski Team
Celebrity Classic

You have read about the disciplined commitment to success of the athletes who make up the U.S. Ski Team, but perhaps you have never envisioned the price one must pay for that success. The gold medal is the goal that the athletes strive for but there is another goal.

That goal is the monies that are required to support the small army of men and women who travel throughout the world chasing their dream. Consider the cost of sending just one athlete back and forth to Europe as many as three times in the course of four months.

The airfare alone is staggering, not to mention food, lodging, and transportation. Now, imagine that figure multiplied by approximately 75 to include the remainder of the team and coaching staff. The price tag now starts to move into the realm of the astronomical.

Can you imagine the budget required for a single season? It takes millions and it takes imagination to create those millions. But, there is an extensive support system behind the Team with the American public as their marketplace. Without this extensive network of friends across the country, the U.S.

Ski Team could not have challenged the Europeans at their own game, on their own turf, and emerged victorious.

That help falls basically into three categories: corporate sponsorship and licensing, private donations, and fundraising activities.

The corporate involvement with the Team has grown to include many companies, both within the realm of the sport itself as well as those outside of skiing. It is a diverse list of companies who help the Team both financially and through their support in various assorted projects.

THE PRICE OF GOLD

SUBARU'S ALAN ROSS

JOHN McMILLIAN AND UTAH'S FIRST FAMILY

Private donations are one of the oldest forms of support for the Ski Team, dating back to the manager advancing his personal funds to pay for return tickets from Europe to the extensive direct mail program that is in place today. Whether it is a five dollar donation from a child in Nebraska or a $100,000 check from a Texas oilman, each dollar helps to bring a U.S. skier one step closer to the top step of an Olympic victory platform.

Finally, there is the extensive network of fundraising events, some of which are pictured on these pages. These events include the annual circuit of ski balls, fun runs, cookbooks, and ski shows as well as major productions such as the Salute To The U.S. Ski Team and the U.S. Ski Team Celebrity Classic. Once again, these events are made possible by the enormous support system of friends from Seattle to Florida and New York to California, who donate their time and energy to help keep the U.S. Ski Team on top of the world.

Events such as the Celebrity Classic and the Salute bring together team members, staff, corporate sponsors, celebrities and friends in an effort not only to raise money but to have a good time as well. Whether it be team parallel racing on the slopes of the Park City Ski Area or a round of golf at the Park Meadows Country Club, a gala ski ball on a cruise ship off the coast of New York or a reception at the White House, all facets of the American public continue to support the U.S. Ski Team in their own way.

The U.S. Ski Team could not have known the success of the past several years had it not been for the support of another team — the team behind the Team. When an American athlete climbs to the top of a victory stand, he or she is carrying the flag for all of us.

U.S. SKI TEAM
GOLD RUSH — 1984

CINDY OAK
AROSA, SUI

THE ADMINISTRATIVE TEAM

INEZ AIMEE
Executive Director

The dawning of the 1984 World Cup campaign will signal Aimee's third season as Executive Director of the U.S. Ski Team and U.S. Ski Educational Foundation. Appointed to the position in mid-summer of 1981, she brings more than 20 years of sports management, marketing, and sales to the Team.

Aimee first joined the fledgling National Football League Films in 1965, shortly after its inception, with the objective of syndicating the first of those programs produced. During her 13 years with NFL Films, she attained the position of Vice President of Sales and Marketing.

The 1984 objective of the administrative offices is to gain even greater public awareness of ski racing as well as the accomplishments of the U.S. Ski Team. This goal can be reached initially through the medium of television, which has the capacity to appeal to contributors on either an individual level or through the licensing of the Ski Team logo and image.

U.S. Ski Team Administrative Directory

Executive Director	Inez Aimee
Executive Assistant	Kristi Scott
Finance Administrator	Jim Huston
Accountant	John Roberts
Account Executive	Anne Burnett
Information Director	John Dakin
Assistant Information Director	Ed Bowers
Administrative Assistant	Marita Viselli
Administrative Secretary	Marlene Nelson
Administrative Secretary	Lea Geary
Administrative Secretary	Daryl Ott
Receptionist	Mary Rose Knowles

U.S. Ski Educational Foundation

Assistant Director	Kae Erickson
Assistant Fundraiser	Lisa Osterstock

Alpine Staff

Alpine Program Director	Bill Marolt
Assistant Alpine Director	Bob Harkins
Administrative Assistant	Cindy Larkin
Alpine Secretary	Anita Storey

Nordic Staff

Nordic Program Director	Jim Page
Assistant Nordic Director	Carol Bradley
Nordic Secretary	Kim Ballou

U.S. Ski Team Coaches Education Program

Alpine Technical Director	Harald Schoenhaar
Nordic Technical Director	Steve Gaskill
Administrative Assistant	Suzette Cantin

INEZ AIMEE　　　**BILL MAROLT**

ALPINE TEAM
THE COACHES: MEN

BILL MAROLT
Alpine Director

Winning is no stranger to Marolt, who enters his fifth year at the helm of the most successful alpine team in U.S. Ski Team history with the 1984 season. The Aspen, Colorado native was elevated to the position of Alpine Director in May of 1979 after serving one season as Director of Development.

As an athlete, Marolt was a three-time national champion and All-American for the University of Colorado, where he claimed four NCAA skiing titles. Following his collegiate career, Marolt moved on to the U.S. Ski Team where he was a member of the 1964 Olympic Team, placing 12th in Giant Slalom, as well as representing the U.S. in the 1962 and 1966 World Championships.

The 40-year-old Marolt served as head coach for the University of Colorado Ski Team from 1969 until 1978 and guided the Buffs to seven consecutive NCAA Skiing Championships from 1972-78, tying the consecutive collegiate skiing title record held by former U.S.Ski Team coach Willy Schaeffler while at the University of Denver. He was chairman of the NCAA Skiing Rules Committee from 1973-78 and has served on the FIS Committee for the Classification of Alpine Racers.

BOB HARKINS
Assistant Alpine Director

Concentrating his efforts primarily on the U.S. Ski Team Development Program as well as assisting Marolt in general Team affairs, Harkins will begin his third season as Assistant Alpine Director in 1984. Prior to this appointment, he served as a development coach for the Team during the 1981 season.

Previous experience includes serving as Head Coach of the Alpental Race Team in Washington state and Athletic Director and Head Alpine Coach for Gould Academy in Bethel, Maine.

KONRAD RICKENBACH
Head Men's Coach

The 28-year-old Rickenbach moves into more of an overall head coaching position with the 1984 season, his fourth at the head of the U.S. men's alpine program. Born in Steinen, Switzerland, he is responsible for the organization and training of the men's team and for the direction of the coaching staff.

A native of Pleasanton, California, Rickenbach began his coaching career in his native Switzerland and headed the China Peak Ski Team in California from 1977-78. Prior to his appointment as Head Men's Coach for the U.S. Team, he served

as men's Europa Cup coach during the 1979 and 1980 seasons.

Rickenbach is single and resides in Midway, Utah.

THEO NADIG
Head Men's Downhill Coach

Nadig enters his first season at the controls of the U.S. men's downhill program with the 1984 season after serving three years as the Europa Cup downhill mentor for the U.S. Team. He assumed the reins of the program from Andreas Rauch at the conclusion of the 1983 season.

A native of Flumserberg, Switzerland, Nadig spent two years working with the Swiss slalom and giant slalom skiers on the World Cup circuit and headed the Swiss Europa Cup effort for four seasons. He is a graduate of the Magglingen Physical Education Institute.

The 39-year-old Nadig is the brother of former World Cup champion Marie-Theres Nadig and he has nurtured the likes of Pirmin Zurbriggen, Peter Luescher, Jacques Luethy, and of course, his sister, to the World Cup circuit. He is married and the father of a son and a daughter.

TOM KELLY
Head Men's Slalom and Giant Slalom Coach

"TK" proved that you can take the man out of the Ski Team but you can't take the Ski Team out of the man as he rejoined the men's staff for the 1982 season after a seven-year leave of absence. During that time, the Squaw Valley native headed up the Olympic Training Center in Squaw Valley.

The 51-year-old Kelly will take over full contol of the slalom and giant slalom programs this coming winter. He first joined the U.S. Team as an assistant women's coach in 1971 and worked with development athletes on the CanAm circuit during the 1972 season. Prior to that, Kelly served as an assistant men's coach for the Canadian National Team from 1968-69.

He is married and the father of two sons.

RUBEN MACAYA
Men's Europa Cup Slalom and Giant Slalom Coach

Macaya will return to his coaching duties this coming season after a back injury sidelined him for the majority of the 1983 campaign and he is eager to continue the progress that U.S. racers have made on the Europa Cup circuit in the past several years.

Originally from Bariloche, Argentina, Macaya was a member of the Argentine National Team from 1966-71 before coming to the United States where he headed the Squaw Valley Racing Team for five years. The 35-year-old Macaya also served as Head Coach of the Lake Tahoe Ski Etude program from June of 1980 until his appointment to the U.S. Team in 1981.

A native of Truckee, California, Macaya is married and the father of a son and a daughter.

ERIK STEINBERG
Assistant Men's Downhill Coach

A member of four NCAA Championship ski teams at the University of Colorado, Steinberg will enter his fourth season as Assistant Downhill Coach, working primarily with the World Cup group.

As an athlete, the Vail, Colorado native skied on the 1972-76 collegiate title teams for the Buffs and competed on the professional ski circuit following his graduation in 1977. He was an NCAA All-American choice in 1974.

The 30-year-old Steinberg conducted his own racing camps in Italy during the summers of 1978 and 1979 and headed the Boulder Alpine Racing Team in 1979. He served as downhill coach for Ski Club Vail during the 1980 season.

TOM CANNON
Assistant Men's Europa Cup Coach

Pressed into service last season when Ruben Macaya sustained a back injury that prevented him from coaching the Europa Cup group, Cannon will begin his first full year as the Assistant Europa Cup Coach with the 1984 season.

The 41-year-old Cannon began his coaching career with the Steamboat Springs Winter Sports Club and has served as a Western Region Associate Coach for the U.S. Team for the past two seasons. Other coaching responsibilities have included the head coaching position at Crystal Mountain, Washington and head women's coach in Squaw Valley in 1981.

A graduate of the University of Colorado in 1970, Cannon resides in Steamboat Springs, Colorado during the off-season. He was married in July of this past summer.

GENE "TOPPER" HAGERMAN
Men's Trainer

The responsibility for keeping the men's alpine team healthy and in top condition will again rest with Hagerman as he begins his second season at the helm of the men's training program. Topper came to the Ski Team last season following two years as co-head of the U.S. Olympic Committee's Sports Physiology Laboratory at the Olympic Training Center in Colorado Springs.

Prior to that appointment, he served four years as head of the Sports Physiology Lab at the USOC's Training Center in Olympic Valley, California. During his six years with the Olympic Committee, the 36-year-old Hagerman conducted physiological evaluations on athletes who represented the U.S. in both Summer and Winter Olympic Games as well as the Pan American Games.

Topper earned his bachelor's degree at the University of Wisconsin La Crosse in 1968 and followed that with a master's degree from Ohio State University in 1974. He was awarded his Ph.D. in 1976, also from Ohio State.

Currently residing in Truckee, California with his wife, Hagerman has been widely published and has also worked extensively with the U.S. Rowing Team.

THE COACHES: WOMEN

MICHEL RUDIGOZ
Head Women's Coach

Heading up one of the most talented women's alpine teams in the world, the 39-year-old Rudigoz will begin his fifth season at the controls of the U.S. women's alpine program with the dawn of the 1984 season.

Originally from Lentilly, France, Rudigoz joined the U.S. Team staff in 1977 as men's downhill coach following five years as coach of the Sun Valley Junior Race Team from 1973-77. Appointed Head Women's Coach in 1980, he engineered the women's Nations Cup victory in 1982.

Now residing in Sun Valley, Idaho, Rudigoz was a French National Ski Instructor and earned the French coaching certificate under Honore Bonnet in 1968. He was the British men's coach from 1968-72 and directed the British Team during the 1970 World Championships and 1972 Olympics.

Rudigoz and wife Maggie are the parents of one son.

ERNST HAGER
Head Women's Downhill Coach

The future looks bright for the U.S. women's downhill program as Hager begins his sixth season of association with the World Cup group.

Originally from Worgl, Austria, Hager began coaching in the U.S. in 1971 at Squaw Valley, California and directed the racing program for Squaw until 1976. He first joined the U.S. Team as Assistant Women's Coach on the CanAm circuit in 1976 and coached the women's Europa Cup group from 1977-78.

The 42-year-old Hager is married and the father of three children. He and his family reside in Squaw Valley during the off-season.

JOHN McMURTRY
Head Women's Slalom and Giant Slalom Coach

McMurtry's eight-year tenure with the U.S. Team was highlighted last season by Tamara McKinney's overall World Cup title and he will enter his fourth season at the controls of the women's technical program with the task of defending that title.

The 33-year-old McMurtry trained as a racer with the Austrian Junior Team from 1966-68 and was a member of the University of Denver Ski Team in 1970 while earning a master's degree from DU.

A native of Englewood, Colorado, McMurtry began his coaching career with Denver University and served as head coach of the China Peak Junior Race Team from 1974-76. He first joined the coaching ranks of the U.S. Team in 1976 and directed the CanAm Team during the 1976-77 seasons before spending four years on the Europa Cup circuit.

During the off-season, McMurtry makes his home in Englewood.

CHIP WOODS
Assistant Women's Coach

The 1984 season will signal Woods' fourth year with the U.S. Team in the position of Assistant Women's Coach, working primarily on the World Cup circuit.

A native of East Burke, Vermont, Woods began his coaching career at Loon Mountain, New Hampshire in 1968 before moving on to Haystack Mountain where he founded the Haystack Ski Educational Foundation in 1971. He served as Director and Head Coach of the Haystack Junior Development Program from 1971-76.

The 36-year-old Woods was both teacher and coach at Northwood School in Lake Placid, New York from 1976-77 and served as head women's coach at Burke Mountain Academy from 1977-79.

During the off season, Woods and his wife enjoy canoe racing and they reside in East Burke with their two children.

BRAD GHENT
Head Women's Europa Cup Coach

The task of preparing the younger U.S. ladies for World Cup competition will again be Ghent's responsibility as he enters his fourth season at the controls of the women's Europa Cup group following a year that saw one of his athletes, Heidi Bowes, advance to the B Team.

A native of Fort Collins, Colorado, Ghent was a four-year letterman for the NCAA Champion University of Colorado Ski Team, graduating from CU in 1976. A former resident of Winter Park, Colorado, he began his coaching career at Winter Park in 1976 and remained at the area until 1980.

The 31-year-old Ghent served as the Director and Head Coach of the Rocky Mountain Competition Division during the 1979-80 season and still managed to accompany the U.S. women on a World Cup trip as an assistant coach.

An avid windsurfer, Ghent resides in Heber, Utah during the off-season.

BILL BOURTON
Assistant Women's Coach

Bourton will enter his second season as assistant coach for the women with the dawning of the 1984 season. His primary responsibilities will be on the World Cup circuit although he served as head alpine coach for the first U.S. Ski Team contingent to ever compete in the World University Games this past season.

A native of Orondo, Washington, Bourton raced for the Pacific Northwest Ski Association before beginning his coaching career at the Mission Ridge Ski Training Academy in 1976. He moved on to the University of Colorado where he spent two years as B Team coach for the Buffs, graduating in 1981.

The 29-year-old Bourton resides in Orondo in the off-season.

JOHN ATKINS
Women's Trainer

Part of the enormous success of the U.S. alpine women over the past several years can be attributed to the efforts of Atkins, both on and off the snow, who starts his sixth season in the role of women's trainer.

The 37-year-old Atkins has a broad background of training and physical conditioning maintenance as well as injury rehabilitation. He was a combat medic in Viet Nam in 1970-71 and worked as an operating room aide at the University of Utah hospital.

A 1969 graduate of California State Polytechnic University and a 1970 honors graduate of the U.S. Army Medical Training Center, Atkins supervises physical conditioning maintenance during the course of the season and advises reconditioning programs during injury rehabilitation. He received his master's degree in Physical Education and Health Science from the University of Utah in 1978 after working as both men's and women's graduate athletic trainer.

A former ski and tennis instructor, Atkins is a black belt karate instructor and has incorporated karate exercises into the overall women's training regimen. He also organized the women's dryland training camp in Hawaii, which will enter its third year in July, obtaining both the facilities and the funding in conjunction with the Huehue Ranch in Kailua Kona. With the help of Philadelphia Stars (USFL) tight end Steve Folsom and Green Bay Packer running back Del Rodgers, Atkins has additionally been able to introduce professional football weight training and agility drills to the women as part of the Hawaii camp.

THE ATHLETES—MEN

PHIL MAHRE

Height—5'9"
Weight—170
Birthdate—May 10, 1957
Birthplace—White Pass, Washington
Residence—Yakima, Washington
Year on National Team—10th

Phil Mahre joined the ranks of the ski racing elite once again in 1983 as he captured his third consecutive overall World Cup title, joining Sweden's Ingemar Stenmark and Gustavo Thoeni of Italy as the only three men in World Cup history to have won a trio of consecutive overall titles. Now, only Thoeni holds more career overall championships with four.

In addition to the overall title, which the 26-year-old Mahre wrapped up with his first individual victory of the winter March 7 in Aspen, Colorado, he also claimed his third consecutive World Cup combined title as well as the giant slalom discipline title with victories in the final three giant slaloms of the season, despite not running a single super giant slalom during the course of the season.

Instead of competing in the controversial new event, Mahre turned his attention to downhill and recorded an impressive fifth place finish in St. Anton, Austria, the best World Cup downhill finish of his nine-year career. Training only for individual races, Phil finished 18th in the final World Cup downhill standings and scored Cup points in six of the nine World Cup downhills that he entered in 1983.

The first American to ever win the overall World Cup title in 1981, Mahre claimed a trio of individual wins in 1983, which brought his total number of career wins to 27 including combineds. He also skied to the slalom championship at the U.S. Alpine National Championships at Copper Mountain, Colorado.

Phil equalled the best Olympic performance by an American male in 1980 at Lake Placid with his silver medal in slalom. He also equalled Bill Kidd's 1970 performance by capturing the FIS Combined gold medal. A two-time Olympian in 1976 and 1980, Phil placed fifth in giant slalom and 18th in slalom in 1976 in Innsbruck, Austria and claimed a second in slalom, tenth in giant slalom, and 14th in downhill at Lake Placid.

First named to the B Team in 1973, he was forced to miss the 1974 season with a broken leg suffered in an avalanche, and a fractured ankle suffered during the pre-Olympic giant slalom at Lake Placid prevented him from completing the 1979 season, a year that still saw him finish third in the final overall World Cup standings.

A member of the A Team since 1976, Phil has also been a member of the 1978 and 1982 World Championship Teams. He and wife Holly became the proud parents of a baby girl, Lindsey, in September of 1982 and the "family" travels the majority of the World Cup circuit with Phil. When not skiing, Mahre enjoys water skiing and motocross riding.

Date/Year	Event	Race	Finish
1983	Overall World Cup Standings		1
	Downhill World Cup Standings		18
	Slalom World Cup Standings		6
	Giant Slalom World Cup Standings		1
	Combined World Cup Standings		1
12/14/82	Courmayeur, Italy	WC SL	3
12/19/82	Val Gardena, Italy	WC DH	18
12/20/82	Val Gardena, Italy	WC DH	20
12/21/82	Madonna di Campiglio, Italy	WC SL	3
1/9/83	Val d'Isere, France	WC DH	14
1/10/83	Val d'Isere, France	WC DH	18
1/11/83	Adelboden, Switzerland	WC GS	11
1/21/83	Kitzbuhel, Austria	WC DH	12
1/22/83	Kitzbuhel, Austria	WC DH	13
1/23/83	Kitzbuhel, Austria	WC SL	3
1/23/83	Kitzbuhel, Austria	WC C	1
1/29/83	Kranjska Gora, Yugoslavia	WC GS	5
2/5/83	St. Anton, Austria	WC DH	5
2/6/83	St. Anton, Austria	WC SL	3
2/6/83	St. Anton, Austria	WC C	1
2/11/83	Markstein, France	WC SL	3
2/11/83	Kitzbuhel/Markstein	WC C	1
2/12/83	Markstein, France	WC SL	5
2/13/83	Todtnau, West Germany	WC GS	4
2/17/83	Copper Mountain, Colorado	U.S. Nat. GS	2
2/18/83	Copper Mountain, Colorado	U.S. Nat. SL	1
2/26/83	Gallivare, Sweden	WC GS	2(T)
2/27/83	Gallivare, Sweden	WC SL	4
3/6/83	Aspen, Colorado	WC DH	9
3/7/83	Aspen, Colorado	WC GS	1
3/8/83	Vail, Colorado	WC GS	1
3/12/83	Lake Louise, Canada	WC DH	13
3/19/83	Furano, Japan	WC GS	1
3/20/83	Furano, Japan	WC SL	6
3/21/83	Furano, Japan	WC P	2

STEVE MAHRE

Height—5'9"
Weight—170
Birthdate—May 10, 1957
Birthplace—White Pass, Washington
Residence—Yakima, Washington
Year on National Team—10th

It has been said that if there were no Phil Mahre, then certainly Steve Mahre would be the best ski racer that the United States has ever produced. However, hampered by a nagging shoulder injury in 1983, Steve's results and final standing did not belie his experience and talent.

The reigning World Championship giant slalom gold medalist captured a pair of slalom wins during the course of the winter of 83, the first coming in Parpan, Switzerland, January 4 and the second coming in St. Anton, Austria on February 11, en route to a twelfth place overall finish on the World Cup season. In addition, he posted the top American finish in the final World Cup slalom standings with a fourth place effort and skied to a 27th place finish in the giant slalom standings.

The shoulder injury occurred during a dual slalom in Flumserberg, Switzerland and given the demanding travel and competition schedule of the World Cup circuit, Steve was never able to give the shoulder the rest that it needed to heal. As a result, he found himself changing his skiing so as not to aggravate the injury further, which meant not always taking the best line through a course.

The giant slalom victory at the World Championships in Schladming, Austria in February of 1982 ended America's search for men's Olympic or World Championship gold in an individual event and came just two weeks after he underwent surgery on both knees. In addition, Steve posted a trio of historic one-two finishes in 1982 along with Phil, marking the first time American men had ever swept the top two places in a World Cup event.

First named to the B Team in 1974, Steve has been a member of both the 1976 and the 1980 Olympic Teams. In 1976 in Innsbruck, Austria, he claimed a 13th place finish in giant slalom while he placed 15th in the giant slalom in 1980 at Lake Placid.

He was elevated to the A Team in 1975 and has competed as a member of the 1978 and 1982 World Championship Teams. In addition, Steven is a three-time U.S. National slalom champion.

During the off-season, Steve can be found water skiing or riding motocross. He is married and wife Debbie and daughter Ginger accompany Steve on various trips throughout the course of the World Cup season.

Date/Year	Event	Race	Finish
1983	Overall World Cup Standings		12
	Slalom World Cup Standings		4
	Giant Slalom World Cup Standings		27
	Combined World Cup Standings		13(T)
12/14/82	Courmayeur, Italy	WC SL	4
12/21/82	Madonna di Campiglio, Italy	WC SL	8
1/4/83	Parpan, Switzerland	WC SL	1
1/11/83	Adelboden, Switzerland	WC GS	18
1/23/83	Kitzbuhel, Austria	WC SL	6
1/30/83	Kranjska Gora, Yugoslavia	WC SL	16
2/5/83	St. Anton, Austria	WC DH	21
2/6/83	St. Anton, Austria	WC SL	1
2/6/83	St. Anton, Austria	WC C	3
2/11/83	Markstein, France	WC SL	11
2/13/83	Todtnau, West Germany	WC GS	20
2/17/83	Copper Mountain, Colorado	U.S. Nat. GS	5
2/26/83	Gallivare, Sweden	WC GS	22
3/7/83	Aspen, Colorado	WC GS	11
3/8/83	Vail, Colorado	WC GS	8
3/19/83	Furano, Japan	WC GS	16
3/21/83	Furano, Japan	WC P	4

MIKE BROWN

Height—5'10"
Weight—160
Birthdate—March 22, 1962
Birthplace—Vail, Colorado
Residence—Vail, Colorado
Year on National Team—3rd

One of the bright spots for the U.S. men's overall alpine effort in 1983, Mike scored the first World Cup points of his career in Aspen, Colorado with a strong 14th place showing. A good three-event skier, Brown showed his prowess at the U.S. Alpine National Championships in Copper Mountain, Colorado as he claimed the combined award with a third place downhill finish coupled with an eighth in giant slalom and a twelfth in slalom.

Billed primarily as an up-and-coming downhiller, Brown was a member of the U.S. downhill contingent that invaded the Europa Cup circuit in January and he finished ninth in the final Europa Cup downhill standings. In addition to his World Cup scoring effort in Aspen, Mike came right back with a strong 18th place result the following weekend in Lake Louise, Canada in the final World Cup downhill event of the season.

The results were just as consistent on the domestic scene as Brown nailed down third place in the final NorAm downhill standings with results such as a third place showing at Crested Butte, Colorado and a third at Copper Mountain prior to the start of the U.S. Nationals.

Date/Year	Event	Race	Finish
1983	Overall World Cup Standings		94(T)
	World Cup Downhill Standings		34
	Overall Europa Cup Standings		56
	Europa Cup Downhill Standings		9
	Overall NorAm Standings		10
	NorAm Downhill Standings		3

JOHN BUXMAN

Height—5'7"
Weight—150
Birthdate—April 10, 1960
Birthplace—Denver, Colorado
Residence—Vail, Colorado
Year on National Team—4th

The frustration of putting two good runs together continued to plague Buxman during the course of the 1983 season as once again, he alternated between the World Cup and the Europa Cup for the majority of the winter.

The season was not without some bright spots, however, as John finished fourth in the slalom at the U.S. Nationals in Copper Mountain, Colorado and then came back with a sixth place Europa Cup slalom finish in Sella Nevea, Italy. In addition, he was victorious in the NorAm slalom finals at Stratton Mountain, Vermont to end the season tied for 20th in the final NorAm point standings.

Bux posted some excellent results during the 1981 campaign, including an eighth place effort in the World Cup slalom in Kitzbuhel, Austria on a tough icy course that even the Mahres failed to negotiate. He also posted a runnerup finish in the slalom at the Europa Cup Finals that season.

First named to the C Team in 1976, John spent three years on the Development Team. Noted for his quickness and balance, he will be among the group of young technical skiers who are looking to provide some depth behind the Mahres.

Date/Year	Event	Race	Finish
1983	Overall Europa Cup Standings		74
	Europa Cup Slalom Standings		38
	Europa Cup Giant Slalom Standings		41
	Overall NorAm Standings		20(T)

ANDY CHAMBERS

Height—5'10"
Weight—170
Birthdate—May 19, 1961
Birthplace—Jackson, Wyoming
Residence—Jackson, Wyoming
Year on National Team—4th

Chambers played the bridesmaid role on the Europa Cup downhill circuit in 1983 to teammate Bill Johnson as he posted a trio of second place results to Johnson's three victories during the course of the winter. As a result, Andy skied his way to the runnerup spot in the final Europa Cup downhill standings and earned a tenth place tie in the final overall Europa Cup point standings on the season.

Andy equalled his top World Cup downhill showing twice in 1983 with a pair of 22nd place finishes, the first in Val d'Isere, France and the second coming in the final World Cup event of the 1983 season in Lake Louise, Canada. In addition to his European exploits, Chambers claimed a fifth place finish in the second NorAm downhill held in Crested Butte, Colorado as well as an eighth place showing in the U.S. National Alpine Championships at Copper Mountain, Colorado. He ended the 1983 campaign ranked in a tie for sixth place in the final NorAm downhill standings.

A product of the Jackson Ski Club and the Intermountain Race Team, Chambers was first named to the National Junior Team in 1980 and posted some of his top Europa Cup results in 1981 and 82 prior to this past season. Andy comes from an athletic family background which includes alpine and Junior National jumping credentials for his father.

When not on snow, Chambers enjoys cycling, climbing and kayaking.

Date/Year	Event	Race	Finish
1983	Overall Europa Cup Standings		10(T)
	Europa Cup Downhill Standings		2
	NorAm Downhill Standings		6(T)

BILL JOHNSON

Height—5'9"
Weight—170
Birthdate—March 30, 1960
Birthplace—Los Angeles, California
Residence—Van Nuys, California
Year on National Team—3rd

Bill gave the traditional European downhill powers someone else to worry about in 1983 as he became the only American to ever win the overall Europa Cup men's title as well as the first American to ever win a Europa Cup discipline title, winning the downhill crown by virtue of victories in three of the four events run and a runnerup effort in the final race.

Then, if that wasn't enough to turn a few heads on both sides of the Atlantic, he returned to the World Cup circuit and promptly recorded the first World Cup points of his young career with an impressive sixth place result in St. Anton, Austria, 31 hundredths of a second behind teammate Phil Mahre in fifth position. The finishing touch came at the U.S. National Alpine Championships in Copper Mountain, Colorado as Johnson bested the rest of the field to nab the U.S. National Downhill title.

Off to somewhat of a slow start at the outset of the season, Johnson changed his body position once he hit the Europa Cup circuit in January, resulting in the trio of downhill victories in the space of five days. He also picked up what were to be the deciding points for the overall Europa Cup title with a second place combined finish that coupled the downhill in Meribel, France with a giant slalom in Lermoos, Austria. It was these points that enabled Bill to maintain his two-point advantage over France's Frank Piccard.

In addition to Johnson's European heroics, he also skied to first and second place NorAm downhill finishes in Crested Butte, Colorado and Copper Mountain, Colorado to finish second in the final NorAm downhill rankings and 15th overall.

Considering the results of the 1983 season, Johnson should spearhead a group of young U.S. downhillers who are looking to make their mark on the international scene in the years to come.

Date/Year	Event	Race	Finish
1983	Overall World Cup Standings		65(T)
	World Cup Downhill Standings		27(T)
	Overall Europa Cup Standings		1
	Europa Cup Downhill Standings		1
	Overall NorAm Standings		15(T)
	NorAm Downhill Standings		2

ANDY LUHN

Height—5'7"
Weight—152
Birthdate—January 3, 1962
Birthplace—Aspen, Colorado
Residence—Bellevue, Idaho
Year on National Team—2nd

Andy got off to a fast start in his rookie season on the World Cup circuit in 1983, finishing a very respectable 26th in Val Gardena, Italy that coupled with an earlier event to rank him 15th in the initial World Cup combined event of the winter and earn him his first World Cup points. He continued this kind of consistency with a trio of top 25 World Cup downhill results until falls in both days of downhill at Kitzbuhel, Austria damaged his ankle and he was unable to compete in the final European portion of the World Cup downhill season.

Luhn returned to action in Copper Mountain, Colorado for the U.S. National Alpine Championships and placed fifth in the Nationals downhill as well as seventh in the NorAm downhill event that preceded the Championships. Back on the World Cup circuit in Aspen, Colorado, he claimed a 34th place result in "America's Downhill" and followed that up the next weekend with a 35th place showing in the final downhill event of the World Cup calendar in Lake Louise, Canada.

A football, baseball and track athlete for Wood River High School, Luhn claimed a third place finish in downhill at the U.S. National Championships in 1980 in Alaska and placed third in the final combined standings at the Nationals that year. In 1982, he alternated between the World Cup and Europa Cup downhill circuits, finishing 15th in a Europa Cup downhill in Meribel, France.

During the off-season, Andy enjoys windsurfing, tennis and volleyball.

Date/Year	Event	Race	Finish
1983	Overall World Cup Standings		101
	World Cup Combined Standings		43

DOUG POWELL

Height—5'9"
Weight—160
Birthdate—August 28, 1957
Birthplace—Morristown, New Jersey
Residence—Peru, Vermont
Year on National Team—6th

Doug literally weathered the storm of the 1983 season as the veteran of a very young U.S. downhill contingent as falls in both the pre-Olympic downhill in Sarajevo and again at Aspen resulted in a fractured nose and cheekbone. Despite these mishaps, Powell was victorious in two of the three NorAm downhills run this past winter to claim the NorAm downhill title.

Although not scoring World Cup points in 1983, Doug posted several good results including an 18th place effort on the second day of downhill in Kitzbuhel, Austria and a 20th place result in the pre-Olympic downhill event as the lone American entrant. His NorAm victories came at Crested Butte, Colorado and at Copper Mountain, Colorado prior to the start of the U.S. Nationals, the latter on the heels of a training fall that carried him into the woods.

Powell moved to the forefront of the U.S. downhill effort in 1982 with the retirement of Andy Mill, Karl Anderson and Pete Patterson but injuries have continued to plague him throughout the course of his career, 1982 being cut short at the World Championships as he aggravated a previous ankle injury and spent the remainder of the season in the U.S.

"Boog" has cracked the top ten of World Cup downhill twice during the course of his five years on the National Team, the first time in 1979 with a tenth place showing at Morzine, France and the second coming in 1981 with a ninth place finish at Aspen. Following the Aspen result, he went on to capture the U.S. National downhill title in Aleyeska, Alaska. His best career World Cup overall finish came in 1981 as he placed 65th overall and was ranked 27th in downhill points.

Given a completely healthy year in 1984, Powell could well be at the head of the surging U.S. downhill program. When not flying down a mountain, Doug enjoys soccer, tennis, golf and swimming.

Date/Year	Event	Race	Finish
1983	NorAm Overall Standings		13
	NorAm Downhill Standings		1
12/5/82	Pontresina, Switzerland	WC DH	55
12/19/82	Val Gardena, Italy	WC DH	30
12/20/82	Val Gardena, Italy	WC DH	35
1/9/83	Val d'Isere, France	WC DH	28
1/21/83	Kitzbuhel, Austria	WC DH	27
1/22/83	Kitzbuhel, Austria	WC DH	18
1/28/83	Sarajevo, Yugoslavia	WC DH	20
2/10/83	Crested Butte, Colorado	NorAm DH	1
2/11/83	Crested Butte, Colorado	NorAm DH	2
2/15/83	Copper Mountain, Colorado	NorAm DH	1
2/16/83	Copper Mountain, Colorado	U.S. Nat. DH	4
3/6/83	Aspen, Colorado	WC DH	21

TIGER SHAW

Height—5'11"
Weight—175
Birthdate—August 24, 1961
Birthplace—Burlington, Vermont
Residence—Stowe, Vermont
Year On National Team—3rd

Even though the 1983 season was marked by individual success for Tiger, perhaps the most memorable was his victory in giarft slalom at the U.S. National Alpine Championships in Copper Mountain, Colorado as he defeated both Phil and Steve Mahre as well as an extremely stróng domestic field to become a national champion. In addition, Shaw added an FIS B giant slalom win to his portfolio and collected a trio of NorAm giant slalom wins in the spring to claim the NorAm giant slalom title and grab the runnerup position in the final overall NorAm standings.

Winning is nothing new to Shaw, who was the 1982 NCAA slalom champion and placed third in giant slalom at the collegiate championships to earn All American status for Dartmouth College and to be named College Skier of the Year by Ski Racing Magazine. During the 1983 season, he skied to an 18th place ranking in the final Europa Cup giant slalom standings and a 28th place overall finish. His top World Cup finish this past winter came in January in Parpan, Switzerland as he skied to a 28th place slalom finish.

A product of the Mt. Mansfield Ski Club in Stowe, Shaw has also earned Junior Skier of the Year honors in 1981 and was named the first annual Rusty Nail Amateur Athlete of the Year. He attends Dartmouth College, majoring in Engineering Science.

One of the top young technical prospects for the U.S., Tiger posted five top 15 European results during the course of 1983, including his FIS B giant slalom win in Madonna di Campiglio, Italy in January. With this kind of consistency and added experience, he may be ready to head to the World Cup circuit on a full-time basis in the not too distant future.

Date/Year	Event	Race	Finish
1983	Overall Europa Cup Standings		28
	Europa Cup Slalom Standings		56
	Europa Cup Giant Slalom Standings		18
	Overall NorAm Standings		2
	NorAm Slalom Standings		7
	NorAm Giant Slalom Standings		1

THE ATHLETES—WOMEN

CHRISTIN COOPER

Height—5'6"
Weight—125
Birthdate—October 8, 1959
Birthplace—Los Angeles, California
Residence—Sun Valley, Idaho
Year on National Team—8th

The 1983 season was to have been the one in which Christin Cooper continued her assault on the women's World Cup circuit. In 1982, Coop had posted the highest finish ever for an American woman in the final overall standings with her third place showing and brought home a trio of medals from the World Championships, another first for an American, male or female. But 1983 ended for Christin January 28 in Les Diablerets, Switzerland when a downhill training fall resulted in a compression fracture of the bone below the knee and she was on her way back to the states and the magic hands of U.S. Team physician Dr. Richard Steadman.

Steadman elevated the bone and held it in place with a bone graft from Cooper's hip and by April, Super Coop was off crutches and engaging in a little cross-country skiing. Prior to the injury, Cooper sat in fifth position in the women's overall World Cup standings and was coming off an impressive second place giant slalom result in St. Gervais, France behind teammate Tamara McKinney. She had also posted a 16th place result in downhill at Sansicario, Italy and coupled that with a third place slalom showing in Piancavallo, Italy to win the second women's World Cup combined event of the 1983 season.

Given a good spring and summer of rehabilitation and training, Cooper is determined to make up for 1983 and the prognosis is good for a full recovery. She showed the stuff she is made of in 1982 at the World Cup in Waterville Valley, New Hampshire when she finished the final six gates of the slalom on one ski and still managed to finish fourth before being disqualified for straddling the gate where she lost the ski.

Despite missing the final two months of the 1983 season, Christin still found herself in 12th position in the final overall women's World Cup standings as well as 12th in giant slalom and 16th in slalom. Her combined win in Piancavallo left her in ninth position in the final combined rankings.

First named to the B Team in 1976, Cooper was elevated to the A Team in 1977 and was selected to represent the U.S. as a member of the Olympic Team in 1980 at Lake Placid. In those Winter Games, she recorded the best finish for an American woman in both the slalom and the giant slalom, finishing eighth in slalom and seventh in giant slalom. She has also been a member of the 1978 and 1982 World Championship Teams for the U.S., earning a bronze medal in the combined at Schladming, Austria in 1982 along with a pair of silver medals in slalom and giant slalom.

During the off-season, Cooper enjoys a variety of activities, including hiking, swimming and dancing.

Date/Year	Event	Race	Finish
1983	Overall World Cup Standings		12
	World Cup Slalom Standings		16
	World Cup Giant Slalom Standings		12
	World Cup Combined Standings		9
12/7/82	Val d'Isere, France	WC DH	43
12/8/82	Val d'Isere, France	WC GS	9
12/8/82	Val d'Isere, France	WC C	13
12/15/82	Sansicario, Italy	WC DH	16
12/17/82	Piancavallo, Italy	WC SL	3
12/17/82	Piancavallo, Italy	WC C	1
1/9/83	Verbier, Switzerland	WC SGS	23
1/10/83	Verbier, Switzerland	WC SGS	11
1/11/83	Davos, Switzerland	WC SL	4
1/14/83	Schruns, Austria	WC DH	34
1/21/83	Megeve, France	WC DH	31
1/22/83	Megeve, France	WC DH	39
1/23/83	St. Gervais, France	WC GS	2
1/28/83	Les Diablerets, Switzerland		Injured

TAMARA McKINNEY

Height—5'4"
Weight—117
Birthdate—October 16, 1962
Birthplace—Lexington, Kentucky
Residence—Squaw Valley, California
Year on National Team—6th

McKinney skied her way into the World Cup record books in 1983, becoming the first American woman to ever win the women's overall World Cup title. In addition, she joined teammate Phil Mahre as overall champion to mark only the third time in World Cup history that skiers from the same nation have claimed the men's and women's overall World Cup titles in the same season.

Tamara started off the 1983 season fast, winning the initial slalom of the winter in Limone, Italy which marked the first World Cup slalom win of her career. She was to post six more World Cup victories before the conclusion of the season, including a one-two giant slalom finish in St. Gervais, France with Christin Cooper as well as winning three of the last four giant slaloms of the season.

In addition to the overall title, McKinney also claimed the World Cup giant slalom championship for the second time in her career, the first coming in 1981. That initial giant slalom honor made her the first American woman since Marilyn Cochran in 1969 to capture that discipline title. She also claimed the runnerup slalom spot in 1983.

On the domestic front, McKinney, who came off of a broken hand that hampered her for most of the 1982 season, captured both the slalom and the giant slalom titles at the U.S. National Alpine Championships in Copper Mountain, Colorado, winning the slalom by close to one and one half seconds and staging a come-from-behind second run effort to claim the giant slalom national title. She was also to post the best World Cup downhill finish of her career in 1983 with a 19th place result in the opening downhill of the winter in Val d'Isere, France.

First named to the Development Team in 1978, McKinney was a member of the 1980 Olympic Team in Lake Placid. In addition, she has been a member of the 1982 World Championship Team for the U.S., placing sixth in giant slalom.

An accomplished equestrian, McKinney enjoys training and riding horses on the family farm in Lexington during the off-season. She is also a good figure skater and uses skating as a diversion from the rigors of the World Cup circuit during the winter.

Date/Year	Event	Race	Finish
1983	Overall World Cup Standings		1
	World Cup Slalom Standings		2
	World Cup Giant Slalom Standings		1
	World Cup Combined Standings		6
12/7/82	Val d'Isere, France	WC DH	19
12/8/82	Val d'Isere, France	WC GS	2
12/8/82	Val d'Isere, France	WC C	2
12/10/82	Limone, Italy	WC SL	1
12/15/82	Sansicario, Italy	WC DH	45
1/9/83	Verbier, Switzerland	WC SGS	3
1/10/83	Verbier, Switzerland	WC SGS	4
1/11/83	Davos, Switzerland	WC SL	1
1/23/83	St. Gervais, France	WC GS	1
1/29/83	Les Diablerets, Switzerland	WC DH	53
1/30/83	Les Diablerets, Switzerland	WC SL	6
1/30/83	Les Diablerets, Switzerland	WC C	6
2/18/83	Copper Mountain, Colorado	U.S. Nat. SL	1
2/19/83	Copper Mountain, Colorado	U.S. Nat. GS	1
3/8/83	Waterville Valley, New Hampshire	WC SL	2
3/9/83	Waterville Valley, New Hampshire	WC GS	1
3/10/83	Waterville Valley, New Hampshire	WC GS	1
3/12/83	Vail, Colorado	WC GS	1
3/18/83	Furano, Japan	WC GS	12
3/20/83	Furano, Japan	WC SL	1
3/21/83	Furano, Japan	WC P	9

MARIA MARICICH

Height—5'6"
Weight—135
Birthdate—March 30, 1961
Birthplace—Sun Valley, Idaho
Residence—Sun Valley, Idaho
Year on National Team—4th

The 1983 World Cup downhill season will always be one of "What If" for Maria Maricich. What if she had not been injured midway through the season after posting some impressive results in Megeve, France. What if she had been able to come back before the conclusion of the season.

Unfortunately, no one will ever know the answers to those questions but they still remain. The past two years have been spent trying to get things back together following a total knee reconstruction as a result of another downhill mishap in Altenmarkt, Austria. But, things had apparently come back together in mid-1983 as Maria shocked the women's World Cup downhill family with a second place finish in Megeve on January 21, a mere 19 hundredths of a second off the winner's time. And to make things more impressive, she accomplished that feat starting 40th in the field. The following day in Megeve, she was again the top American finisher, this time in 17th position.

But then came Les Diablerets, Switzerland. The same course had already taken Christin Cooper from the American camp for the remainder of the season with a knee injury prior to the actual race day and midway down the course on race day, Maricich suffered a fall that resulted in a broken collarbone and torn ligaments in her thumb. Both girls returned to the U.S. to sit out the rest of the season.

Named to the National Team in 1981, Maria has been a member of the 1982 World Championship Team and placed 26th in downhill at the championships in Schladming, Austria. Prior to her result at Megeve this past season, Maricich's top World Cup downhill finish came in the form of a point scoring 15th place result in Piancavallo, Italy during the 1981 season. She skied to a sixth place downhill finish at the U.S. National Downhill Championships in Sugarloaf, Maine in 1982.

During the off-season, Maria is attending classes at the University of Utah in Salt Lake City and given her performances in 1983, the coming season may well be the answer to "What If" as she moves into the first seed for downhill.

Date/Year	Event	Race	Finish
1983	Overall World Cup Standings		48
	World Cup Downhill Standings		20(T)
12/7/82	Val d'Isere, France	WC DH	47
12/15/82	Sansicario, Italy	WC DH	33
1/14/83	Schruns, Austria	WC DH	43
1/21/83	Megeve, France	WC DH	2
1/22/83	Megeve, France	WC DH	17
1/29/83	Les Diablerets, Switzerland	WC DH	Injured

CINDY NELSON

Height—5'6"
Weight—140
Birthdate—August 19, 1955
Birthplace—Duluth, Minnesota
Residence—Reno, Nevada
Year on National Team—13th

The European press calls her "Die Alte Amerikanerin", American race fans and teammates know her as "Nellie", and the world of international ski racing counts her as one of the greats. But, no matter what you call her, Cindy Nelson has distinguished herself as not only one of the best ski racers this country has ever produced, but one of the great athletes as well.

At 27-years-old and competing as the oldest woman on the World Cup circuit in 1983, Nellie showed the "youngsters" how it should be done January 10 in Verbier, Switzerland as she took the second day of super giant slalom, the World Cup's newest event, and turned it into a perfect run according to some World Cup veterans and the seventh win of her illustrious career.

Once again, as it has been so many times during the course of her career, consistency was the name of the game as Cindy failed to finish in just two of the 28 races she entered in 1983. Still racing in all three disciplines, she has been proclaimed as the unofficial World Cup queen of super giant slalom, having won the trial event prior to the 1982 World Cup Finals as well

as winning and placing fourth in the two days at Verbier this past season.

Nelson scored an impressive second place ranking in the final World Cup giant slalom standings behind teammate Tamara McKinney in 1983 as well as collecting the seventh spot in the final overall standings, 25th in downhill, 39th in slalom and finished the season tied for ninth in the World Cup combined point standings. She was the top U.S. woman finisher in the pre-Olympic downhill, the only women's event able to be held in Sarajevo, Yugoslavia in 1983, placing seventh.

When not racing, her hobbies include fishing, biking, tennis and photography.

Date/Year	Event	Race	Finish
1983	Overall World Cup Standings		7
	World Cup Downhill Standings		25
	World Cup Slalom Standings		39
	World Cup Giant Slalom Standings		2
	World Cup Combined Standings		9(T)
12/7/82	Val d'Isere, France	WC DH	15
12/8/82	Val d'Isere, France	WC GS	25
12/8/82	Val d'Isere, France	WC C	9
12/10/82	Limone, Italy	WC SL	20
12/15/82	Sansicario, Italy	WC DH	23
12/17/82	Piancavallo, Italy	WC SL	41
12/17/82	Sansicario,/Piancavallo	WC C	16
1/9/83	Verbier, Switzerland	WC SGS	4
1/10/83	Verbier, Switzerland	WC SGS	1
1/16/83	Schruns, Austria	WC SL	20
1/21/83	Megeve, France	WC DH	21
1/22/83	Megeve, France	WC DH	28
1/22/83	Schruns/Megeve	WC C	6
1/23/83	St. Gervais, France	WC GS	10
1/29/83	Les Diablerets, Switzerland	WC DH	13
1/30/83	Les Diablerets, Switzerland	WC SL	17
1/30/83	Les Diablerets, Switzerlnd	WC C	4
2/5/83	Sarajevo, Yugoslavia	WC DH	7
2/15/83	Copper Mountain, Colorado	NorAm DH	3
2/16/83	Copper Mountain, Colorado	U.S. Nat. DH	4
2/18/83	Copper Mountain, Colorado	U.S. Nat. SL	6
2/19/83	Copper Mountain, Colorado	U.S. Nat. GS	3
2/19/83	Copper Mountain, Colorado	U.S. Nat. C	1
3/5/83	Mont Tremblant, Canada	WC DH	17
3/6/83	Mont Tremblant, Canada	WC GS	11
3/9/83	Waterville Valley, New Hampshire	WC GS	5
3/10/83	Waterville Valley, New Hampshire	WC GS	3
3/12/83	Vail, Colorado	WC GS	2
3/18/83	Furano, Japan	WC GS	6
3/20/83	Furano, Japan	WC SL	15
3/21/83	Furano, Japan	WC P	5

B-TEAM—WOMEN

DEBBIE ARMSTRONG

Height—5'5"
Weight—137
Birthdate—December 6, 1963
Birthplace—Salem, Oregon
Residence—Seattle, Washington
Year on National Team—2nd

One of the very pleasant surprises that the U.S. Alpine Women's Program experienced in 1983, Debbie scored the first World Cup points of her young career December 8 with a 14th place showing in the World Cup giant slalom opener in Val d'Isere, France and the results continued to roll in. She finished the 1983 season scoring Cup points in eight races over the course of the winter.

Coming off a broken leg suffered in Schaldming, Austria in 1982 after having been named to the World Championship Team, Armstrong stunned the World Cup downhill circuit with a fifth place finish in Les Diablerets, Switzerland, starting in the third seed, along with a seventh place showing in Sansicario, Italy, starting 40th in the field. She finished the 1983 season as the top ranked U.S. woman in the World Cup downhill standings, holding down 19th position.

On the domestic scene, she claimed the runnerup spot in the U.S. Nationals giant slalom at Copper Mountain, Colorado to Tamara McKinney after leading the overall World Cup champion following the first run. She also finished second in the combined event behind Cindy Nelson.

A product of the Alpental Race Program, Armstrong was named to the U.S. National Junior Team for 1982. While a student at Garfield High School, Debbie was named the Most Valuable Player for two years in both basketball and soccer.

Coming from a diverse family background where both parents teach skiing, Debbie spent her seventh grade year living in Malaysia.

Date/Year	Event	Race	Finish
1983	Overall World Cup Standings		33(T)
	World Cup Downhill Standings		19
	World Cup Giant Slalom Standings		26
	World Cup Combined Standings		20
12/8/82	Val d'Isere, France	WC GS	14
12/8/82	Val d'Isere, France	WC C	11
12/15/82	Sansicario, Italy	WC DH	7
12/17/82	Sansicario/Piancavallo	WC C	11
1/10/83	Verbier, Switzerland	WC SGS	13
1/23/83	St. Gervais, France	WC GS	22
1/29/83	Les Diablerets, Switzerland	WC DH	5
2/15/83	Copper Mountain, Colorado	NorAm DH	5
2/16/83	Copper Mountain, Colorado	U.S. Nat. DH	10
2/18/83	Copper Mountain, Colorado	U.S. Nat. SL	7
2/19/83	Copper Mountain, Colorado	U.S. Nat. GS	2
2/19/83	Copper Mountain, Colorado	U.S. Nat. C	2
3/5/83	Mont Tremblant, Canada	WC DH	14
3/6/83	Mont Tremblant, Canada	WC GS	19
3/8/83	Waterville Valley, New Hampshire	WC SL	27
3/9/83	Waterville Valley, New Hampshire	WC GS	28
3/12/83	Vail, Colorado	WC GS	12

HEIDI BOWES

Height—5'7"
Weight—130
Birthdate—December 9, 1962
Birthplace—Steamboat Springs, Colorado
Residence—Steamboat Springs, Colorado
Year on National Team—3rd

Heidi has been on the verge for the last several seasons and 1983 was the breakthrough year as she makes the move to B Team status for the 1984 season after a pair of successful campaigns on the Europa Cup circuit. The tip of the iceberg could well be her first Europa Cup victory which occurred at the beginning of February in Semmering, Austria in giant slalom en route to a ninth place overall finish in the final women's Europa Cup standings.

Bowes alternated between the World Cup circuit and Europa Cup during the course of last winter, her top World Cup showing coming as a 29th place slalom finish in Limone, Italy. On the home front, she claimed the runnerup spot in slalom behind Tamara McKinney at the U.S. Alpine Nationals at Copper Mountain, Colorado while posting an 11th place downhill showing.

A product of the Steamboat Springs Winter Sports Club, Bowes finished 1982 in second place in the NorAm giant slalom standings and she placed second overall in the 1981 Elbert Series standings with ten top three finishes.

Heidi began competitive ski racing at the age of three and lists pottery, art and knitting as her hobbies outside of skiing. She intends on making college part of her future and would like to investigate a career in Sports Physiology.

Date/Year	Event	Race	Finish
1983	Overall Europa Cup Standings		9
	Europa Cup Slalom Standings		10
	Europa Cup Giant Slalom Standings		10
12/8/82	Val d'Isere, France	WC GS	53
12/10/82	Limone, Italy	WC SL	29
12/15/82	Sansicario, Italy	WC DH	66
2/2/83	Semmering, Austria	EC GS	1
2/15/83	Copper Mountain, Colorado	NorAm DH	6
2/16/83	Copper Mountain, Colorado	U.S. Nat. DH	11
2/18/83	Copper Mountain, Colorado	U.S. Nat. SL	2
2/26/83	Immenstadt, West Germany	EC SL	7
2/27/83	Immenstadt, West Germany	EC SL	3
3/10/83	Bled, Yugoslavia	EC GS	17
3/14/83	Abetone, Italy	EC SL	7
3/18/83	Pamparova, Bulgaria	EC SL	7

HOLLY FLANDERS

Height—5'6"
Weight—143
Birthdate—December 26, 1957
Birthplace—Arlington, Massachusetts
Residence—Deerfield, New Hampshire
Year on National Team—7th

The 1982 World Cup downhill runnerup had her share of problems this past winter returning to the form that brought her within one race of the top of the downhill standings. Holly was able to record a pair of World Cup scoring results in 1983, the first coming as an eighth-place effort in Megeve, France and the second coming at the pre-Olympics in Sarajevo, Yugoslavia with a 13th place result.

Once back in the states, the results looked more like the Holly of a year ago as she captured the NorAm downhill that was run prior to the start of the U.S. National Alpine Championships in Copper Mountain, Colorado and then earned the runnerup spot in the Nationals downhill.

During 1982, Holly became the first American since Cindy Nelson to win a World Cup downhill in the last ten years in Bad Gastein, Austria and then followed that up with the second World Cup victory of her career in Arosa, Switzerland, a win that sparked an historic one-two-six U.S. finish with Nelson and Cindy Oak.

First named to the Development Team in 1976, Flanders worked her way to the B Team in 1977 and the 1979 season found her as a member of the A Team. She was selected to represent the U.S. in the 1980 Olympics at Lake Placid and placed 14th in the downhill. In addition, she was a member of the 1982 World Championship Team for the U.S. and skied to a ninth place downhill finish in Schladming, Austria.

Holly is a product of Burke Mountain Academy and has attended Middlebury College. An accomplished windsurfer in the off-season, Holly also spends time competing in bicycle races throughout the state of New Hampshire and the surrounding area.

Date/Year	Event	Race	Finish
1983	Overall World Cup Standings		54(T)
	World Cup Downhill Standings		26(T)
12/7/82	Val d'Isere, France	WC DH	36
12/15/82	Sansicario, Italy	WC DH	36
1/9/83	Verbier, Switzerland	WC SGS	27
1/10/83	Verbier, Switzerland	WC SGS	30
1/21/83	Megeve, France	WC DH	8(T)
1/22/83	Megeve, France	WC DH	29(T)
2/5/83	Sarajevo, Yugoslavia	WC DH	13
2/15/83	Copper Mountain, Colorado	NorAm DH	1
2/16/83	Copper Mountain, Colorado	U.S. Nat. DH	2
2/18/83	Copper Mountain, Colorado	U.S. Nat. SL	18
2/19/83	Copper Mountain, Colorado	U.S. Nat. GS	9

PAM FLETCHER

Height—5'6"
Weight—132
Birthdate—January 30, 1963
Birthplace—Concord, Massachusetts
Residence—Acton, Massachusetts
Year on National Team—4th

Life on the World Cup circuit might have been tough for Fletcher in her rookie season on the White Circus but there was no substitute for being home as she captured the downhill title at the U.S. National Championships in Copper Mountain, Colorado, outdistancing the likes of Holly Flanders, Cindy Nelson and Cindy Oak. With that win under her belt, Pam went on to score the first World Cup points of her young career with a seventh place downhill result in Mont Tremblant, Canada, the final downhill stop for the women in 1983.

A three-time NorAm downhill champion in 1981, 82 and 83, Fletcher placed tenth and third respectively the last two years in the women's overall NorAm standings. A product of Stratton Mountain School, Pam was named to the National Junior Team in 1981.

With added confidence down the stretch this past winter and a full year of World Cup experience under her belt, Pam could well become a force to be reckoned with on the World Cup women's downhill circuit in the near future.

Date/Year	Event	Race	Finish
1983	Overall World Cup Standings		58(T)
	World Cup Downhill Standings		30
	Overall NorAm Standings		10
	NorAm Downhill Standings		1
12/15/82	Sansicario, Italy	WC DH	37
1/22/83	Megeve, France	WC DH	37
2/5/83	Sarajevo, Yugoslavia	WC DH	40
2/15/83	Copper Mountain, Colorado	NorAm DH	4
2/16/83	Copper Mountain, Colorado	U.S. Nat. DH	1
2/18/83	Copper Mountain, Colorado	U.S. Nat. SL	15
3/5/83	Mont Tremblant, Canada	WC DH	7

HEIDI PREUSS

Height—5'4"
Weight—140
Birthdate—March 18, 1961
Birthplace—Laconia, New Hampshire
Residence—Lakeport, New Hampshire
Year on National Team—8th

The comeback trail got a little easier for Heidi in 1983 as she had a trio of World Cup scoring races during the course of the winter, her top finishes coming in the form of a pair of 13th place results, the first in giant slalom in St. Gervais, France and the second coming in slalom at Les Diablerets, Switzerland.

Injuries have been a nagging part of Preuss' career on the U.S. Team as she missed all of the 1978 season with a back injury and underwent extensive knee surgery following a fall at the finish line of the U.S. Nationals downhill in 1980. She then promptly suffered a second knee injury the following season while competing at Aspen.

On the domestic scene in 1983, Heidi recorded a fifth place finish in slalom at the U.S. Nationals in Copper Mountain, Colorado along with a strong showing in NorAm competition, including a giant slalom win in Bromont, Canada and a trio of second place efforts, also in giant slalom.

Highlighting her career was a fourth place result in the 1980 Olympic downhill in Lake Placid which proved to be the highest finish for a U.S. alpine woman during the course of the Winter Games. In addition, she also skied her way to the finals of the World Cup parallel competition in 1979, losing out in the final run to Austria's legendary Annemarie Moser-Proell. The 1980 season saw her ranked seventh in the final World Cup downhill standings and 11th overall.

Named to the Development Team in 1976, Heidi advanced to the B Team the following year and moved to the A Team in 1978. She was named Ski Racing's Junior Alpine Competitor of the Year in 1977 after claiming the CanAm Series overall, slalom and giant slalom championships.

During the off-season, Heidi attends the University of Utah in Salt Lake City and she lists windsurfing, soccer and tennis as hobbies.

Date	Event	Race	Finish
1983	Overall World Cup Standings		64(T)
	World Cup Slalom Standings		35(T)
	World Cup Giant Slalom Standings		29(T)
12/10/82	Limone, Italy	WC SL	21(T)
1/9/83	Verbier, Switzerland	WC SGS	15
1/10/83	Verbier, Switzerland	WC SGS	17
1/23/83	St. Gervais, France	WC GS	13
1/30/83	Les Diablerets, Switzerland	WC SL	13
2/18/83	Copper Mountain, Colorado	U.S. Nat. SL	5
3/9/83	Waterville Valley, New Hampshire	WC GS	24
3/10/83	Waterville Valley, New Hampshire	WC GS	24
3/12/83	Vail, Colorado	WC GS	35

U.S. OLYMPIC AND WORLD CHAMPIONSHIP ALPINE RESULTS
(Includes top 10 finishes if available)

1936 Olympics
Innsbruck, Austria

Dick Durrance, 10th Combined

1937 World Championships
Chamonix, France

Clarita Heath, 4th Downhill

1938 World Championships
Engelberg, Switzerland

Marion McKean, 6th Downhill

1948 Olympics
St. Moritz, Switzerland

Gretchen Fraser, 1st Slalom
2nd Combined
Jack Reddish, 7th Slalom

1950 World Championships
Aspen, Colorado

Jack Reddish, 4th Slalom
Katy Rudolph, 5th Downhill
Andrea Mead, 6th Slalom

1952 Olympics
Oslo, Norway

Andrea Mead Lawrence, 1st Slalom
1st Giant Slalom
Bill Beck, 5th Downhill
Imogene Opton, 5th Slalom
Katy Rudolph, 5th Giant Slalom
Brooks Dodge, 6th(T) Giant Slalom
9th Slalom

1954 World Championships
Are, Sweden

Jannette Burr, 3rd Giant Slalom
4th Downhill
Brooks Dodge, 4th Combined
Katy Rudolph, 5th Combined

1956 Olympics
Cortina d'Ampezzo, Italy

Brooks Dodge, 4th Slalom
15th Giant Slalom
Andrea Mead Lawrence
4th Giant Slalom

1958 World Championships
Bad Gastein, Austria

Sally Deaver, 2nd Giant Slalom
Buddy Werner, 4th Slalom
5th Giant Slalom

1960 Olympics
Squaw Valley, California

Penny Pitou, 2nd Downhill
2nd Giant Slalom
Betsy Snite, 2nd Slalom
4th Giant Slalom
Tom Corcoran, 4th Giant Slalom
9th Slalom
Rennie Cox, 9th Slalom

1962 World Championships
Chamonix, France

Barbara Ferries, 3rd Downhill
5th Giant Slalom
Joan Hannah, 3rd Giant Slalom
Buddy Werner, 5th Giant Slalom
Jimmie Heuga, 5th Combined
Linda Meyers, 5th Combined
Jean Saubert, 6th Giant Slalom

1964 Olympics
Innsbruck, Austria

Billy Kidd, 2nd Slalom
3rd Combined
7th Giant Slalom
Jean Saubert, 3rd Slalom
3rd Giant Slalom
4th Combined
Jimmie Heuga, 3rd Slalom
Buddy Werner, 8th Slalom

1966 World Championships
Portillo, Chile

Penny McCoy, 3rd Slalom
Jimmie Heuga, 4th Combined
6th Slalom
Jean Saubert, 4th Slalom
Cathy Allen, 5th Slalom
Suzy Chaffee, 5th Downhill

1968 Olympics
Grenoble, France

Spider Sabich, 5th Slalom
Billy Kidd, 5th Giant Slalom
Jimmie Heuga, 7th Slalom
10th Giant Slalom
Rick Chaffee, 9th Slalom

1970 World Championships
Val Gardena, Italy

Billy Kidd, 1st Combined
3rd Slalom
5th(T) Downhill
Barbara Anne Cochran, 2nd Slalom
4th Combined
9th Giant Slalom
Marilyn Cochran, 3rd Combined
6th Slalom
6th Giant Slalom
9th Downhill
Judy Nagel, 5th Slalom

1972 Olympics
Sapporo, Japan

Barbara Anne Cochran, 1st Slalom
Susie Corrock, 3rd Downhill
        9th(T) Slalom
Patty Boydstun, 8th Slalom
Bob Cochran, 8th Downhill
Tyler Palmer, 9th Slalom

1974 World Championships
St. Moritz, Switzerland

Barbara Anne Cochran
        6th Giant Slalom
Marilyn Cochran, 8th Giant Slalom

1976 Olympics
Innsbruck, Austria

Cindy Nelson, 3rd Downhill
        4th Combined
Lindy Cochran, 6th Slalom
Greg Jones, 9th Giant Slalom
        3rd Combined
Phil Mahre, 5th Giant Slalom
Andy Mill, 6th Downhill
Mary Seaton, 10th Slalom

1978 World Championships
Garmisch-Partenkirchen,
West Germany

Pete Patterson, 3rd Combined
        8th Giant Slalom
Phil Mahre, 5th Giant Slalom
Cindy Nelson, 2nd Combined
        7th Downhill
Heidi Preuss, 4th Downhill
Pete Patterson, 5th Downhill
Christin Cooper, 7th Giant Slalom
        8th Slalom

1980 Olympics
Lake Placid, New York

Phil Mahre, 1st Combined, 2nd Slalom
Cindy Nelson, 2nd Combined, 7th Downhill
Heidi Preuss, 4th Downhill
Pete Patterson, 5th Downhill
Christin Cooper, 7th Giant Slalom, 8th Slalom

1982 World Championships
Schladming, Austria

Steve Mahre, 1st Giant Slalom
Christin Cooper, 2nd Slalom
        2nd Giant Slalom
        3rd Combined
Cindy Nelson, 2nd Downhill

1983 WORLD CUP MEN'S FINAL STANDINGS
(Following thirty-two events and five combineds)

OVERALL

1.	PHIL MAHRE, USA	285
2.	Ingemar Stenmark, Swe.	218
3.	Andreas Wenzel, Lie.	176
4.	Marc Girardelli, Lux.	168
5.	Peter Lluescher, Sui.	164
6.	Pirmin Zurbriggen, Sui.	161
7.	Peter Mueller, Sui.	125
8.	Max Julen, Sui.	116
9.	Franz Gruber, Aut.	112
	Bojan Krizaj, Yug.	112
12.	STEVE MAHRE, USA	108
65.	BILL JOHNSON, USA	10
94.	MIKE BROWN, USA	2
	TRIS COCHRANE, USA	2
101.	ANDY LUHN, USA	1

DOWNHILL
(11 Events)

1.	Franz Klammer, Aut.	95
2.	Conradin Cathomen, Sui.	92
3.	Harti Weirather, Aut.	74
4.	Erwin Resch, Aut.	73
5.	Urs Raeber, Sui.	72
	Peter Lluescher, Sui.	72
7.	Peter Mueller, Sui	71
8.	Ken Read, Can.	69
9.	Todd Brooker, Can.	67
10.	Helmut Hoeflehner, Aut.	65
18.	PHIL MAHRE, USA	28
27.	BILL JOHNSON, USA	10
34.	MIKE BROWN, USA	2

SLALOM
(11 Events)

1.	Ingemar Stenmark, Swe.	110*
	Stig Strand, Swe.	110
3.	Andreas Wenzel, Lie.	92
4.	STEVE MAHRE, USA	80
5.	Bojan Krizaj, Yug.	78
6.	PHIL MAHRE, USA	75
7.	Marc Girardelli, Lux.	69
8.	Paolo DeChiesa, It.	67
9.	Franz Gruber, Aut.	66
10.	Christian Orlainsky, Aut.	62

GIANT SLALOM
(10 Events)

1.	PHIL MAHRE, USA	107
2.	Ingemar Stenmark, Swe.	100
	Max Julen, Sui.	100
4.	Pirmin Zurbriggen, Sui.	90
5.	Hans Enn, Aut.	83
6.	Marc Girardelli, Lux.	52
7.	Peter Lluescher, Sui.	51
8.	Jure Franko, Yug.	50
	Robert Erlacher, It.	50
10.	Jacques Luethy, Sui.	44

COMBINED
(5 Combineds)

1.	PHIL MAHRE, USA	75
2.	Pirmin Zurbriggen, Sui.	47
	Marc Girardelli, Lux.	47
4.	Peter Lluescher, Sui.	41
5.	Andreas Wenzel, Lie.	40
6.	Silvano Meli, Sui.	29

7.	Urs Raeber, Sui	27
	Peter Mueller, Sui.	27
9.	Franz Heinzer, Sui.	25
10.	Bruno Kernen, Sui.	22
12.	STEVE MAHRE, USA	15
41.	TRIS COCHRANE, USA	2
43.	ANDY LUHN, USA	1

NATION'S CUP
(Men)

1.	Switzerland	1210
2.	Austria	944
3.	Sweden	464
4.	UNITED STATES	440
5.	Italy	364

NATIONS CUP
(Overall)

1.	Switzerland	1882
2.	Austria	1517
3.	UNITED STATES	978
4.	France	690
5.	Italy	569

*Stenmark awarded slalom title because of more World Cup victories than Strand.

1983 WORLD CUP WOMEN'S FINAL STANDINGS
(Following twenty-six events and four combineds)

OVERALL

1.	TAMARA McKINNEY, USA	225
2.	Hanni Wenzel, Lie.	193
3.	Erika Hess, Sui.	192
4.	Elisabeth Kirchler, Aut.	163
5.	Maria Walliser, Sui.	135
6.	Irene Epple, BRD	117
7.	CINDY NELSON, USA	115
8.	Olga Charvatova, Tch.	111
9.	Marile Epple, BRD	108
10.	Doris DeAgostini, Sui.	96
12.	CHRISTIN COOPER, USA	87
33.	DEBBIE ARMSTRONG, USA	41
48.	MARIA MARICICH, USA	20
54.	HOLLY FLANDERS, USA	11
58.	PAM FLETCHER, USA	9
64.	HEIDI PREUSS, USA	7
66.	EVA TWARDOKENS, USA	5

DOWNHILL
(8 Events)

1.	Doris DeAgostini, Sui.	105
2.	Maria Walliser, Sui.	97
3.	Elisabeth Kirchler, Aut.	76
4.	Caroline Attia, Fra.	66
5.	Laurie Graham, Can.	63
6.	Elisabeth Chaud, Fra.	50
7.	Jana Gantnerova-Soltysova, Tch.	47
8.	Claudine Emonet, Fra.	44
9.	Lea Soelkner, Aut.	40
10.	Ariane Ehrat, Sui.	39
19.	DEBBIE ARMSTRONG, USA	22
20.	MARIA MARICICH, USA	20
25.	CINDY NELSON, USA	13
26.	HOLLY FLANDERS, USA	11
30.	PAM FLETCHER, USA	9

SLALOM
(9 Events)

1.	Erika Hess, Sui	110
2.	TAMARA McKINNEY, USA	105
3.	Maria Rosa Quario, It.	89
4.	Hanni Wenzel, Lie.	82
5.	Roswitha Steiner, Aut.	70
6.	Anni Kronbichler, Aut.	66
7.	Malgorzata Tlalka, Pol.	65
8.	Dorata Tlalka, Pol.	54
9.	Daniela Zini, It.	47
10.	Petra Wenzel, Lie.	46
16.	CHRISTIN COOPER, USA	27
35.	HEIDI PREUSS, USA	3
39.	CINDY NELSON, USA	1

GIANT SLALOM
(9 Events)

1.	TAMARA McKINNEY, USA	120
2.	CINDY NELSON, USA	83
3.	Marile Epple, BRD	81
4.	Erika Hess, Sui.	78
5.	Hanni Wenzel, Lie.	77

6.	Fabienne Serrat, Fra.	68
7.	Irene Epple, BRD	65
8.	Anne Flore Rey, Fra.	64
9.	Elisabeth Kirchler, Aut.	46
10.	Maria Walliser, Sui.	40
12.	CHRISTIN COOPER, USA	32
26.	DEBBIE ARMSTRONG, USA	9
29.	HEIDI PREUSS, USA	4

COMBINED
(4 Combineds)

1.	Hanni Wenzel, Lie.	52
2.	Elisabeth Kirchler, Aut.	47
3.	Erika Hess, Sui	35
4.	Irene Epple, BRD	32
5.	Olga Charvatova, Tch.	31
6.	TAMARA McKINNEY, USA	30
7.	CINDY NELSON, USA	29
	Sylvia Eder, Aut.	29
9.	CHRISTIN COOPER, USA.	28
10.	Heidi Wiesler, BRD	22
	Brigette Oertli, Sui.	22
20.	DEBBIE ARMSTRONG, USA	10
24.	EVA TWARDOKENS, USA	5

NATIONS CUP
(Women)

1.	Switzerland	672
2.	France	574
3.	Austria	573
4.	UNITED STATES	538
5.	West Germany	378

YEAR BY YEAR WORLD CUP OVERALL RESULTS

Year Men

1967　1. Jean Claude Killy, Fra.
　　　2. Heini Messner, Aut.
　　　3. Guy Perillat, Fra.

1968　1. Jean Claude Killy, Fra.
　　　2. Dumeng Giovanoli, Sui.
　　　3. Herbert Huber, Aut.
　　　7. BILLY KIDD, USA

1969　1. Karl Schranz, Aut.
　　　2. Jean Noel Augert, Fra.
　　　3. Reinhard Tristcher, Aut.

1970　1. Karl Schranz, Aut.
　　　2. Patrick Russell, Fra.
　　　3. Gustavo Thoeni, It.

1971　1. Gustavo Thoeni, It.
　　　2. Henri Duvillard, Fra.
　　　3. Patrick Russell, Fra.
　　　10. TYLER PALMER, USA

1972　1. Gustavo Thoeni, It.
　　　2. Henri Duvillard, Fra.
　　　3. Edmund Bruggermann, Sui
　　　9. MIKE LAFFERTY, USA

1973　1. Gustavo Thoeni, It.
　　　2. David Zwilling, Aut.
　　　3. Roland Collombin, Sui.
　　　8. BOB COCHRAN, USA.

1974　1. Piero Gros, It.
　　　2. Gustavo Thoeni, It.
　　　3. Hans Hinterseer, Aut.

1975　1. Gustavo Thoeni, It.
　　　2. Ingemar Stenmark, Swe.
　　　3. Franz Klammer, Aut.

1976　1. Ingemar Stenmark, Swe.
　　　2. Piero Gros, It.
　　　3. Gustavo Thoeni, It.

1977　1. Ingemar Stenmark, Swe.
　　　2. Klaus Heidegger, Aut.
　　　3. Franz Klammer, Aut.
　　　9. PHIL MAHRE, USA

1978　1. Ingemar Stenmark, Swe.
　　　2. PHIL MAHRE, USA
　　　3., Andreas Wenzel, Lie.

1979　1. Peter Luescher, Sui.
　　　2. Leonard Stock, Aut.
　　　3. PHIL MAHRE, USA
　　　10. STEVE MAHRE, USA

1980　1. Andreas Wenzel, Lie.
　　　2. Ingemar Stenmark, Swe.
　　　3. PHIL MAHRE, USA
　　　12. STEVE MAHRE, USA

1981　1. PHIL MAHRE, USA
　　　2. Ingemar Stenmark, Swe.
　　　3. Alexander Zhirov, USSR
　　　4. STEVE MAHRE, USA

1982　1. PHIL MAHRE, USA
　　　2. Ingemar Stenmark, Swe.
　　　3. STEVE MAHRE, USA

1983　1. PHIL MAHRE, USA
　　　2. Ingemar Stenmark, Swe.
　　　3. Andreas Wenzel, Lie.
　　　12. STEVE MAHRE, USA

Year Women

1967　1. Nancy Greene, Can.
　　　2. Marielle Goitschel, Fra.
　　　3. Annie Famose, Fra.

1968　1. Nancy Greene, Can.
　　　2. Isabelle Mir, Fra.
　　　3. Florence Steurer, Fra.
　　　9. KIKI CUTTER, USA

1969 1. Gertrud Gabl, Aut.
      2. Florence Steurer, Fra.
      3. Wilfrud Drexel, Aut.
      4. KIKI CUTTER, USA
      9. JUDY NAGEL, USA

1970 1. Michele Jacot, Fra.
      2. Francoise Macchi, Fra.
      3. Florence Steurer, Fra.
      5. BARBARA COCHRAN,
         USA
      6. JUDY NAGEL, USA

1971 1. Annemarie Proell, Aut.
      2. Michele Jacot, Fra.
      3. Isabelle Mir, Fra.
      8. BARBARA COCHRAN
         USA

1972 1. Annemarie Proell, Aut
      2. Francoise Macchi, Fra.
      3. Britt Lafforgue, Fra.

1973 1. Annemarie Proell, Aut.
      2. Monika Kaserer, Aut.
      3. Patricia Emonet, Fra.
      8. MARILYN COCHRAN,
         USA

1974 1. Annemarie Proell, Aut.
      2. Monika Kaserer, Aut.
      3. Hanni Wenzel, Lie.

1975 1. Annemarie Moser-
         Proell, Aut.
      2. Hanni Wenzel, Lie.
      3. Rosi Mittermaier,
         BRD
      8. CINDY NELSON, USA

1976 1. Rosi Mittermaier
         BRD
      2. Lise-Marie Morerod, Sui
      3. Monika Kaserer, Aut.
      8. CINDY NELSON, USA

1977 1. Lise-Marie Morerod,
         Sui.
      2. Annemarie Moser-
         Proell, Aut.
      3. Monika Kaserer, Aut.

1978 1. Hanni Wenzel, Lie.
      2. Annemarie Moser-
         Proell, Aut.
      3. Lise-Marie Morerod,
         Sui.
      5. CINDY NELSON, USA
      13. BECKY DORSEY, USA
      15. ABBI FISHER, USA

1979 1. Annemarie Moser-
         Proell, Aut.
      2. Hanni Wenzel, Lie.
      3. Irene Epple, BRD
      4. CINDY NELSON, USA

1980 1. Hanni Wenzel, Lie.
      2. Annemarie Moser-
         Proell, Aut.
      3. Marie-Theres Nadig,
         Sui.
      10. CINDY NELSON, USA
      12. HEIDI PREUSS, USA
      14. TAMARA McKINNEY,
         USA

1981 1. Marie-Theres Nadig,
         Sui.
      2. Erika Hess, Sui.
      3. Hanni Wenzel, Lie.
      4. CHRISTIN COOPER,
         USA
      6. TAMARA McKINNEY,
         USA
      8. CINDY NELSON, USA
      19. HOLLY FLANDERS,
         USA

1982 1. Erika Hess, Sui.
      2. Irene Epple, BRD
      3. CHRISTIN COOPER,
         USA
      5. CINDY NELSON, USA
      9. TAMARA McKINNEY,
         USA
      12. HOLLY FLANDERS,
         USA

1983 1. TAMARA McKINNEY,
         USA
      2. Hanni Wenzel, Lie.
      3. Erika Hess, Sui.
      7. CINDY NELSON, USA
      12. CHRISTIN COOPER,
         USA

YEAR BY YEAR WORLD CUP DISCIPLINE RESULTS

MEN

1967 DH J.C. Killy, Fra.
      SL J.C. Killy, Fra
      GS J.C. Killy, Fra

1968 DH G. Nenning, Aut.
      SL D. Giovanoli, Sui
      GS J.C. Killy, Fra.

1969 DH K. Schranz, Aut.
      SL J.N. Augert, Fra.
      GS K. Schranz, Aut.

1970 DH K. Schranz, Aut.
         K. Cordin, Aut.
      SL P. Russell, Fra.
         A. Penz, Fra.
      GS G. Thoeni, It.

1971 DH B. Russi, Sui.
      SL J.N. Augert, Fra.
      GS P. Russell, Fra.

1972 DH B. Russi, Sui.
      SL J.N. Augert, Fra.
      GS G. Thoeni, It.

1973 DH R. Collombin, Sui.
      SL G. Thoeni, It.
      GS H. Hinterseer, Aut.

1974 DH R. Collombin, Sui.
      SL G. Thoeni, It.
      GS P. Gros, It.

1975 DH F. Klammer, Aut.
      SL I. Stenmark, Swe.
      GS I. Stenmark, Swe.

1976 DH F. Klammer, Aut.
      SL I. Stenmark, Swe.
      GS I. Stenmark, Swe.

1977 DH F. Klammer, Aut.
      SL I. Stenmark, Swe.
      GS H. Hemmi, Sui.

1978 DH F. Klammer, Aut.
      SL I. Stenmark, Swe.
      GS I. Stenmark, Swe.

1979 DH P. Mueller, Sui.
      SL I. Stenmark, Swe.
      GS I. Stenmark, Swe.

1980 DH P. Mueller, Sui.
      SL I. Stenmark, Swe.
      GS I. Stenmark, Swe.

1981 DH H. Weirather, Aut.
      SL I. Stenmark, Swe.
      GS I. Stenmark, Swe.

1982 DH S. Podborsky, Can.
      SL P. MAHRE, USA
      GS P. MAHRE, USA

1983 DH F. Klammer, Aut.
      SL I. Stenmark, Swe.
      GS P. MAHRE, USA

YEAR BY YEAR WORLD CUP DISCIPLINE RESULTS

WOMEN

1967	DH	M. Goitschel, Fra.
	SL	M. Goitschel, Fra.
	GS	N. Greene, Can.
1968	DH	I. Mir, Fra.
	SL	M. Goitschel, Fra.
	GS	N. Greene, Can.
1969	DH	W. Drexel, Aut.
	SL	G. Gabl, Aut.
	GS	M. COCHRAN, USA
1970	DH	I. Mir, Fra.
	SL	I. Lafforgue, Fra.
	GS	M. Jacot, Fra.
1971	DH	A. Moser, Aut.
	SL	B. Lafforgue, Fra.
	GS	A. Moser, Aut.
1972	DH	A. Moser, Aut.
	SL	B. Lafforgue, Fra.
	GS	A. Moser
1973	DH	A. Moser, Aut.
	SL	P. Emonet, Fra.
	GS	M. Kaserer, Aut.
1974	DH	A. Moser, Aut.
	SL	C. Zechmeister, BRD
	GS	H. Wenzel, Lie.
1975	DH	A. Moser, Aut.
	SL	L.M. Morerod, Sui.
	GS	A. Moser, Aut.
1976	DH	I. Habersatter, Aut.
	SL	R. Mittermaier, BRD
	GS	L.M. Morerod, Sui.
1977	DH	I. Habersatter, Aut.
	SL	L.M. Morerod, Sui.
	GS	L.M. Morerod, Sui.
1978	DH	A. Moser, Aut.
	SL	H. Wenzel, Lie.
	GS	L.M. Morerod, Sui.
1979	DH	A. Moser, Aut.
	SL	R. Sackl, Aut.
	GS	C. Kinshofer, BRD
1980	DH	M.T. Nadig, Sui.
	SL	P. Pelen, Fra.
	GS	H. Wenzel, Lie.
1981	DH	M.T. Nadig, Sui.
	SL	E. Hess, Sui.
	GS	T. McKINNEY, USA
1982	DH	M.C. Gros-Gaudenier, Fra.
	SL	E. Hess, Sui.
	GS	I. Epple, BRD
1983	DH	D. DeAgostini, Sui.
	SL	E. Hess, Sui.
	GS	T. McKINNEY, USA

1983 EUROPA CUP FINAL STANDINGS

OVERALL

1. BILL JOHNSON, USA	115
2. Frank Piccard, Fra.	113
3. Ernst Riedelsperger, Aut.	103
4. Jonas Nilsson, Swe.	97
5. Paul Arne Skajem, Nor.	96
10. ANDY CHAMBERS, USA.	75
28. TIGER SHAW, USA.	42
52. JACE ROMICK, USA	23
56. MIKE BROWN, USA	21
61. DAN STRIPP, USA	19
65. DOUG LEWIS, USA	17
74. JOHN BUXMAN, USA	15

DOWNHILL

1. BILL JOHNSON, USA	95
2. ANDY CHAMBERS, USA	60
3. Henri Feige, Fra.	59
4. Frank Piccard, Fra.	39
5. Hans Zehenther, BRD	25
7. JACE ROMICK, USA	23
9. MIKE BROWN, USA.	21
11. DOUG LEWIS, USA	17
24. TRIS COCHRANE, USA	6

SLALOM

1. Peter Mally, It.	83
2. Jonas Nilsson, Swe.	78
3. Gunnar Neurisser, Swe.	75
4. Eric Pechoux, Fra.	67
5. Roberto Grigas, It.	58
Helmut Gstrein, Aut.	58
24. DAN STRIPP, USA	19
38. JOHN BUXMAN, USA	10
56. TIGER SHAW, USA	5

GIANT SLALOM

1. Gunther Mader, Aut.	80
2. Alexander Zhirov, USSR	67
3. Ernst Riedelsperger, Aut.	64
4. Martin Hangl, Sui.	50
5. Yves Tavernier, Fra.	46
11. TIGER SHAW, USA	37
48. JOHN BUXMAN, USA	5

WOMEN

OVERALL

1. Christine Von Gruenigen, Sui.	160
2. Brigette Gadient, Sui.	147
3. Corinne Schmidhauser, Sui.	107
4. Paola Marciandi, It.	101
5. Alexandra Marasova, Tch.	98
9. HEIDI BOWES, USA	71
27. REBECCA SIMNING, USA	34
31. LYNDA McGEHEE, USA	29
50. BETH MADSEN, USA.	12
71. EVA PFOSI, USA	5

DOWNHILL

1. Veronika Wallinger, Aut.	50
2. Elisabeth Warter, Aut.	30
Patricia Kaestle, Sui.	30
Roberta Berbenni, It.	30
5. Rosemarie Dreier, Aut.	24

SLALOM

1. Christine Von Gruenigen, Sui.	87
2. Brigette Gadient, Sui.	75
3. Ivana Valesova, Tch.	66
4. Corinne Schmidhauser, Sui.	60
5. Alexandra Marasova, Tch.	58
10 HEIDI BOWES, USA	46
21. LYNDA McGEHEE, USA	16
29. REBECCA SIMNING, USA.	10
37. EVA PFOSI, USA	5
41. BETH MADSEN, USA	3

GIANT SLALOM

1. Christine Von Gruenigen, Sui.	69
2. Brigette Gadient, Sui.	66
3. Paola Marciandi, It.	52
4. Manuela Ruef, Aut.	49
5. Alexandra Marasova, Tch.	48
10. HEIDI BOWES, USA	25
12. REBECCA SIMNING, USA	24
20. LYNDA McGEHEE, USA	13
30. BETH MADSEN, USA	9

U.S. NATIONAL CHAMPIONS 1966-83

MEN

DOWNHILL

1966	Hanspeter Rohr, Sui
1967	Dennis McCoy, USA
1968	Scott Henderson, Can.
1969	Spider Sabich, USA
1970	Rod Taylor, USA
1971	Bob Cochran, USA
1972	Steve Lathrop, USA
1973	Bob Cochran, USA
1974	(Cancelled)
1975	Andy Mill, USA
1976	Greg Jones, USA
1977	(Cancelled)
1978	Karl Anderson, USA
1979	Sepp Ferstl, BRD
1980	Davé Irwin, Can.
1981	Doug Powell, USA
1982	Steve Hegg, USA
1983	Bill Johnson, USA

SLALOM

1966	Guy Perillat, Fra.
1967	Jimmie Heuga, USA
1968	Rick Chaffee, USA
1969	Bob Cochran, USA
1970	Bob Cochran, USA
1971	Otto Tschudi,Nor.
1972	Terry Palmer, USA
1973	Masayoki Kashiwagi. Jpn.
1974	Cary Adgate, USA
1975	Steve Mahre, USA
1976	Cary Adgate, USA
1977	Cary Adgate, USA
1978	Phil Mahre, USA
1979	Cary Adgate, USA
1980	Steve Mahre, USA.
1981	Steve Mahre, USA
1982	Francois Jodoin, Can.
1983	Phil Mahre

GIANT SLALOM

1966	Jean Claude Killy, Fra.
1967	Dumeng Giovanoli, Sui.
1968	Rick Chaffee, USA
1969	Hank Kashiwa, USA
1970	Tyler Palmer, USA
1971	Bob Cochran, USA
1972	Jim Hunter, Can.
1973	David Currier, USA
1974	Bob Cochran, USA
1975	Phil Mahre, USA
1976	Geoff Bruce, USA
1977	Phil Mahre, USA
1978	Phil Mahre, USA
1979	Phil Mahre, USA
1980	Peter Monod, Can.
1981	Phil Mahre, USA
1982	(Cancelled)
1983	Tiger Shaw

WOMEN

DOWNHILL

1966	Madeleine Wuillord, Sui.
1967	Nancy Greene, Can.
1968	Ann Black, USA
1969	Ann Black, USA
1970	Ann Black, USA
1971	Cheryl Bechtdolt, USA
1972	Stephanie Forrest, USA
1973	Cindy Nelson, USA

1974	(Cancelled)
1975	Gail Blackburn, USA
1976	Susie Patterson, USA
1977	(Cancelled)
1978	Cindy Nelson, USA
1979	Irene Epple, BRD
1980	Cindy Nelson, USA
1981	Holly Flanders, USA
1982	Cindy Oak, USA
1983	Pam Fletcher, USA

WOMEN

SLALOM

1966	Marielle Goitschel, Fra.
1967	Penny McCoy, USA
1968	Judy Nagel, USA
1969	(Cancelled)
1970	Patty Boydstun, USA
1971	Barbara Cochran, USA
1972	Marilyn Cochran, USA
1973	Lindy Cochran, USA
1974	Susie Patterson, USA
1975	Cindy Nelson, USA
1976	Cindy Nelson, USA
1977	Christin Cooper, USA
1978	Becky Dorsey, USA
1979	Cindy Nelson, USA
1980	Christin Cooper, USA
1981	Cindy Nelson, USA
1982	Tamara McKinney, USA
1983	Tamara McKinney, USA

GIANT SLALOM

1968	Nancy Greene, Can.
1969	Barbara Cochran, USA
1970	Susie Corrock, USA
1971	Laurie Kreiner, Can.
1972	Sandra Poulsen, USA
1973	Debi Handley, USA
1974	Marilyn Cochran, USA
1975	Becky Dorsey, USA
1976	Lindy Cochran, USA
1977	Becky Dorsey, USA
1978	Becky Dorsey, USA
1979	Vicki Fleckenstein, USA
1980	Christin Cooper, USA
1981	Tamara McKinney, USA
1982	(Cancelled)
1983	Tamara McKinney, USA

JIM PAGE

NORDIC TEAM THE COACHES

JIM PAGE
Nordic Director

Charged with administering one of the most talented groups of nordic skiers in U.S. Ski Team history, Page enters his fourth season at the helm of the U.S. Nordic Program. First named to the Ski Team staff in 1979 as Assistant Team Director and Nordic Combined Coach, "Pagie" has guided the nordic team to such heights as Bill Koch's Nordic World Cup championship in 1982 and Kerry Lynch's triumphs this past winter as well as an emergence of the American ski jumpers as an international power.

Originally from Lake Placid, New York, Page won a trio of NCAA skiing titles for Dartmouth College as an athlete from 1960-63. The three-time NCAA All-American moved on to the U.S. Team where he was a member of the nordic combined team during the 1964 and 1965 seasons and named to the Olympic Team for the 1964 Games in Innsbruck, Austria.

The 42-year-old Page headed the Dartmouth ski program and his Big Green teams won a pair of EISA championships and one NCAA title in his four-year stint, earning him EISA Coach of the Year honors in 1974.

Page counts a long association with nordic skiing, including a three-year tenure as USSA Nordic Technical Committee Chairman. He is also a member of the U.S. Olympic Committee's Development Committee.

CAROL BRADLEY
Assistant Nordic Director

Bradley begins her third year in the position of Assistant Nordic Director with the opening of the 1984 season and her ninth year as a member of the U.S. Nordic Team staff.

Originally from Huntington Park, California, Bradley first got a taste of competition as an equestrian, showing horses extensively throughout Southern California. At the 1980 Winter Olympics in Lake Placid, New York, she was selected to be the Women's Administrator for the U.S. delegation to the Winter Games.

Her duties include coordination of the nordic team office, staff, and athletes and she resides in Park City, Utah.

MIKE GALLAGHER
Head Men's Cross-Country Coach

The task of building on the past two seasons' remarkable men's cross-country performances falls to Gallagher, who begins his fourth season at the controls of the U.S. men's cross-country program with the 1984 season.

As an athlete, the 42-year-old Gallagher can claim one of the most notable careers in the history of U.S. nordic skiing, spanning 11 years and a trio of Olympic and World Championship appearances. During his competition days, he also racked up a total of 13 individual national championships.

Following his retirement from the U.S. Team as a competitor, the University of Colorado product served as a teacher in the Rochester, Vermont school system while working in the area of product development and racer service for Edsbyn and Elan. A graduate of Castleton State College, he had a teaching stint at his alma mater as well as Johnson State College for two years while still competing as a member of the National Team.

Gallagher and wife Sarah reside in Pittsfield, Vermont and are the parents of two sons.

ROBERT "RUFF" PATTERSON
Head Women's Cross-Country Coach

The U.S. Women's Cross-Country program will enter its second year apart from the men's program with the 1984 season and Patterson begins his sixth year of association with the U.S. Team, likewise, his second as Head Women's Cross-Country coach.

Prior to assuming the head coaching responsibilities, the 29-year-old Patterson served as Assistant Cross-Country Coach to Gallagher, his primary responsibilities concerning the ladies team.

Formerly the head coach of the Sun Valley Nordic Ski Program, the Sun Valley native earned his bachelor's degree from the University of Colorado in molecular biology with an emphasis in chemistry and psychology. While at Colorado, he was an alpine and nordic skier for the Buffs and is an accomplished tennis and soccer player.

Patterson resides in Sun Valley during the off-season where he enjoys river rafting.

GREG WINDSPERGER
Head Jumping Coach

The past season may well be only the tip of the U.S. jumping iceberg as Windsperger prepares for his fourth year in charge of the American ski jumping fortunes.

The 31-year-old Windsperger was named to the B Team in 1969 and earned a spot on the A Team in 1972, the first alternate to the Olympic jumping squad that same year. He was a member of the 1974 World Championship Team as well as the 1976 Olympic contingent and carried A Team status until his retirement in 1977.

A summa cum laude graduate of the University of Northern Michigan, "Winnie" served as assistant jumping coach for his alma mater and led the Wildcats to the 1980 NCAA Jumping Championship.

Windsperger gave up a management position with AIRTEX Industries in Minneapolis following the 1980 Olympics to assume the head coaching responsibilities with the U.S. Team.

Windsperger and wife Mary reside in Mounds View, Minnesota and are the parents of one son.

JOE LAMB
Head Nordic Combined Coach

Lamb, who enters his second season in charge of the U.S. Nordic Combined fortunes, will have the distinction of being the first U.S. World Cup Nordic Combined head man as the sport receives World Cup status for the coming winter.

An associate coach for two seasons before taking over the program, the Lake Placid, New York native helped Kerry Lynch to the best season ever for a U.S. nordic combined skier this past winter.

As an athlete, Lamb was a member of the U.S. Nordic Combined Team from 1971-74 and was named to the 1972 Olympic Team for the Games in Sapporo, Japan. A 1978 graduate of the University of Vermont, Lamb was a combined skier for the Catamounts and coached the UVM jumpers for one season following graduation. As a junior coach for the U.S. Team, he headed the U.S. nordic combined contingent to the World Junior Championships in Murau, Austria during the 1982 season.

Lamb and wife Elisabeth reside in Lake Placid.

PHIL PECK
Assistant Men's Cross-Country Coach

The 1984 season will signal Peck's second in the position of assistant to Mike Gallagher in the World Cup men's cross-country program.

The 28-year-old Peck skied for Nordic Director Jim Page while at Dartmouth College from 1976-78 and was a member of the Dartmouth team that tied the University of Colorado for the NCAA crown in 1976. Also, as an athlete, Peck claimed the men's overall Dannon Series title during the 1982 season.

Following graduation from Dartmouth in 1978 with a degree in history, the Framingham, Massachusetts native conducted racing programs for Edsbyn and Elan, continuing as a competitor on the domestic circuit. He joined the U.S. Team this past season and travelled with the men on the World Cup circuit.

Peck resides in Juneau, Alaska during the off-season.

ERLING RIMESLATTEN
Assistant Jumping Coach

The U.S. jumpers made great strides this past winter, thanks in part to the knowledge and guidance brought to the program by Rimeslatten, who enters his second campaign as Assistant Jumping Coach in 1984.

A top assistant for the Norwegian National Team, the 36-year-old Rimeslatten has also served as Educational Consultant for Norwegian coaches since 1976 and was assistant jumping coach from 1980-82. He is currently in his second year of a two-year appointment to the United States and will return to Norway following the 1984 Olympics.

A native of Drobak, Norway and a former Norwegian National Team member, Rimeslatten will assist Windsperger in coaching the top U.S. World Cup jumpers and will review coaches education programs and athlete training in this country.

Rimeslatten and wife Annbjorg reside in Burnsville, Minnesota and are the parents of two daughters.

PETER ASHLEY
Assistant Women's Cross-Country Coach

Ashley steps into a new role with the 1984 season as he takes over the job of Assistant Women's Cross-Country Coach after serving four years as National Junior Team Coach. The reorganization within the cross-country program will allow the top junior skiers to compete with the seniors.

The 33-year-old Ashley is the former coach of the Jackson Nordic Program in Jackson, Wyoming, long a top feeder program for the U.S. nordic effort. A graduate of the University of Colorado, Ashley was a five-time member of the Rocky Mountain Junior National Team and has served as chairman of the USSA Junior Committee. In addition, he organized the Nordic Junior National Championships in Jackson in 1978.

During the off-season, Ashley resides in Jackson and runs float trips down the Snake River.

DOUG PETERSON
Nordic Combined Cross-Country Coach

Peterson will be the newest addition to the U.S. Nordic Staff for the 1984 season as he begins his first season as special cross-country coach for the nordic combined group. A former U.S. National Cross-Country Team member for eight years, his competitive career came to a close in 1982 when he suffered a cracked vertebrae in his neck in a training fall in West Yellowstone, Montana.

A 1976 graduate of Dartmouth College, Peterson spent the 1983 season as assistant men's cross-country coach for the Canadian National Team under former U.S. coach Marty Hall. He was named to his current position in the summer of 1983.

As an athlete, Peterson was a member of the 1976 and 1980 Olympic Teams for the U.S. as well as the 1978 World Championship Team. He began skiing competitively in 1971, primarily to stay in shape for kayaking. When not coaching, the Minneapolis native still enjoys kayaking as well as hunting. He resides in Hanover, New Hampshire in the off-season.

GARY LARSON
Assistant Cross-Country Coach

The development of cross-country athletes on the domestic level will again be the primary responsibility of Larson, who begins his fourth season as a member of the U.S. nordic staff.

The 31-year-old Larson has a broad background in both alpine and nordic skiing, having been team captain of the University of Minnesota-Duluth as an alpine racer as well as head coach of the UMD program for four years following graduation.

A native of Duluth, Larson was the 1979 USSA National Veterans 15 kilometer champion and has been a member of the Central Division senior Cross-Country squad since 1979. He was appointed as coach for the Central Division for the 1981 U.S. Nationals along with being elected to the AIAW National Ski Committee.

Recently married this past June, Larson and wife April reside in Duluth.

REX BELL
National Junior Jumping Coach and Domestic Jump Team Coordinator

Bell enters his third year in the position of National Junior Jumping Team Coach with the 1984 season as well as serving double duty as Jumping Team Coordinator. His duties will include acting as liaison to USSA clubs and divisions, organizing coaches education programs and coaching the top U.S. junior ski jumpers.

The Brattleboro, Vermont native served as Eastern Regional jumping coach from 1978-80 and was selected as the Assistant Jumping Venue Manager for the Lake Placid Olympics. Prior to his appointment to the U.S. Team, he was Nordic Program Administrator for the Eastern Ski Association and was a member of the Eastern Ski Jumping Committee from 1976-80.

The 31-year-old Bell is a product of the University of New Hampshire where he developed into a top intercollegiate ski jumper. Following graduation, he remained at UNH to coach the jumping team which, under his guidance, became the best collegiate jumping team at the 1975 NCAA Championships, and he was named the EISA Coach of the Year in 1976.

PETER GRAVES
Domestic Cross-Country Coordinator

The 1984 season will signal the third for Graves as Cross-Country Coordinator in charge of the domestic scene, working with development athletes throughout the United States.

A native of Wayzata, Minnesota, Graves was a member of the 1970 Eastern Junior National Cross-Country Team and the Eastern Senior Nordic Training squad. A product of Fort Lewis College in Durango, Colorado, Graves was a four-year nordic skier for the Raiders and competed under former U.S. Olympic coach Adolph Kuss.

Following his competitive career, Graves turned to broadcasting with television and radio sports. He served as ABC's color commentator for cross-country at the 1980 Olympics and has covered nordic events for both NBC's Sportsworld and ESPN. In addition, he served five years as Director of Marketing and Racing for NorTur, Inc. and has worked with Edsbyn on racing development.

1983 U.S. CROSS-COUNTRY TEAM

MEN

TIM CALDWELL

Height—6'0"
Weight—175
Birthdate—February 4, 1954
Birthplace—Brattleboro, Vermont
Residence—Putney, Vermont
Year on National Team—14th

Even though Tim Caldwell carries the most seniority of any member of the U.S. Ski Team, Alpine or Nordic, his results in 1983 definitely bear out the fact that some things do get better with age. With 13 years of international experience under his belt, "TC" came on strong down the stretch to record a 25th place final ranking in the overall World Cup point standings.

The highlight of Tim's season came on home ground as he sprinted to the runnerup spot in the World Cup 15 kilometer event in Anchorage, Alaska, defeating a very strong international field, including teammate Bill Koch, to finish less than a minute behind the winner. This finish also marked Caldwell as the U.S. National 15K champion as that race was run in conjunction with the World Cup, and two days later, he skied to a fourth place showing in the U.S. National 30 kilometer event.

In addition to his World Cup finish in Anchorage, Caldwell scored Cup points in four other races this season, being the only other American to score points besides Bill Koch in both Kovgolova, Soviet Union and Falun, Sweden. He also posted a 19th place result in the pre-Olympic 30 kilometer competition in Sarajevo, Yugoslavia.

During the 1982 season, Caldwell skied to a 15th place showing in the World Championship 50K in Oslo, Norway, the best finish for any U.S. skier in that event, and claimed the U.S. National 50K title as well.

Named to the U.S. Team for the 1971 season, Tim has been a member of the 1972, 1976 and 1980 Olympic Teams. His top finish came in the Winter Games in 1980 in Lake Placid where he placed 25th in the 15 kilometer race. He also claimed a 27th place finish in the 30K in Innsbruck, Austria in 1976. He has represented the U.S. in the 1974, 78 and 82 Nordic World Championships, finishing 20th in the 15K at Lahti, Finland in 1978 in addition to his result from Oslo in 1982.

Beginning the sport at the age of two and skiing competitively at age 12, the son of 1972 Olympic coach John Caldwell has racked up a long list of accomplishments that include the Beck Memorial Trophy for best international results by a U.S. skier in 1973 and 1977. He is an eight-time national champion and tied for the overall Dannon series title in 1980.

During the off-season, the Dartmouth College graduate enjoys playing the violin and a multitude of outdoor activities. He spent the summer of 1982 working with U.S. Ski Team Sports Medicine Nordic Coordinator Brian Sharkey at the University

of Montana in Missoula and lightened his competition load in 1981 to teach at Vermont Academy.

Date/Year	Event	Race	Finish
1983	Overall World Cup XC Standings		25
12/18/82	Davos, Switzerland	WC 15K	70
2/10/83	Sarajevo, Yugoslavia	WC 15K	80
2/12/83	Sarajevo, Yugoslavia	WC 30K	19
2/19/83	Kovgolova, Soviet Union	WC 50K	19
2/26/83	Falun, Sweden	WC 30K	14
3/4/83	Lahti, Finland	WC 15K	25
3/12/83	Oslo, Norway	WC 50K	28
3/19/83	Anchorage, Alaska	WC 15K	2
3/21/83	Anchorage, Alaska	U.S. Nat 30K	4
3/27/83	Labrador City, Canada	WC 30K	20

AUDUN ENDESTAD

Height—6'1"
Weight—175
Birthdate—January 19, 1953
Birthplace—Bryggja, Norway
Residence—Fairbanks, Alaska
Year on National Team—3rd

Having proven his skiing prowess in the longer races, Audun is now trying to adapt himself to the shorter events as he enters his second season as a full-time World Cup competitor. A two-time overall champion on the Great American Ski Chase Series, he scored the first World Cup points of his career this past March with a 19th place showing in the 50 kilometer event in Oslo, Norway.

A distinguished skier on the European marathon circuit as well, Audun alternated between that circuit and the World Cup tour during the 1982 season and placed third in the prestigious Engadin Ski Marathon in Switzerland as well as the 55-kilometer Norwegian Birkebeiner while placing second in the men's 50 kilometer race at the U.S. National Championships that same year.

He showed his strength and stamina this past season as he won the initial leg of the Great American Ski Chase, a 50K race at Devils Thumb Ranch in Colorado just after returning from the first World Cup tour. One week later, he placed second to Bill Koch in the 50K race at the U.S. Nationals and followed that up less than a week later with a first and second place showing in World Cup tryout races that insured a return trip to Europe with the World Cup contingent.

A member of the 1982 World Championship Team, Audun hopes to make 1984 his first Olympic berth for the U.S.

Date/Year	Event	Race	Finish
1983	Overall World Cup XC Standings		63
11/22/82	Labrador City, Canada	9.2K	3
11/25/82	Labrador City, Canada	10K	2
12/12/82	San Bernadino, Switzerland	FIS 15K	4
12/14/82	Madonna di Campiglio, Italy	FIS 15K	53
12/18/82	Davos, Switzerland	WC 15K	47
1/14/83	Reit im Winkl, West Germany	WC 15K	28
1/22/83	Devils Thumb Ranch, Colorado	GASC 50K	1
1/29/83	Sherman Hollow, Vermont	U.S. Nat. 50K	2
1/31/83	Waitsfield, Vermont	WC Tryout 15K	1
2/2/83	Sherman Hollow, Vermont	WC Tryout 15K	2
2/10/83	Sarajevo, Yugoslavia	WC 15K	49

2/12/83	Sarajevo, Yugoslavia	WC 30K	21
2/26/83	Falun, Sweden	WC 30K	50
3/4/83	Lahti, Finland	WC 15K	49
3/12/83	Oslo, Norway	WC 50K	19
3/19/83	Anchorage, Alaska	WC 15K	24
3/21/83	Anchorage, Alaska	U.S. Nat. 30K	5
3/27/83	Labrador City, Canada	WC 30K	21

JIM GALANES

Height—6'1"
Weight—170
Birthdate—August 28, 1956
Birthplace—Brattleboro, Vermont
Residence—Brattleboro, Vermont
Year on National Team—11th

The 1983 season proved to be an up and down one for Galanes, who finished the winter ranked 26th in the final overall World Cup nordic point standings. Off to a fast start at the outset of the season, Jim placed sixth in Reit im Winkl, West Germany in the second World Cup 15 kilometer competition and followed that up with an eighth place showing in the pre-Olympic 30 kilometer event in Sarajevo, Yugoslavia.

The second half of the season proved to not be as productive for Galanes, although he did pick up more Cup points with his 18th place result in the World Cup 15K in Anchorage, Alaska and a runnerup showing in the U.S. National 30 kilometer race. Early season results included a pair of wins, the first in the Labrador West Fall Series in Labrador City, Canada and the second coming in the form of a 30 kilometer FIS victory in Valsassina, Italy.

Six years ago, Jim made a dramatic switch from nordic combined skiing to concentrate solely on the cross-country aspect of the sport. As a nordic combined skier for the U.S. Team, he distinguished himself as one of the best international competitors with his victory in Reit im Winkl in 1978. He was the U.S. Nordic Combined champion for both 1977 and 1978.

A member of both the 1976 and 1980 Olympic Teams, Galanes competed as a nordic combined skier in Innsbruck, Austria, placing 17th in the combined event at the Winter Games. His cross-country had come to the forefront in 1980 at Lake Placid and he finished 20th in the 50 kilometer competition as well as 33rd in the 15K and 41st in the 30K. He has also been a member of the 1978 and 1982 World Championship Teams for the U.S., placing 14th in the 30 kilometer race in Oslo, Norway in 1982 and 22nd in the 15K.

A competitive skier at the age of 10, Jim is married to the former Lynn Spencer, a member of the U.S. women's cross-country team for the past eight years. During the off-season, he enjoys cycling and rowing.

Date/Year	Event	Race	Finish
1983	Overall World Cup XC Standings		26
11/22/82	Labrador City, Canada	9.2K	1
12/14/82	Madonna di Campiglio, Italy	FIS 15K	6
12/28/82	Valsassina, Italy	FIS 10K	2
12/30/82	Valsassina, Italy	FIS 30K	1
1/8/83	Zernez, Switzerland	FIS 10K	2
1/14/83	Reit im Winkl, West Germany	WC 15K	6
1/18/83	Zermatt, Switzerland	FIS 10K	7

1/21/83	Brusson, Italy	FIS 15K	4
2/12/83	Sarajevo, Yugoslavia	WC 30K	8
2/16/83	Falun, Sweden	WC 30K	27
3/4/83	Lahti, Finland	WC 15K	27
3/19/83	Anchorage, Alaska	WC 15K	18
3/21/83	Anchorage, Alaska	U.S. Nat. 30K	2

BILL KOCH

Height—5'10"
Weight—150
Birthdate—June 7, 1955
Birthplace—Brattleboro, Vermont
Residence—Eugene, Oregon
Year on National Team—13th

The 1983 World Cup cross-country season was one week too long as far as the American faithful were concerned as reigning World Cup Champion Bill Koch was unable to hold off a rejuvenated Alexander Zavjalov and a surging Gunde Svan and finished the winter in third place in the overall final standings. Neverthless, Koch's performance this past season was very respectable given the fact that he lost the majority of the month of November, a critical training month, to a virus and still led the World Cup standings into the final race of the season.

En route to that final ranking, Koch skied to victory in the pre-Olympic 30 kilometer competition and claimed both the 50 kilometer and 30 kilometer U.S. National championships. In addition, he added a pair of individual wins in FIS events in San Bernadino, Switzerland and Zernez, Switzerland.

Deservingly regarded as one of the best U.S. skiers of all time, Koch set nordic standards for years to come in 1982 when he won the final race of the World Cup season and became the first American to ever win the overall Nordic World Cup title. On the road to that historic plateau, he also became the first American to ever win a World Cup cross-country race in Europe and ended the 1982 season with four World Cup individual wins to his credit and seven overall triumphs, including repeating as the U.S. National Champion in the 15 kilometer event. As icing on the cake, Bill also skied to a bronze medal in the 30 kilometer competition at the Nordic World Championships, becoming the only American to ever win a World Championship medal for nordic skiing.

Koch first made the history books in 1976 when he first stood the nordic world on its collective ear by claiming a silver medal in the Winter Olympic 30 kilometer event in Innsbruck, Austria, making him the only U.S. male to have ever won an Olympic medal in a nordic event. He took a year off from the World Cup circuit in 1981 to follow the marathon trail and was victorious in the Engadin Marathon in Switzerland and finished seventh that same year in the Vasa Loppet, which fielded perhaps the strongest group of international cross-country skiers ever assembled.

In an interesting twist for cross-country skiing, Bill set world speed records for 50 kilometers (1 hour, 59 minutes and 47 seconds), and 30 kilometers, (1 hour, 11 minutes and 45 seconds) in a solo attempt on an isolated pond near Marlboro, Vermont in 1981.

Bill began skiing at the age of two and was selected as a nordic combined skier for the 1972 U.S. Ski Team as a 17-year-old. He just missed making the U.S. Olympic Team that season but went on to become a member of the 1976 and 1980 teams for the Winter Games. In addition to his medal-winning performance in the 30K in Innsbruck, Bill placed sixth in the 15 kilometer competition and 13th in the 50K. In Lake Placid, Bill recorded the best U.S. finish in both the 15K and the 50K,, finishing 16th and 13th respectively. He has also represented the U.S. at the Nordic World Championships in 1974, 78 and 82, placing 21st in the 15K event in Oslo last season in addition to his bronze-medal effort in the 30K.

Kochie became a "westerner" this past summer as he and wife Katie (Tobey), a former U.S. Cross-Country team member, moved to Eugene, Oregon from Putney, Vermont. The Koch's have two daughters, Leah and Elisabeth. The past several summers have been spent designing cross-country trails in Labrador City, Canada.

Date/Year	Event	Race	Finish
1983	Overall World Cup XC Standings		3
12/18/82	Davos, Switzerland	WC 15K	4
1/14/83	Reit im Winkl, West Germany	WC 15K	2
1/29/83	Sherman Hollow, Vermont	U.S. Nat. 50K	1
2/10/83	Sarajevo, Yugoslavia	WC 15K	35
2/12/83	Sarajevo, Yugoslavia	WC 30K	1
2/19/83	Kovgolova, Soviet Union	WC 50K	4
2/26/83	Falun, Sweden	WC 30K	8
3/4/83	Lahti, Finland	WC 15K	20
3/19/83	Anchorage, Alaska	WC 15K	3
3/21/83	Anchorage, Alaska	U.S. Nat. 30K	1
3/27/83	Labrador City, Canada	WC 30K	9

CRAIG WARD

Height—6'1"
Weight—190
Birthdate—February 15, 1954
Birthplace—Cleveland, Ohio
Residence—Lake Placid, New York
Year on National Team—7th

Craig skied his way on to the U.S. World Cup Team for the return to Europe in January this past season with results such as a trio of wins at the Gitchi-Gami Games in Telemark, Wisconsin in December and strong showings in the World Cup tryout races. He scored World Cup points in the pre-Olympic 30 kilometer competition in Sarajevo, Yugoslavia, placing 12th, and finished tied for 48th position in the final World Cup nordic standings.

In addition to his European efforts, Craig placed second and third in a pair of Labrador West Fall Series races in November and claimed a win in the 15 kilometer race held in Sherman Hollow, Vermont in early February that was one of the qualification races for the return trip to Europe with the World Cup group.

Named to the 1980 Olympic Team for Lake Placid as an alternate, Ward did not compete in the Winter Games. He was also a member of the 1978 and 1982 World Championship Teams, placing 50th in the 15 kilometer race in Oslo, Norway in 1982.

Alternating between the marathon circuit and the World Cup in 1982, Ward finished an impressive seventh in the 42-kilometer Engadin Marathon in Switzerland. He also posted a pair of third place showings in the 30 and 50 kilometer races at the U.S. Nationals that same year.

A graduate of Middlebury College in Environmental Studies and Biology in 1976, Ward skied for former U.S. Nordic Director John Bower and was co-captain of the 1976 Panther team that represented the school in NCAA Championship competition.

Date/Year	Event	Race	Finish
1983	Overall World Cup XC Standings		48(T)
11/25/82	Labrador City, Canada	9.2K	3
11/27/82	Labrador City, Canada	15K	2
12/15/82	Telemark, Wisconsin	Karhu 10K	1
12/16/82	Telemark, Wisconsin	Gitchi-Gami 15K	1
12/19/82	Telemark, Wisconsin	Gitchi-Gami 20K	1
1/8/83	Zernez, Switzerland	FIS 10K	7
1/14/83	Reit im Winkl, West Germany	WC 15K	73
1/18/83	Zermatt, Switzerland	FIS 10K	13
1/21/83	Brusson, Italy	FIS 15K	27
1/31/83	Waitsfield, Vermont	WC Tryout 15K	3
2/2/83	Sherman Hollow, Vermont	WC Tryout 15K	1
2/12/83	Sarajevo, Yugoslavia	WC 38K	12
2/26/83	Falun, Sweden	WC 30K	51
3/4/83	Lahti, Finland	WC 15K	39
3/12/83	Oslo, Norway	WC 50K	63
3/19/83	Anchorage, Alaska	WC 15K	27
3/27/83	Labrador City, Canada	WC 30K	27

B-TEAM—MEN

HOWIE BEAN

Height—5'9"
Weight—150
Birthdate—July 8, 1956
Birthplace—Wolfeboro, New Hampshire
Residence—Wolfeboro, New Hampshire
Year on National Team—3rd

Howie once again showed his penchant for the longer races in 1983 as he captured the overall title on the Great American Ski Chase Series, recording wins in the North American Vasa (50K), the Dannon Yellowstone Rendezvous (50K), and the Royal Gorge California Vasa (50K), en route to the championship. In addition, he was the first American finisher in the American Birkebeiner in fifth position, a mere 31 seconds behind the winner after 50 kilometers.

Following a short stint with the World Cup group in December and January, Howie concentrated his efforts on the Ski Chase, but he returned to the international scene for the final World Cup event of the season in Labrador City, Canada and picked up Cup points for an 18th place showing in the 30 kilometer race to earn a 61st place ranking in the final overall World Cup standings. He ended the 1983 season with a pair of runnerup finishes in the North American Cross-Country Championships, also staged in Labrador City.

A graduate of the University of New Hampshire, Bean was tabbed as a top prospect while still a student and spent two years on the Development Team before earning National Team status in 1982. He gained his first World Cup points during the 1981 season while competing in Norway and Sweden and continues to make the adjustment to the World Cup circuit on a more permanent basis.

Date/Year	Event	Race	Finish
1983	Overall World cup XC Standings		61(T)
	Overall GASC Standings		1
11/22/82	Labrador City, Canada	9.2K	4
11/25/82	Labrador City, Canada	10K	4
11/27/82	Labrador City, Canada	15K	1
12/12/82	San Bernadino, Switzerland	FIS 15K	8
12/18/82	Davos, Switzerland	WC 15K	90
1/8/83	Zernez, Switzerland	FIS 10K	8
1/14/83	Reit im Winkl, West Germany	WC 15K	45
1/31/83	Waitsfield, Vermont	WC Tryout 15K	2
2/4/83	Stowe, Vermont	WC Tryout 15K	2
2/12/83	Traverse City, Michigan	GASC 50K	1
2/26/83	Telemark, Wisconsin	GASC 50K	5
3/12/83	West Yellowstone, Montana	GASC 50K	1
3/20/83	Soda Springs, California	GASC 50K	1
3/27/83	Labrador City, Canada	WC 30K	18
3/29/83	Labrador City, Canada	NA Champ 15K	2
3/31/83	Labrador City, Canada	NA Champ 30K	2

DAN SIMONEAU

Height—5'9"
Weight—165
Birthdate—January 9, 1959
Birthplace—Farmington, Maine
Residence—Eugene, Oregon
Year on National Team—9th

The cards were not stacked in Dan's favor in 1983 following his performance in 1982 that saw him finish seventh in the final overall World Cup nordic point standings. He never really got untracked during this past winter and finished the season tied for the 54th position in the final World Cup rankings.

Struggling throughout the majority of the winter, Simmy posted his lone World Cup point scoring result when the tour made its way to the U.S. with a 14th place showing in the 15 kilometer event in Anchorage, Alaska. Being home seemed to agree with Dan as he went out two days later and placed third in the U.S. Nationals 30 kilometer race. In addition, he posted a 24th place effort in the pre-Olympic 30K competition in Sarajevo, Yugoslavia.

His seventh place finish in 1982 ranks as the highest finish for an American male whose last name is not Koch and he and Bill Koch teamed up for the first ever one-two U.S. cross-country finish in World Cup history that same year in Falun, Sweden. He was to score Cup points in five races that year.

The University of Oregon student became the first American male skier to ever compete in the Soviet Union in 1981 along with teammate Judy Endestad and head coach Mike Gallagher when they traveled to Kovgolova. Dan was the fourth non-Russian to finish the 30 kilometer event, his 13th place showing outdistancing the likes of Norway's Oddvar Braa and Sweden's Thomas Wassberg. In the 15 kilometer race, he was 20th overall and the third westerner to cross the finish line.

The ninth-year National Team member has five Junior National titles to his credit in addition to being named a High School All-American in 1976 and listed in the Who's Who of American High Schools. He dominated the junior class at the U.S. Nationls in 1978, winning both the 10K and 15K races, but was hampered by chronic lower back problems during the 1979 season.

He came back strong in 1980 and was named to the Olympic Team for Lake Placid, although he did not compete. That same season, he tied Tim Caldwell for the overall point lead in the Dannon Race Series. He has also been a member of the World Junior Championship Team in 1979 as well as the Nordic World Championship Team in 1982, finishing 30th in the 30K and 21st in the 50K.

During the off-season, Dan continues his education at the University of Oregon.

Date/Year	Event	Race	Finish
1983	Overall World Cup XC Standings		54(T)
11/22/82	Labrador City, Canada	9.2K	5
12/12/82	San Berandino, Switzerland	FIS 15K	5
12/18/81	Davos, Switzerland	WC 15K	35
1/8/83	Zernez, Switzerland	FIS 10K	4
1/14/83	Reit im Winkl, West Germany	WC 15K	40
1/18/83	Zermatt, Switzerland	FIS 10K	5
1/21/83	Brusson, Italy	FIS 15K	12
2/10/83	Sarajevo, Yugoslavia	WC 15K	50
2/12/83	Sarajevo, Yugoslavia	WC 30K	24
2/26/83	Falun, Sweden	WC 30K	31
3/19/83	Anchorage, Alaska	WC 15K	14
3/21/83	Anchorage, Alaska	U.S. Nat. 30K	3

WOMEN

JUDY ENDESTAD

Height—5'2"
Weight—115
Birthdate—April 9, 1958
Birthplace—Fairbanks, Alaska
Residence—Fairbanks, Alaska
Year on National Team—6th

Judy found herself in a rut during most of the 1983 season, but a rather nice rut as far as the U.S. Ski Team was concerned—one of scoring World Cup points on a consistent basis. Of the ten World Cup events that she entered this past winter, Judy scored Cup points in seven of them, five of those coming in the form of 16th place results.

Those results marked Judy as the top U.S. female on the World Cup circuit in 1983 and she ended the season tied for 20th in the final standings. She broke the 16th place jinx on home turf, posting a ninth place showing in the 10 kilometer event in Anchorage, Alaska, to notch the best World Cup finish in her career, and then came back the following day to capture the U.S. National championship in the 5 kilometer event. Her finish in the 10K also tabbed her as the U.S. National Champion at that distance.

Other top international results last season included a pair of second place finishes in FIS races in Italy as she chose to stay in Europe to train and compete rather than coming home for the Christmas break. The domestic scene was again good for Judy as she finished near the top in every race she entered in North America.

Named to the B Team in 1979, Judy was a member of the first American nordic group to compete in the Soviet Union in 1981 as she and teammate Dan Simoneau traveled to Kovgolova with head coach Mike Gallagher to compete in a pair of races during the latter part of February. Her finishes (33rd and 36th) were considered very strong for a skier with limited international experience and provided a preview for what was to come.

A competitive skier at the age of 16, Judy has completed two years at Harvard University, competing for the Harvard Ski Team both years and finishing fifth in the 5K race in the 1978 AIAW National Championships. Her future plans include finishing her degree and possibly going on to law school.

Date/Year	Event	Race	Finish
1983	Overall World Cup XC Standings		20(T)
11/22/82	Labrador City, Canada	6.2K	4
11/25/82	Labrador City, Canada	5K	2
11/27/82	Labrador City, Canada	10K	2
12/12/82	Madonna di Campiglio, Italy	WC 5K	16
12/18/82	Davos, Switzerland	FIS 5K	16
12/28/82	Valsassina, Italy	FIS 5K	2
12/30/82	Valsassina, Italy	FIS 10K	2
1/8/83	Klingenthal, East Germany	WC 10K	24
1/14/83	Stachy Zadov, Czechoslovakia	WC 10K	27
2/10/83	Sarajevo, Yugoslvia	WC 5K	31
2/20/83	Kovgolova, Soviet Union	WC 20K	16
2/25/83	Falun, Sweden	WC 10K	16
3/5/83	Lahti, Finland	WC 5K	16
3/12/83	Oslo, Norway	WC 20K	16
3/20/83	Anchorage, Alaska	WC 10K	9
3/21/83	Anchorage, Alaska	U.S. Nat. 5K	1
3/26/83	Labrador City, Canada	WC 10K	15

LYNN SPENCER-GALANES

Height—5'4"
Weight—117
Birthdate—June 6, 1954
Birthplace—Anchorage, Alaska
Residence—Brattleboro Vermont
Year on National Team—9th

One of the top performers year in and year out for the U.S. cross-country women, Lynn had problems getting untracked this past winter until late in the season when the World Cup tour moved to North America. Once back on home ground, she posted scoring results with her 17th place finish in the World Cup 10 kilometer competition in her native Anchorage and then ended the year with a ninth place result in the 10K in Labrador City, Canada, the top U.S. finish on the day.

Lynn started fast in 1983, posting wins in her first two outings in the Labrador West Fall Series but struggled once she got to Europe. She posted a 38th place showing in the pre-Olympic 5 kilometer competition in Sarajevo, Yugoslavia and claimed a 25th place result in the FIS 10K race that was held on the Olympic course. She ended the year on an up note with a victory in the 5 kilometer event at the North American Cross-Country Championships in Laborador City.

During the course of the 1982 season, Lynn was honored by *Sports Illustrated* in their Faces in the Crowd section following her victories in all three individual races at the U.S. Nationals. She was the highest finisher for the U.S. that season in the final women's World Cup standings in 43rd spot despite missing the final two races of the season due to illness.

A late starter by international standards, Lynn did not begin competing until her senior year in high school. Despite that fact, she was a member of the 1976 and 1980 Olympic Teams, claiming a 31st place finish in the 10K race in Lake Placid in 1980. In addition, she has been a member of both the 1978 and 1982 World Championship Teams for the U.S., her top finish coming in the form of a pair of 25th place results in the 5 and 10 kilometer races in 1978 in Lahti, Finland.

Married to National Team member Jim Galanes, Lynn will be attempting to make her third Olympic Team this coming season and will begin her sixth year on the World Cup circuit. An eye injury in 1972 temporarily halted her skiing career and she missed much of 1977 due to illness, but she came back strong in 1978, winning the National 10K championship at the U.S. Nationals.

Jim and Lynn reside in Brattleboro in the off-season, but do much of their training in Alaska.

Date/Year	Event	Race	Finish
1983	Overall World Cup XC Standings		31(T)

CHRISSY LEWIS

Height—5'8"
Weight—130
Birthdate—April 20, 1961
Birthplace—Denver, Colorado
Residence—Parshall, Colorado
Year on National Team—5th

Chrissy earned a spot on the U.S. World Cup group for the pre-Olympics and the final portion of the European tour by virtue of some strong domestic and Scandinavian results during the first half of the winter. In her first 13 races of the 1983 season, she never finished below seventh, including a pair of wins in World Cup tryout races held in Vermont.

A former All-American skier for Middlebury College in 1981, Chrissy qualified for a trip to Norway in January and competed in a series of five Norwegian races, claiming a pair of second and third place showings during the course of the trip. Her first World Cup start came in Sarajevo, Yugoslavia in the pre-Olympic 5 kilometer competition in which she placed 47th in the field.

Following Sarajevo, she joined the U.S. contingent at the World University Games in Sofia, Bulgaria and placed seventh in the women's 10 kilometer event and 12th in the 5K. She finished out the final European tour with the World Cup group and then returned to the states to post the best World Cup finish of her career with a 25th place showing in the 10K in Anchorage, Alaska, following that up the next day with a fourth in the U.S. Nationals 5K.

A member of the Junior Development Team from 1978 to 1980, she joined the Senior Development group in 1981. She is currently attending Denver University and pursuing a degree in Accounting with junior status. Her immediate plans call for working toward that degree from D.U. in the off-season.

Named the Outstanding Athlete in Colorado by the YWCA in 1979 and 1980, Chrissy enjoys knitting and tennis when not competing or studying.

Date/Year	Event	Race	Finish
11/22/82	Labrador City, Canada	6.2K	1
11/27/82	Labrador City, Canda	10K	1
12/12/82	Madonna di Campiglio, Italy	WC 5K	28
12/28/82	Valsassina, Italy	FIS 5K	4
12/30/82	Valsassina, Italy	FIS 10K	8
1/14/83	Stachy-Zadov, Czechoslovakia	WC 10K	26
2/10/83	Sarajevo, Yugoslavia	WC 5K	38
2/12/83	Sarajevo, Yugoslavia	FIS 10K	25
2/20/83	Kovgolova, Soviet Union	WC 20K	29
2/25/83	Falun, Sweden	WC 10K	39
3/20/83	Anchorage, Alaska	WC 10K	17
3/21/83	Anchorage, Alaska	U.S. Nat. 5K	5
3/26/83	Labrador City, Canada	WC 10K	9
3/29/83	Labrador City, Canada	NA Champ. 5K	1

Date/Year	Event	Race	Finish
11/28/82	Jackson, Wyoming	5.4K	1
12/16/82	Telemark, Wisconsin	Gitchi-Gami 10K	3
12/19/82	Telemark, Wisconsin	Gitchi-Gami 5K	7
1/8/83	Oslo, Norway	FIS 5K	6
1/15/83	Hof, Norway	FIS 5K	3
1/16/83	Oslo, Norway	FIS 27K	2
1/22/83	Oslo, Norway	FIS 5K	2
1/23/83	Sognzann, Norway	FIS 27K	3
1/31/83	Waitsfield, Vermont	WC Tryout 5K	1
2/2/83	Sherman Hollow, Vermont	WC Tryout 10K	1

2/10/83	Sarajevo, Yugoslavia	WC 5K	47
2/19/83	Sofia, Bulgaria	FIS Univ. 10K	7
2/22/83	Sofia, Bulgaria	FIS Univ. 5K	12
3/5/83	Lahti, Finland	WC 5K	40
3/12/83	Oslo, Norway	WC 20K	42
3/20/83	Anchorage, Alaska	WC 10K	25
3/21/83	Anchorage, Alaska	U.S. Nat. 5K	4

SUE LONG

Height—5'5"
Weight—123
Birthdate—April 4, 1960
Birthplace—Glen Ridge, New Jersey
Residence—Manchester Center, Vermont
Year on National Team—2nd

Sue skied her way on to the World Cup group for the initial trip to Europe by virtue of her performances in early-season races and then continued to prove herself as the season went along, becoming a permanent fixture on the tour. She recorded a pair of Cup scoring results in her rookie season, the first in Anchorage, Alaska with a 20th place showing in the 10 kilometer competition, and the second the following week with a 19th place in the final 10K race of the season in Labrador City, Canada. Her efforts earned her a tie for 45th place in the final World Cup point rankings.

A product of the Stratton Mountain School in alpine skiing and a graduate of Middlebury College, Long exhibited considerable poise in her first year of international competition as she joined the ranks of the younger skiers who are building the future talent base for the U.S. women's team.

An accomplished cross-country foot runner as well, she was named All New England in 1981 as well as earning All-American honors by virtue of a third place finish in the NCAA Division III National Championships that year. She also competed on snow for Middlebury College for two seasons and was named to the Collegiate All East Team in 1982.

Her future plans may include a career in animal science and during the off-season, Sue enjoys hiking, swimming and knitting.

Date/Year	Event	Race	Finish
1983	Overall World Cup XC Standings		45(T)
11/22/82	Labrador City, Canada	6.2K	10
11/25/82	Labrador City, Canada	5K	4
11/27/82	Labrador City, Canada	10K	3
12/12/82	Madonna di Campiglio, Italy	WC 5K	41
12/28/82	Valsassina, Italy	FIS 5K	10
12/30/82	Valsassina, Italy	FIS 10K	11
1/8/83	Klingenthal, East Germany	WC 10K	38
1/14/83	Stachy-Zadov, Czechoslovakia	WC 10K	37
1/31/83	Waitsfield, Vermont	WC Tryout 5K	2
2/2/83	Sherman Hollow, Vermont	WC Tryout 10K	2
2/10/83	Sarajevo, Yugoslavia	WC 5K	48
2/19/83	Sofia, Bulgaria	FIS Univ. 10K	10
2/22/83	Sofia, Bulgaria	FIS Univ. 5K	11
3/5/83	Lahti, Finland	WC 5K	37
3/12/83	Oslo, Norway	WC 20K	27
3/20/83	Anchorage, Alaska	WC 10K	20
3/21/83	Anchorage, Alaska	U.S. Nat. 5K	10
3/26/83	Labrador City, Canada	WC 10K	19
3/29/83	Labrador City, Canada	NA Champ. 5K	5
3/31/83	Labrador City, Canada	NA Champ. 10K	4

THE ATHLETES: JUMPING

JON DENNEY

Height—5'10"
Weight—162
Birthdate—March 13, 1960
Birthplace—Duluth, Minnesota
Residence—Duluth, Minnesota
Year on National Team—7th

A dislocated shoulder suffered at Christmas-time slowed Jon's progress in 1983 but the youngest of the three Denney brothers to compete for the U.S. Ski Team came back to put together a pair of World Cup scoring efforts and finish tied for 49th in the final World Cup standings. His top finish this past winter came in the form of a tenth place result on the 90 meter hill in Lahti, Finland while the second scoring finish came on the 120 meter hill in Vikersund, Norway with a 15th place effort.

A student at the University of Minnesota-Duluth, Denney was named to the U.S. contingent to the World University Games in Bulgaria this past season and placed seventh on the 70 meter hill in Sofia. He competed on the World Cup circuit when the tour moved to North America and then rejoined the team for the last half of the season.

Jon surprised everyone in 1977 when he qualified for the early trip to Europe and the Intersport Springertournee while still a member of the Junior Team. That same year, he captured the U.S. Junior National jumping title, capping a year that saw all three Denneys win national championships. This past year, he placed seventh and fourth respectively in the 70 and 90 meter competitions at the U.S. Nationals.

Majoring in Electrical Engineering at UMD, Denney assisted in the design of the "ski jumping bus" that allows jumpers to practice flight positions while driving down the highway. The bus is open in the front and back and the jumpers are suspended from a harness inside the vehicle and their movements and positions can be monitored while the air flowing through simulates flight.

First named to the Ski Team in 1978, Jon began skiing at the age of three and joined competitive circles the following year. His immediate plans include the completion of his degree.

Date/Year	Event	Hill	Finish
1983	Overall World Cup Jumpings Standings		49(T)
	Second Period Standings		36(T)
11/30/82	Steamboat Springs, Colorado	WC Tryouts 70M	2
12/11/82	Lillehammer, Norway	EC 70M	40
12/13/82	Lillehammer, Norway	EC 70M	31
1/15/83	Lake Placid, New York	WC 90M	25
1/16/83	Lake Placid, New York	WC 90M	16
1/22/83	Thunder Bay, Canada	WC 70M	33
1/23/83	Thunder Bay, Canada	WC 90M	44
1/29/83	Eau Claire, Wisconsin	U.S. Nat. 70M	7
2/5/83	Westby, Wisconsin	U.S. Nat. 90M	4
2/18/83	Vikersund, Norway	WC 120M	22
2/19/83	Vikersund, Norway	WC 120M	15
2/20/83	Vikersund, Norway	WC 120M	18
3/6/83	Lahti, Finland	WC 90M	10
3/11/83	Baerum, Norway	WC 90M	25
3/13/83	Oslo, Norway	WC 90M	26
3/18/83	Harrachov, Czechoslovakia	120M	25
3/19/83	Harrachov, Czechoslovakia	120M	26
3/20/83	Harrachov, Czechoslovakia	120M	25
3/26/83	Planica, Yugoslavia	WC 70M	39
3/27/83	Planica, Yugoslavia	WC 90M	28

JEFF HASTINGS

Height—5'8"
Weight—150
Birthdate—June 25, 1959
Birthplace—Mountain Home, Idaho
Residence—Norwich, Vermont
Year on National Team—4th

Jeff proved to the Europeans that his strong finish down the stretch in 1982 was no fluke as he picked up where he left off in 1983 and recorded one of the best overall World Cup point standings. He spearheaded the emergence of a group of young U.S. ski jumpers in 1983, along with teammate Mike Holland, that saw eight different Americans score World Cup points during the course of the winter.

Off to a fast start in 1983, Hastings posted the best World Cup result of his career with a second place effort in Engelberg, Switzerland, a mere one and a half points off the winner's total, although they jumped equal distances. Results such as this and a third place showing in the first day of competition on the 90 meter hill in Lake Placid moved Jeff to an eighth place ranking following the conclusion of the first period of World Cup competition.

The lone U.S. jumper to compete in the pre-Olympic competition in Sarajevo, Yugoslavia, Hastings placed ninth in the 70 meter competition, although the meet was not scored as a World Cup. On the home front, he posted back-to-back wins on the 90 meter hill in Westby, Wisconsin, the first win enabling him to retain his U.S. National title he won last season.

A product of the Ford Sayre Ski Program, which has yielded many top U.S. competitors, Hastings finished seventh in the final second period standings in 1982, scoring World Cup points in six of the final seven events. In 1983, he had scoring results in eight of the 19 events he entered. A graduate of Williams College, Hastings just missed a berth on the 1980 U.S. Olympic Team but was named to the 1982 World Championship Team and placed 15th in the 90 meter competition in Oslo, Norway.

One of the most colorful members of the U.S. Team, Jeff began competing at the age of nine and he was one of the first members of the U.S. Ski Team to earn placement in the U.S. Olympic Committee's job opportunity program, landing a summer job with the Sheraton Corporation in Denver.

During the off-season, Jeff enjoys lacrosse and fly fishing.

Date/Year	Event	Hill	Finish
1983	Overall World Cup Jumpings Standings		11(T)
	First Period Standings		8
	Second Period Standings		21(T)
12/11/82	Lillehammer, Norway	EC 70M	16
12/12/82	Lillehammer, Norway	EC 70M	7
12/18/82	Cortina, Italy	WC 72M	44
12/22/82	Lake Placid, New York	WC Tryout 90M	2
12/30/82	Oberstdorf, West Germany	WC 90M	32
1/1/83	Garmisch, West Germany	WC 85M	25

Date	Location	Event	Finish
1/4/83	Innsbruck, Austria	WC 86M	19
1/8/83	Harrachov, Czechoslovakia	WC 90M	7
1/9/83	Harrachov, Czechoslovakia	WC 90M	19
1/15/83	Lake Placid, New York	WC 90M	3
1/16/83	Lake Placid, New York	WC 90M	47
1/22/83	Thunder Bay, Canada	WC 70M	4
1/23/83	Thunder Bay, Canada	WC 90M	8
1/26/83	St. Moritz, Switzerland	WC 70M	34
1/28/83	Gstaad, Switzerland	WC 70M	7
1/30/83	Engelberg, Switzerland	WC 90M	2
2/5/83	Westby, Wisconsin	U.S. Nat. 90M	1
2/6/83	Westby, Wisconsin	90M	1
2/12/83	Sarajevo, Yugoslavia	FIS 70M	9
2/25/83	Falun, Sweden	WC 70M	21
2/27/83	Falun, Sweden	WC 90M	35
3/11/83	Baerum, Norway	WC 90M	20
3/13/83	Oslo, Norway	WC 90M	6
3/26/83	Planica, Yugoslavia	WC 70M	8
3/27/83	Planica, Yugoslavia	WC 90M	32

MIKE HOLLAND

Height—5'10"
Weight—153
Birthdate—December 9, 1961
Birthplace—Barre, Vermont
Residence—Norwich, Vermont
Year on National Team—2nd

If the U.S. Ski Team had a "Cinderella Award", it would most certainly go to Mike Holland in 1983 as he literally skied his way to becoming one of the top U.S. ski jumpers this past winter. Classified as a Development Team member at the start of the season, Holland finished the winter as the second highest American point scorer on the World Cup circuit with a 15th place overall ranking in the final World Cup points list.

Holland began the season as part of a training group that was sent to Norway for early Europa Cup competition. When the dust had settled, Holland was on his way to Cortina and a regular spot with the World Cup group for the remainder of the season.

Mike's highest World Cup finish was to come on home turf as he recorded a fourth place showing off the 90 meter hill in Lake Placid during the first day of World Cup competition. He scored his initial Cup points in the second leg of the Intersport Springertournee in Garmisch, West Germany with a 12th place effort on the 85 meter hill. In the 22 World Cup events that Mike entered in 1983, he picked up points in 12 of them, including a string of five in a row during the course of January.

On the domestic front, Mike placed third in the 90 meter competition at the U.S. Nationals and added another third place finish to his list of accomplishments on the 70 meter hill at the Shell Cup in Thunder Bay. His top international showing came on the 120 meter hill at the World Ski Flying Championships in Harrachov, Czechoslovakia when he soared 177 meters to set a new personal best while falling just four meters short of the hill record that was set that same day.

A student at the University of Vermont in Mechanical Engineering, Mike is a product of the Ford Sayre jumping program.

When not flying down the hill, Mike enjoys scuba diving, water skiing and photography.

Date/Year	Event	Hill	Finish
1983	Overall World Cup Jumping Standings		15
	First Period Standings		15
	Second Period Standings		14
12/18/82	Cortina, Italy	WC 72M	22
1/1/83	Garmisch, West Germany	WC 85M	12
1/4/83	Innsbruck, Austria	WC 86M	234
1/8/83	Harrachov, Czechoslovakia	WC 90M	16
1/9/83	Harrachov, Czechoslovakia	WC 90M	6
1/15/83	Lake Placid, New York	WC 90M	4
1/16/83	Lake Placid, New York	WC 90M	11
1/22/83	Thunder Bay, Canada	WC 70M	9
1/23/83	Thunder Bay, Canada	WC 90M	6
1/26/83	St. Moritz, Switzerland	WC 70M	17
2/5/83	Westby, Wisconsin	U.S. Nat. 90M	3
2/18/83	Vikersund, Norway	WC 120M	9
2/19/83	Vikersund, Norway	WC 120M	5
2/20/83	Vikersund, Norway	WC 120M	6
2/25/83	Falun, Sweden	WC 70M	15
2/27/83	Falun, Sweden	WC 90M	7
3/11/83	Baerum, Norway	WC 90M	12
3/18/83	Harrachov, Czechoslovakia	120M	15
3/19/83	Harrachov, Czechoslovakia	120M	2
3/20/83	Harrachov, Czechoslovakia	120M	14
3/27/83	Planica, Yugoslavia	WC 90M	23

MARK KONOPACKE

Height—5'10"
Weight—160
Birthdate—April 26, 1963
Birthplace—Iron Mountain, Michigan
Residence—Kingsford, Michigan
Year on National Team—2nd

A discretionary choice to the 1983 jumping team, Mark showed the coaches that their faith in him was not unfounded this past winter as he scored the first World Cup points of his career with an 11th place showing in the first day on the 90 meter hill in Lake Placid. In addition, he captured the U.S. National 70 meter championship and skied to the runnerup position a week later in the 90 meter competition.

Solid results in Lake Placid in January in the Europa Cup Tryout competition earned him a spot on the team that competed on the Europa Cup circuit in the Dreilander Tournee. Konopacke ended the tour ranked 15th in the final Dreilander standings.

He was later named to the World University Games Team for the U.S., the first time an American contingent has ever participated in the Games, and he responded with a bronze medal effort in the 70 meter competition, one of only two U.S. skiers to win medals at the Games.

A product of one of the most active ski jumping areas of the country, Iron Mountain, Mark and his brother Mike have spearheaded the effort to supply more upper peninsula jumpers to the U.S. Team.

Date/Year	Event	Hill	Finish
1983	Overall World Cup Jumping Standings		55(T)
	First Period Standings		42(T)
1/15/83	Lake Placid, New York	WC 90M	11
1/16/83	Lake Placid, New York	Wc 90M	17
1/29/83	Ea Claire, Wisconsin	U.S. Nat. 70M	1
2/5/83	Westby, Wisconsin	U.S. Nat. 90M	2
2/27/83	Sofia, Bulgaria	FIS Univ. 70M	3

DENNIS McGRANE

Height—5'9"
Weight—137
Birthdate—July 7, 1962
Birthplace—Denver, Colorado
Residence—Littleton, Colorado
Year on National Team—3rd

McGrane alternated between school and training during the fall but came on in a big way early, winning both a U.S.—Canadian meet in Steamboat Springs, Colorado on his first day on-snow, and then capturing the 90 meter honors in the World Cup Tryouts in Lake Placid.

Dennis picked up his first World Cup points in 1983 when the tour moved to North America, finishing 12th in the first day of jumping in Lake Placid.

The Dartmouth College student is a product of the Winter Park Ski Jumping program and was the U.S. Junior National jumping champion in 1979. First named to the Junior Team in 1977, McGrane has been a member of two World Junior Championship Teams in 1979 and 1980 and moved to the National Team midway through the 1982 season.

Date/Year	Event	Hill	Finish
1983	Overall World Cup Jumping Standings		57(T)
	First Period Standings		44
12/11/82	Steamboat Springs, Colorado	US/Can. 70M	1
12/22/82	Lake Placid, New York	WC Tryout 90M	1
1/6/83	Bischofshofen, Austria	WC 90M	18
1/9/83	Harrachov, Czecoslovakia	WC 90M	16
1/15/83	Lake Placid, New York	WC 90M	12
1/22/83	Thunder Bay, Canada	WC 70M	25
2/27/83	Falun, Sweden	WC 90M	25

REED ZUEHLKE

Height—5'9"
Weight—149
Birthdate—October 26, 1960
Birthplace—Eau Claire, Wisconsin
Residence—Eau Claire, Wisconsin
Year on National Team—7th

Reed continued his progress toward the upper echelon of World Cup jumpers in 1983 as he recorded the best World Cup finish of his career with an impressive sixth place effort on the 90 meter hill in Lake Placid in the first day of World Cup competition. In addition, he collected Cup points for his 14th place result at the World Cup Finals in Planica, Yugoslavia, also off the 90 meter hill.

He got off to a fast start in 1983, winning the 70 meter competition at the World Cup Tryouts in Steamboat Springs, Colorado and collecting consistent results in Lake Placid for the second set of tryout jumps following several Europa Cup meets in Norway. He entered the World Cup arena for the events in Lake Placid in mid-January and Thunder Bay, Canada and then rejoined the team for the final events of the season.

On the domestic front, Zuehlke placed third in the U.S. Nationals 70 meter competition and claimed the top spot in the jumping segment of the U.S. Nordic Combined Nationals. He was selected to represent the U.S. at the World University Games in Sofia Bulgaria and placed fourth off the 70 meter hill at the Games. He just missed additional World Cup points with his 17th place effort on the 90 meter jump at Thunder Bay.

A member of the U.S. Olympic contingent in 1980 at Lake Placid, Reed placed 45th in the 90 meter competition at the Winter Games. He has also been a member of the 1982 World Championship Team and claimed a 40th place 70 meter finish. He captured the 70 meter title at the U.S. Nationals that same season.

The University of Wisconsin-Eau Claire student comes by his talents honestly as his father Keith was a top ski jumper for the U.S. in the late 1950's. Reed first gained national attention in 1978 when he consistently outperformed many of the Team veterans in early season competition and qualified for the early trip to Europe. A knee injury suffered during the Springertournee sidelined him for the remainder of the season.

During the off-season, Reed enjoys wood working, water skiing and motorcycles.

Date/Year	Event	Hill	Finish
1983	Overall World Cup Jumping Standings		42(T)
	First Period Standings		36(T)
	Second Period Standings		48(T)
11/30/82	Steamboat Springs, Colorado	WC Tryout 70M	1
12/11/82	Lillehammer, Norway	EC 70M	22
12/12/82	Lillehammer, Norway	EC 70M	46
12/22/82	Lake Placid, New York	WC Tryout 90M	4
1/15/83	Lake Placid, New York	WC 90M	6
1/16/83	Lake Placid, New York	WC 90M	22
1/22/83	Thunder Bay, Canada	WC 70M	31
1/23/83	Thunder Bay, Canada	WC 90M	17
1/29/83	Eau Claire, Wisconsin	U.S. Nat. 70M	3
2/5/83	Westby, Wisconsin	U.S. Nat. 90M	10
2/19/83	Iron Mountain, Michigan	90M	2
2/20/83	Iron Mountain, Michigan	90M	2
2/27/83	Sofia, Bulgaria	FIS Univ. 70M	4
3/13/83	Oslo, Norway	WC 90M	58
3/26/83	Planica, Yugoslavia	WC 70M	25
3/27/83	Planica, Yugoslavia	WC 90M	14

B-TEAM

LANDIS ARNOLD

Height—5'11"
Weight—170
Birthdate—August 6, 1960
Birthplace—Boulder, Colorado
Residence—Tabernash, Colorado
Year on National Team—3rd

Landis spent the majority of the 1983 season on the domestic circuit, joining the World Cup group for the February and March portion of the tour. In addition, he represented the U.S. at the World University Games in Sofia, Bulgaria, placing eighth on the 70 meter hill at the Games.

Following a steady start when his first six results were among the top eight, Landis joined the team in Lake Placid for the first ever World Cup jumping event in the U.S. and just missed World Cup points on the second day of competition on the 90 meter hill placing 18th. He rejoined the team for ski flying in Vikersund, Norway and Harrachov, Czechoslovakia and recorded his top international finish in Harrachov, skiing to a tenth place tie on the 120 meter hill, although the Czechoslovakia jumping was not World Cup.

On the home front in 1983, Arnold placed ninth in the 70 meter competition at the U.S. Nationals and claimed a sixth place showing in the 90 meter championships. His top finish of 1983 came in the form of a runnerup performance in a U.S.-Canada meet in Steamboat Springs, Colorado on the 90 meter hill.

A product of the Winter Park Ski Club, Landis currently attends Dartmouth College and is majoring in Geography and Environmental Studies. He hopes to have his bachelor's degree by August. During his stay at Dartmouth, he has been a member of both the ski team and the kayaking squad, earning NCAA All-American status in 1980 with his fifth place jumping finish in the national championships. In addition, he has also been honored as the Best Rocky Mountain Jumper in 1977 and 1978 as well as the Best Dartmouth Skier in 1980.

Future plans include graduate school in either law or business and possibly coaching. During the off-season, Landis enjoys the study of native cultures, photography and kayaking.

Date/Year	Event	Hill	Finish
11/30/82	Steamboat Springs, Colorado	WC Tryout 70M	5
12/11/82	Steamboat Springs, Colorado	US/Can. 70M	4
12/12/82	Steamboat Springs, Colorado	US/Can. 90M	2
12/22/82	Lake Placid, New York	WC Tryout 90M	8
1/1/83	Lake Placid, New York	EC Tryout 70M	7
1/2/83	Lake Placid, New York	EC Tryout 70M	3
1/15/83	Lake Placid, New York	WC 90M	27
1/16/83	Lake Placid, New York	WC 90M	18
1/22/83	Thunder Bay, Canada	WC 70M	39
1/23/83	Thunder Bay, Canada	WC 90M	39
1/29/83	Eau Claire, Wisconsin	U.S. Nat. 70M	9
2/5/83	Westby, Wisconsin	U.S. Nat. 90M	6
2/18/83	Vikersund, Norway	WC 120M	24
2/19/83	Vikersund, Norway	WC 120M	44
2/10/83	Vikersund, Norway	WC 120M	17
2/27/83	Sofia, Bulgaria	FIS Univ. 70M	8
3/13/83	Oslo, Norway	WC 90M	65
3/18/83	Harrachov, Czechoslovakia	120M	17
3/19/83	Harrachov, Czechoslovakia	120M	10(T)
3/20/83	Harrachov, Czechoslovakia	120M	36

CHRIS HASTINGS

Height—5'7"
Weight—150
Birthdate—August 17, 1964
Birthplace—Hanover, New Hampshire
Residence—Norwich, Vermont
Year on National Team—1st

Chris will join brother Jeff on the U.S. Team this season following a strong showing in 1983 that included capturing the U.S. Junior National 90 meter jumping championship as well as a runnerup performance on the 70 meter hill. One of the top junior competitors the past several seasons, Chris will try his hand at international competition on more of a full-time basis in the years to come.

His first World Cup competition came this past winter as he competed in the North American events in Lake Placid and Thunder Bay, Canada. His top showing came in the form of a 37th place finish on the 90 meter hill at Lake Placid on the second day of competition. In addition, he was selected to the initial U.S. contingent to compete in the World University Games in Sofia, Bulgaria, placing 13th in the 70 meter jumping competition.

A freshman at St. Lawrence University, Chris accompanied a junior group to Scandinavia during the 1982 season and posted some impressive results, including a victory in Kaustinen, Finland. If any of Jeff's influence has rubbed off on Chris, the U.S. ski jumping program is in good hands for the future.

Date/Year	Event	Hill	Finish
12/22/82	Lake Placid, New York	WC Tryout 90M	7
1/1/83	Lake Placid, New York	EC Tryout 70M	2
1/2/83	Lake Placid, New York	EC Tryout 70M	10
1/16/83	Lake Placid, New York	WC 90M	37
1/23/83	Thunder Bay, Canada	WC 90M	43
1/29/83	Eau Claire, Wisconsin	U.S. Jr Nat. 70M	2
2/5/83	Westby, Wisconsin	U.S. Jr Nat. 90M	1
2/27/83	Sofia, Bulgaria	FIS Univ. 70M	13

ZANE PALMER

Height—6'1"
Weight—173
Birthdate—February 27, 1961
Birthplace—Kremmling, Colorado
Residence—Kremmling, Colorado
Year on National Team—2nd

A knee injury sidelined Zane for the second half of the season in 1983 following some strong Europa Cup showings and his first exposure to World Cup competition. He sustained the injury during the second day of World Cup competition on the 90 meter hill in Thunder Bay, Canada.

Prior to the mishap, Zane qualified for the January Europa Cup trip to Middle Europe and posted a ninth place finish in the Dreilander Tournee event in Planica, Yugoslavia and coupled that with a third place effort in Tarvisio, Italy to finish sixth in the final Tournee standings, the top American in the final rankings.

Zane entered the World Cup ranks when the tour moved to North America, his top finish coming in the second day of jumping on the 90 meter hill at Lake Placid with a 23rd place finish. The following weekend in Thunder Bay saw the end of his season.

A member of the Steamboat Springs Winter Sports Club, Zane posted an individual win in the Brattleboro Open Tournament in 1982 on the 70 meter hill as well as claiming second and third place finishes in the jumping portion of the U.S. National Nordic Combined Championships. A four-year member of the U.S. Junior Development Team, Palmer was named to the Who's Who in American High School Students while attending West Grand High School.

During the off-season, Zane participates on the rodeo circuit, riding bareback horses and bulls. In addition, he enjoys hunting and fishing.

Date/Year	Event	Hill	Finish
11/30/82	Steamboat Springs, Colorado	WC Tryout 70M	7
12/12/82	Steamboat Springs, Colorado	US/Can. 90M	6
12/22/82	Lake Placid, New York	WC Tryout 90M	10
1/1/83	Lake Placid, New York	EC Tryout 70M	5
1/2/83	Lake Placid, New York	EC Tryout 70M	4
1/8/83	Planica, Yugoslavia	EC 70M	9
1/9/83	Villach, Austria	EC 70M	21
1/10/83	Tarvisio, Italy	EC 70M	3
1/15/83	Lake Placid, New York	WC 90M	29
1/16/83	Lake Placid, New York	WC 90M	23
1/22/83	Thunder Bay, Canada	WC 70M	35
1/23/83	Thunder Bay, Canada	WC 90M	Injured

NILS STOLZLECHNER

Height—6'1"
Weight—158
Birthdate—May 5, 1962
Birthplace—Salzburg, Austria
Residence—Sun Valley, Idaho
Year on National Team—2nd

Nils waited until the end of the 1983 season to crack the top 15 of a World Cup event and earn the first Cup points of his career with a 12th place showing on the 70 meter hill in Planica, Yugoslavia at the World Cup Finals. A strong early season in 1982 earned him the final jumping spot on the U.S. World Championship Team and this past winter's results netted him a tie for the 57th spot overall in the final World Cup standings as a part-time World Cup competitor.

An Austrian native, Stolzlechner's top result in 1983 came in the form of a runnerup performance on the 70 meter hill in Ishpeming, Michigan in the Paul Diepila Memorial Tournament, 15 points behind Manfred Steiner of Austria. He also claimed a fifth place finish in the U.S. Nationals 70 meter competition.

A top alpine skier as well, Nils competed in the North American World Cup jumping events and headed to Europe for the first time last winter to compete in the World Ski Flying championships in Harrachov, Czechoslovakia, finishing 29th overall in the competition. During the summer, he returns to Austria to train and joined his teammates for summer training on plastic in Middle Europe.

During the off-season, Nils enjoys flying of another sort as he has his pilots license. He also enjoys windsurfing, golf and tennis and future educational plans include aeronautical school.

Date/Year	Event	Hill	Finish
1983	Overall World Cup		
	Jumping Standings		57(T)
	Second Period Standings		41(T)
11/30/82	Steamboat Springs, Colorado	WC Tryout 70M	6
12/11/82	Steamboat Springs, Colorado	US/Can. 70M	6
12/22/82	Lake Placid, New York	WC Tryout 90M	6
1/15/83	Lake Placid, New York	WC 90M	35
1/16/83	Lake Placid, New York	WC 90M	32
1/22/83	Thunder Bay, Canada	WC 70M	44
1/23/83	Thunder Bay, Canada	WC 90M	35
1/29/83	Eau Claire, Wisconsin	U.S. Nat. 70M	5
2/19/83	Iron Mountain, Michigan	90M	3
2/26/83	Ishpeming, Michigan	70M	2
2/27/83	Ishpeming, Michigan	70M	5
3/18/83	Harrachov, Czechoslovakia	120M	31
3/19/83	Harrachov, Czechoslovakia	120M	36
3/20/83	Harrachov, Czechoslovakia	120M	27
3/26/83	Planica, Yugoslavia	WC 70M	12
3/27/83	Planica, Yugoslavia	WC 90M	27

JEFF VOLMRICH

Height—6'2"
Weight—195
Birthdate—January 22, 1964
Birthplace—Pittsburgh, Pennsylvania
Residence—Lake Placid, New York
Year on National Team—1st

One of the top junior jumpers in the U.S. over the last several winters, Volmrich makes the move up to the National Team with the outset of the 1984 season based on his performances in 1983.

Those results included five individual victories throughout the course of the winter. Among those wins, Jeff captured the U.S. Junior National 70 meter crown in Eau Claire, Wisconsin and placed third in the 90 meter championships in Westby, Wisconsin the following week.

A student at St. Lawrence University, Volmrich was selected to the U.S. World Junior Championship Team in 1982 and placed 30th on the 70 meter hill in Murau, Austria. In addition, he claimed the top spot in both days of jumping at the U.S. Junior Nordic Combined Championships that same season.

Jeff got his first taste of World Cup competition this past season, placing 47th and 41st on the 90 meter hill in Lake Placid. A talented athlete, Jeff is one of the young ski jumpers who are providing the talent base for the U.S. Ski Team as they continue to develop into an international jumping power.

Date/Year	Event	Hill	Finish
1/1/83	Lake Placid, New York	EC Tryout 70M	1
1/2/83	Lake Placid, New York	EC Tryout 70M	5
1/15/83	Lake Placid, New York	WC 90M	47
1/16/83	Lake Placid, New York	WC 90M	41
1/29/83	Eau Claire, Wisonsin	U.S. Jr Nat. 70M	1
2/5/83	Westby, Wisconsin	U.S. Jr Nat. 90M	3
2/6/83	Westby, Winsconsin	90M	1
2/26/83	Ishpeming, Michigan	70M	1
2/27/83	Ishpeming, Michigan	70M	1

THE ATHLETES: NORDIC COMBINED

KERRY LYNCH

Height—5'10"
Weight—155
Birthdate—July 31, 1957
Birthplace—Denver, Colorado
Residence—Silver Creek, Colorado
Year on National Team—8th

Kerry added his name to the U.S. nordic history books in 1983 with the best performance ever for a U.S. Nordic Combined skier. His efforts this past winter earned him a third place finish in the final "official unofficial" nordic combined standings, holding the overall lead until the final tournee of the season.

En route to his historic results, Kerry posted a pair of individual tournee wins during the course of the winter, the first coming in Lahti, Finland and the second at the prestigious Holmenkollen Ski Festival in Oslo, Norway.

This second win in Oslo also made nordic history as it marked only the second time in the 100-year history of the Holmenkollen competition that an American has ever won an individual event in Oslo. The first win came in 1968 when former U.S. Nordic Director John Bower captured the Kings Cup, signifying nordic combined supremacy at Holmenkollen. Sitting in 11th place following the jumping portion of the Oslo tournee, Lynch won the cross-country portion by a foot over Norway's powerful Thomas Sandberg to claim the Kings Cup by two tenths of a point.

In addition to his wins, Lynch also claimed the runnerup position in Sapporo, Japan and placed tenth in the pre-Olympic competition in Sarajevo, Yugoslavia, winning the cross-country segments in both events. On the home front, he regained his U.S. National Nordic Combined title in 1983, defeating teammate Pat Ahern, who was the 1982 champion, outdistancing Kerry by a mere two tenths of a point.

In 1981, Lynch won the Nordic Combined International Tournee in Reit im Winkl, West Germany which, until his heroics this past season, marked the most significant U.S. nordic combined performance since Bower in 1968. That same year, he sparked the U.S. Team to a second place finish in a combined meet in Nesselwang, West Germany and captured his first U.S. National title.

Named to the U.S. Olympic Team for 1980, Kerry placed 20th in the jumping portion and 12th in cross-country to rank 18th in the final standings at Lake Placid. A member of the U.S. Nordic World Championship Team in 1982, he experienced an off day in jumping but came back to finish second in cross-country to earn a 14th place overall standing in

Oslo. In the team combined competition, he sprinted to the fastest middle lap time in the cross-country relay which proved to be the second fastest lap of the entire race, lifting the U.S. team into seventh place in the final team standings.

When not skiing, Kerry is an accomplished musician and will spend much of the spring recuperating from knee surgery. With the 1984 season signaling World Cup status for nordic combined, Lynch has to be considered as one of the favorites to claim the first World Cup Nordic Combined championship.

Date/Year	Event	Race	Finish
12/12/82	Steamboat Springs, Colorado	NC Tryout	1
12/16/82	Steamboat Springs, Colorado	NC Tryout	1
12/30/82	Oberweissenthal, West Germany	NC Tournee	11
1/16/83	Reit im Winkl, West Germany	NC Tournee	7
1/22/83	Saporo, Japan	NC Tournee	2
1/29/83	Eau Claire, Wisconsin	U.S. Nat. 70M	2
1/29/83	Eau Claire, Wisconsin	U.S. Nat. 70M	6
1/30/83	Eau Claire, Wisconsin	U.S. Nat. NC 15K	1
1/30/83	Eau Claire, Wisconsin	U.S. Nat. NC	1
2/10/83	Sarajevo, Yugoslavia	NC Tournee	10
2/26/83	Falun, Sweden	NC Tournee	4
3/4/83	Lahti, Finland	NC Tournee	1
3/13/83	Oslo, Norway	NC Tournee	1

B-TEAM

PAT AHERN

Height—6'0"
Weight—160
Birthdate—November 10, 1960
Birthplace—Breckenridge, Colorado
Residence—Breckenridge, Colorado
Year on National Team—4th

Pat got back on track in 1983 following a broken collarbone that cut short his 1982 season at the World Championships. Fueled by a strong 12th place showing in Sapporo, Japan, Pat skied his way to a 29th place showing in the final Nordic Combined International Tournee standings.

His top international result this past winter came in the form of an eighth place overall finish in Falun, Sweden. Sitting in 12th position following the jumping segment, Ahern went out the following day and won the cross-country portion to boost him to the eighth place result. In addition, he posted a 22nd place in pre-Olympic nordic combined action in Sarajevo, Yugoslavia.

On the home front in 1983, Ahern lost his U.S. National title to Kerry Lynch, although Pat finished third in the jumping portion and second in cross-country. He also recorded second and third place overall finishes in the nordic combined tryouts held in Steamboat Springs, Colorado.

A product of Summit High School, Ahern was a member of the Rocky Mountain Junior National Team from 1975-78 and won the Nordic Combined Championship in 1977 and 1978. His tenth place result in the World Junior Championships in 1980 was the best result ever for an American in that event and in 1979, he won the Winterstart Series and narrowly missed making the U.S. Olympic Team.

Having completed one year at the University of Alaska-Anchorage, Pat enjoys hiking and backpacking during the off-season.

Date/Year	Event	Race	Finish
12/12/82	Steamboat Springs, Colorado	NC Tryout	2
12/16/82	Steamboat Springs, Colorado	NC Tryout	3
12/30/82	Oberweissenthal, West Germany	NC Tournee	24
1/16/83	Reit im Winkl, West Germany	NC Tournee	40
1/22/83	Sapporo, Japan	NC Tournee	12
1/29/83	Eau Claire, Wisconsin	U.S. Nat NC 70M	3
1/30/83	Eau Claire, Wisconsin	U.S. Nat. NC 15K	2
1/30/83	Eau Claire, Wisconsin	U.S. Nat. NC	2
2/10/83	Sarajevo, Yugoslavia	NC Tournee	22
2/26/83	Falun, Sweden	NC Tournee	8
3/13/83	Oslo, Norway	NC Tournee	26

MATT BYERLY

Height—5'8"
Weight—155
Birthdate—January 8, 1963
Birthplace—Davenport, Iowa
Residence—Silverthorne, Colorado
Year on National Team—3rd

Matt showed good progress during 1983, and continued as one of the top junior nordic combined skiers in the U.S.,

winning the 70 meter jumping portion of the U.S. Junior National Nordic Combined Championships and finishing fifth overall.

In addition, Byerly was selected to represent the U.S. in the World Junior Championships in Kupio, Finland and placed 31st in the final overall standings. He made his debut on the international tournee circuit in Falun, Sweden and placed 16th in the final rankings as the U.S. experienced one of the best days in nordic combined team history.

A graduate of Summit High School, Matt placed second in the Junior National Championships in 1980 as well as in the 1981 Junior Olympics. Also during the 1980 season, he won the Rocky Mountain Combined Championship to earn the Bookstrom Award for Outstanding Nordic Combined Skier, an award that he was to receive in 1981 as well.

Date/Year	Event	Race	Finish
12/12/82	Steamboat Springs	NC Tryout	5
12/16/82	Steamboat Springs, Colorado	NC Tryout Jr.	1
1/16/83	Reit im Winkl, West Germany	NC Tournee Jr.	24
1/29/83	Eau Claire, Wisconsin	U.S. Jr. Nat 70M	1
1/30/83	Eau Claire, Wisconsin	U.S. Jr. Nat 15K	8
1/30/83	Eau Claire, Wisconsin	U.S. Jr. Nat	5
2/26/83	Falun, Sweden	NC Tournee	16
3/11/83	Kupio, Finland	World Jr. NC	31

MIKE RANDALL

Height—5'9"
Weight—140
Birthdate—March 27, 1962
Birthplace—Cloquet, Minnesota
Residence—Cloquet, Minnesota
Year on National Team—3rd

Mike's second year on the National Team this past season was highlighted by a 14th place showing at the Swedish Ski Games in Falun, Sweden as the U.S. Nordic Combined Team posted one of its top showings with all four skiers in the top 16. In addition, he skied to a fourth place overall finish in the U.S. National Championships, placing seventh in jumping and third in the cross-country segment of the competition.

The only mid-western nordic combined skier to make the U.S. Team in the past ten years, Mike has represented the U.S. in both the World Championships in Oslo, Norway in 1982 and the World Junior Championships in Murau, Austria the same season. Stepping in to replace Pat Ahern in Oslo, Mike recorded a 33rd place overall finish while collecting a 34th place overall showing in the junior championships.

A 1980 graduate of Cloquet High School, he won the Central Division Combined Championship from 1978 to 1980 and was a three-time winner of the Cloquet Ski Team's Outstanding Skier Award.

Date/Year	Event	Race	Finish
12/12/82	Steamboat Springs, Colorado	NC Tryout	3
12/16/82	Steamboat Springs, Colorado	NC Tryout	2
1/29/83	Eau Claire, Wisconsin	U.S. Nat NC 70M	7
1/30/83	Eau Claire, Wisconsin	U.S. Nat NC 15K	3
1/30/83	Eau Claire, Wisconsin	U.S. Nat NC	4
2/26/83	Falun, Sweden	NC Tournee	14
3/13/83	Oslo, Norway	NC Tournee	27

U.S. OLYMPIC AND WORLD CHAMPIONSHIP NORDIC RESULTS
(Includes finishes in top 25 if available)

1924 Olympics
Chamonix, France

Anders Haugen, 3rd Special Jumping
    21st Nordic Combined
Sigurd Overbye,
    11th Nordic Combined
    19th Special Jumping
LeMoine Batson,
    14th Special Jumping
Harry Lein, 16th Special Jumping
John Carelton,
    22nd Nordic Combined

1928 Olympics
St. Moritz, Switzerland

Rolf Monsen, 6th Special Jumping
Charles Proctor,
    14th Special Jumping
Anders Hagen, 18th Special Jumping
    25th Nordic Combined

1932 Olympics
Lake Placid, New York

Casper Oimen, 5th Special Jumping
Rolf Monsen, 9th Nordic combined
Pedar Falstad, 13th Special Jumping
Ed Blood, 14th Nordic Combined
Richard Parsons, 15th Special Jumping
Lloyd Ellingson,
    16th Nordic Combined
Nils Blackstrom, 19th 50 Km XC
Robert Reid, 20th 50Km Xc
Norton Billings, 21st 50 Km Xc
Olle Zetterstrom, 23rd 18 Km XC
John Eriksen, 25th Nordic Combined

1936 Olympics
Garmisch-Partenkirchen,
West Germany

Sverre Fredheim,
    11th Special Jumping
Caspar Oimen, 13th Special Jumping
Karl Satre, 18th 50 Km Xc
Roy Mikkelsen, 23rd Special Jumping

1948 Olympics
St. Moritz, Switzerland

Gordon Wren, 5th Special Jumping
Sverre Fredheim
    12th Special Jumping
Joe Perrault, 15th Special Jumping

1950 World Championships
Lake Placid, New York

Art Devlin, 6th Special Jumping

1952 Olympics
Oslo, Norway

Ted Farwell, 11th Nordic combined
Keith Wengenman,

12th Special Jumping
Art Devlin, 15th Special Jumping
Art Tokle, 18th special Jumping
Tom Jacobs, 21st Nordic Combined
John Caldwell,
    22nd Nordic Combined

1956 Olympics
Cortina d'Ampezzo, Italy

Art Devlin, 21st Special Jumping
Marvin Crawford,
    23rd Nordic Combined

1960 Olympics
Squaw Valley, California

Ansten Samuelstuen,
    7th Special Jumping
Mack Miller, 17th 50 Km XC
    22nd 15Km SC

1964 Olympics
Innsbruck, Austria

John Balfanz, 10th 70M Jumping
Gene Kotlarek, 15th 70M Jumping
    24th 90M Jumping
John Bower, 15th Nordic Combined
Ansten Samuelstuen,
    23rd 70M Jumping

1968 Olympics
Grenoble, France

John Bower, 13th Nordic Combined
Mike Gallagher, 22nd 50 Km XC
George Krog, 22nd Nordic Combined

1970 World Championships
Vysoke Tatry, Czechoslovakia

Bob Gray, 22nd 50 Km XC
Greg Swor, 24th 70M Jumping
Martha Rockwell, 25th 5 Km XC

1972 Olympics
Sapporo, Japan

Martha Rockwell, 16th 10 KM XC
    18th 5 Km XC
Mike Deveka, 21st Nordic Combined
Gene Morgan, 24th 50 Km XC
Ron Steele, 25th 90M Jumping

1974 World Championships
Falun, Sweden

Martha Rockwell, 20th 20 Km XC
    22nd 5 Km XC

1976 Olympics
Innsbruck, Austria

Bill Koch, 2nd 30 Km XC
    6th 15 Km XC
    13th 50 Km XC
    3rd fastest time in relay
Jim Galanes, 17th Nordic Combined
Men's XC Relay Team, 6th
Jim Denney, 17th 90M Jumping

1978 World Championships
Lahti, Finland

Women's XC Relay Team, 8th
Men's XC Relay Team, 9th
Stan Dunklee, 11th 50 Km SC
Jim Denney, 14th 70M Jumping
Bill Koch, 15th 15 Km XC
Walter Malmquist,
    20th Nordic Combined

1980 Olympics
Lake Placid, New York

Women's XC Relay Team, 7th
Men's XC Relay Team, 8th
Jim Denney, 8th 90M Jumping
Walter Malmquist,
    12th Nordic combined
Bill Koch, 13th 50Km XC
    16th 15 Km XC
Jeff Davis, 17th 70M Jumping
Kerry Lynch, 18th Nordic Combined

1982 World Championships
Oslo, Norway

Bill Koch, 3rd 30Km XC
    21st 15 Km XC
Team Jumping, 6th
Nordic Combined Team, 7th
Men's XC Relay Team, 8th
Women's XC Relay Team,00th
Jim Galanes, 14th 30Km XC
    22nd 15 Km XC
Kerry Lynch, 15th Nordic Combined
Tim Caldwell, 15th 50Km XC
    25th 30 Km XC
Jeff Hastings, 15th 90M Jumping
John Broman, 16th 90M Jumping
Dan Simoneau, 21st 50 Km XC
Leslie Bancroft, 24th 10 Km XC

149

1983 WORLD CUP FINAL STANDINGS

(Following ten events for both men and women)

MEN

1.	Alexander Zavjalov, USSR	122
2.	Gunde Svan, Swe.	116
3.	BILL KOCH, USA	114
4.	Jan Lindvall, Nor.	96
5.	Thomas Wassberg, Swe.	94
6.	Pal G. Mikkelsplass, Nor.	85
7.	Yuri Burlakov, USSR	82
8.	Vladimir Nikitin, USSR	79
9.	Nikolai Zimjatov, USSR	74
10.	Andreas Gruenenfelder, Sui.	71

WOMEN

1.	Marja-Liisa Hamalainen, Fin.	144
2.	Brit Pettersen, Nor.	136
3.	Kveta Jeriova, Tch.	126
4.	Blanka Paulu, Tch.	121
5.	Anne Jahren, Nor.	114
6.	Lubov Liadova, USSR	87
7.	Inger-Helene Nybratten, Nor.	80
8.	Raisa Smetanina, USSR	79
9.	Anna Pasiarova, Tch.	73
10.	Marie Johansson-Risby, Swe.	62

NATIONS CUP
MEN

1.	USSR	529
2.	Norway	510
3.	Sweden	322
5.	UNITED STATES	213

WOMEN

1.	Norway	671
2.	USSR	414
3.	Czechoslovakia	390
7.	UNITED STATES	69

OVERALL

1.	Norway	1181
2.	USSR	943
3.	Finland	520
4.	Sweden	427
5.	Czechoslovakia	419
6.	UNITED STATES	282
7.	Switzerland	176
8.	West Germany	121
9.	Italy	118
10.	East Germany	115

1983 WORLD CUP FINAL JUMPING STANDINGS

(Following twenty-six events)

1.	Matti Nykaenen, Fin.	277
2.	Horst Bulau, Can.	260
3.	Armin Kogler, Aut.	211
4.	Olav Hansson, Nor.	186
5.	Per Bergeruud, Nor.	137
6.	Steiner Braaten, Nor.	126
7.	Pentti Kokkonen, Fin.	115
8.	Ole Bremseth, Nor.	99
9.	Richard Schallert, Aut.	98
10.	Jari Puikkonen, Fin.	97
11.	JEFF HASTINGS, USA	93
15.	MIKE HOLLAND, USA	83
42.	REED ZUEHLKE, USA	12
49.	JON DENNEY, USA	7
53.	JOHN BROMAN, USA	6
55.	MARK KONOPACKE, USA	5
57.	DENNIS McGRANE, USA	4
	NILS STOLZLECHNER, USA	4

NATIONS CUP

1.	Norway	859
2.	Finland	696
3.	Austria	644
4.	Canada	387
5.	East Germany	267
6.	UNITED STATES	221
7.	Czechoslovakia	164
8.	Yugoslavia	84
9.	West Germany	72
10.	Italy	51

1983 FINAL NORDIC COMBINED STANDINGS

(Following seven events)

1.	Uwe Dotzauer, DDR	1278.26
2.	Gunther Schmieder, DDR	1271.85
3.	KERRY LYNCH, USA	1268.60
4.	Espen Andersen, Nor.	1259.75
5.	Tom Sandberg, Nor.	1233.00
29.	PAT AHERN, USA	1130.53
34.	MIKE RANDALL, USA	1075.49
54.	MATT BYERLY, USA	693.12

YEAR-BY-YEAR OVERALL WORLD CUP RESULTS

(Standings are unofficial prior to 1979 season)

CROSS COUNTRY

Year	Men
1974	1. Ivar Formo, Nor.
	2. Juha Mieto, Fin.
	3. Edi Hauser, Sui.
1975	1. Oddvar Braa, Nor.
	2. Odd Martinsen, Nor.
	3. Juha Mieto, Fin.
1976	1. Juha Mieto, Fin.
	2. Arto Koivisto, Fin.
	3. Ivar Formo, Nor.
	8. BILL KOCH, USA
1977	1. Thomas Wassberg, Swe.
	2. Juha Mieto, Fin.
	3. Thomas Magnusson, Swe.
1978	1. Sven-Ake Lundback, Swe.
	2. Lars-Erik Eriksen, Nor.
	3. Magne Myrmo, Nor.
1979	1. Oddvar Braa, Nor.
	2. Lars-Erik Eriksen, Nor.
	3. Sven-Ake Lundback, Swe.
1980	1. Juha Mieto, Fin.
	2. Thomas Wassberg, Swe.
	3. Lars-Erik Eriksen, Nor.
1981	1. Alexander Zavjalov, USSR
	2. Oddvar Braa, Nor.
	3. Ove Aunli, Nor.
1982	1. BILL KOCH, USA
	2. Thomas Wassberg, Swe.
	3. Harri Kirvesniemi, Fin.
	7. DAN SIMONEAU, USA
	23. JIM GALANES, USA
	28. TIM CALDWELL, USA
1983	1. Alexander Zavjalov, USSR
	2. Gunde Svan, Swe.
	3. BILL KOCH, USA

Year	Women
1979	1. Galina Kulakova, USSR
	2. Raisa Smetanina, USSR
	3. Zinndia Amosova, USSR
	7. ALLISON OWEN-SPENCER, USA
1981	1. Raisa Smetanina, USSR
	2. Berit Aunli, Nor.
	3. Kveta Jeriova, Tch.
1982	1. Berit Aunli, Nor.
	2. Brit Pettersen, Nor.
	3. Kveta Jeriova, Tch.
1983	1. Marja-Liisa Hamalainen, Fin.
	2. Brit Pettersen, Nor.
	3. Kveta Jeriova, Tc.

JUMPING

1981	1. Armin Kogler, Aut.
	2. Roger Ruud, Nor.
	3. Horst Bulau, Can.
1982	1. Armin Kogler, Aut.
	2. Hubert Neuper, Aut.
	3. Horst Bulau, Can.
1983	1. Matti Nykaenen, Fin.
	2. Horst Bulau, Can.
	3. Armin Kogler, Aut.

U.S. NATIONAL NORDIC CHAMPIONS—1964-83

MEN

15K

1964	Peter Lahdenpera, USA
1965	David Rikert, USA
1966	Mike Gallagher, USA
1967	Mike Gallagher, USA
1968	(Not Available)
1969	Clark Matis, USA
1970	Mike Gallagher, USA
1971	Mike Elliott, USA
1972	Mike Elliott, USA
1973	Tim Caldwell, USA
1974	Larry Martin, USA
1975	Bill Koch, USA
1976	Kevin Swigert, USA
1977	Stan Dunklee, USA
1978	Stan Dunklee, USA
1979	Bill Koch, USA
1980	Bill Koch, USA
1981	Bill Koch, USA
1982	Bill Koch, USA
1983	Tim Caldwell, USA

30K

1964	Ed Demers, USA
1965	Bill Spencer, USA
1966	Mike Elliott, USA
1967	Mike Gallagher, USA
1968	(Not Available)
1969	(Not Available)
1970	Mike Gallagher, USA
1971	Mike Gallagher, USA
1972	Mike Elliott, USA
1973	Bob Gray, USA
1974	Mike Devecka, USA
1975	Tim Caldwell, USA
1976	Kevin Swigert, USA
1977	Tim Caldwell, USA
1978	Bob Treadwell, USA
1979	Tim Caldwell, USA
1980	Stan Dunklee, USA
1981	Bill Koch, USA
1982	Stan Dunklee, USA
1983	Bill Koch, USA

50K

1971	Bob Gray, USA
1972	Bob Gray, USA
1973	Joe McNulty, USA
1974	Ron Yeager, USA
1975	Tim Caldwell, USA
1976	Stan Dunklee, USA
1977	Stan Dunklee, USA
1978	Kevin Swigert, USA
1979	Stan Dunklee, USA
1980	Jim Galanes, USA
1981	Tim Caldwell, USA
1982	Tim Caldwell, USA
1983	Bill Koch, USA

WOMEN

5K

1969	Martha Rockwell, USA
1970	Martha Rockwell, USA
1971	Sharon Firth, Can.
1972	Martha Rockwell, USA
1973	Martha Rockwell, USA

1974	Martha Rockwell, USA
1975	Martha Rockwell, USA
1976	Jana Hlavaty, USA
1981	Alison Owen-Spencer, USA
1982	Lynn Galanes, USA
1983	Judy Endestad, USA

7.5K

1977	Shirley Firth, Can.
1978	Alison Spencer, USA
1979	Alison Owen-Spencer, USA
1980	Alison Owen-Spencer, USA

10K

1969	Martha Rockwell, USA
1970	Martha Rockwell, USA
1971	Martha Rockwell, USA
1972	Martha Rockwell, USA
1973	Martha Rockwell, USA
1974	Martha Rockwell, USA
1975	Martha Rockwell, USA
1976	Jana Hlavaty, USA
1977	Sharon Firth, Can.
1978	Lynn VonderHeide, USA
1979	Alison Owen-Spencer, USA
1980	Alison Owen-Spencer, USA
1981	Alison Owen-Spencer, USA
1982	Lynn Galanes, USA
1983	Judy Endestad, USA

15K

1974	Martha Rockwell, USA

20K

1977	Shirley Firth, Can.
1978	Alison Owen-Spencer, USA
1979	Beth Paxson, USA
1980	Betsy Haines, USA
1981	Lynn Galanes, USA
1982	Lynn Galanes, USA
1983	Pam Weiss, USA

JUMPING

1964	John Balfanz, USA
1965	David Hicks, USA
1966	Gene Kotlarek, USA
1967	Gene Kotlarek, USA
1968	Jay Martin, USA
1969	Adrian Watt, USA
1970	Bill Bakke, USA
1971	Jerry Martin, USA
1972	Greg Swor, USA
1973	Jerry Martin, USA
1974	Ron Steele, USA
1975	Jerry Martin, USA
1976	Jim Denney, USA
1977	Jim Denney, USA
1978	Mike Devecka, USA
1979	Jeff Davis, USA
1980	Walter Malmquist, USA
1981	Horst Bulau, Can. (70M)
	Horst Bulau, Can. (90m)
1982	Reed Zuehlke, USA (70M)
	Jeff Hastings, USA (90M)
1983	Mark Konopacke, USA (70M)
	Jeff Hastings, USA (90M)

NORDIC COMBINED

1964	Jim Balfanz, USA
1965	David Rikert, USA

1966	John Bower, USA
1967	John Bower, USA
1968	John Bower, USA
1969	Jim Miller, USA
1970	Jim Miller, USA
1971	Bob Kendall, USA
1972	Mike Devecka, USA
1973	Teyck Weed, USA
1974	Bruce Cunningham, USA
1975	Mike Devecka, USA
1976	Jim Galanes, USA
1977	Jim Galanes, USA
1978	Jim Galanes, USA
1979	Mike Devecka, USA
1980	Walter Malmquist, USA
1981	Kerry Lynch, USA
1982	Pat Ahern, USA
1983	Kerry Lynch, USA

U.S. SKI TEAM ALUMNI LIST

This list has been made possible through the time and research of the National Ski Hall of Fame in Ishpeming, Michigan and the U.S. Ski Team.

Legend: A-Alpine, XC-Cross-Country, J-Jumping, NC-Nordic Combined, and (D)-Deceased

AKERS, CHARLES   XC
Olympic Team: 1960
ADGATE, CARY   A
A Team: 1974-80
B Team: 1973
C Team: 1972
Olympic Team: 1976, 80
FIS Team: 1974, 78
AHERN, PAT   NC
A Team: 1980-
B Team: 1978-79
FIS Team: 1982
ALLEN, WENDY   A
Ski Team: 1968
ALLSOP, MICHAEL   A
A Team: 1965
AMICK, DON H.   A
A Team: 1948
Olympic Team: 1948
ANDERSEN, ERLING   XC
A Team: 1919-36
Olympic Team: 1932
ANDERSON, KARL   A
A Team: 1975-78, 79-80
B Team: 1972-75, 78, 80-81
Olympic Team: 1976, 80
FIS Team: 1978
ANDERSON, KATHY (SHERWOOD)   XC
B Team: 1973-75
FIS Team: 1974
ARMSTRONG, DEBBIE   A
B Team;   1984-
ARNOLD, LANDIS   J
B Team: 1981-
C Team: 1980
AROYO, BARBARA (FERRIES)   A
A Team: 1964
Olympic Team: 1964
FIS Team: 1962
ATKINS, MARY LEE   XC
A Team: 1972-74
B Team: 1971
FIS Team: 1974
AUSEKLIS, NANCY (SISE)   A
A Team: 1961-62
FIS Team: 1962
AXELSON, CHRIS   NC
B Team: 1979-80

B

BACKSTROM, NILS   XC
Olympic Team: 1932, 36
BAKKE, WILLIAM   J
A Team: 1965-72
Olympic Team: 1968
FIS Team: 1970
BALBUENA, CHERYL (BECHDOLT)   A
A Team: 1969-70
B Team: 1971-72
BALFANZ, JOHN C.   J
A Team: 1962-68
Olympic Team: 1964-68
FIS Team: 1962, 66
BANCROFT, LESLIE   XC
A Team: 1978-83
Olympic Team:1980
FIS Team: 1982

BARBER, MERRILL H. (MEZZY) J
A Team: 1937-56
C Team: 1953
Olympic Team: 1948, 52
FIS Team: 1940, 50
BARRETT, PENNY (McCOY) A
A Team: 1965-69
FIS Team: 1966
BARRIER, JAMES A
Olympic Team: 1960
BARROWS, JIM A
A Team: 1965-70
Olympic Team: 1968
FIS Team: 1966
BATSON, LEMOINE J
A Team: 1923-40
Olympic Team: 1924, 32
BAXTER, RUTH XC
A Team: 1978-79
B Team: 1979-80
BEAN, HOWARD JR. XC
B Team: 1979-
C Team: 1981
BEAR, LEITH LENDE A
B Team: 1974-77
BECK, WILLIAM A
A Team: 1951-57
Olympic Team: 1952-56
FIS Team: 1954
BELL, ROBBY J. A
A Team: 1969-70
B Team: 1968
BERG, MARY A
FIS Team: 1950
BERMAN, SARA MAE XC
A Team: 1968-69
BERRY, SCOTT J
A Team: 1970-72
Olympic Team: 1972
BIEDERMANN, RON A
A Team: 1975-79
B Team: 1974
FIS Team: 1978
BIETILA, RALPH J
Olympic Team: 1948, 52
FIS Team: 1950
BIETILA, ROY J
FIS Team: 1940
BIETILA, WALTER J
Olympic Team: 1936, 40, 48
BILLINGS, NORTON XC
Olympic Team: 1932
BLACK, ANN A
A Team: 1967-70
B Team: 1965-67
BLACKBURN, GAIL A
B Team: 1972-78
C Team: 1971
BLANN, SHERRY (MORRIS) A
A Team: 1968-70
B Team: 1966-68
C Team: 1963-66
BLATT, BOB A
Olympic Team: 1948
FIS Team: 1940
BLATT, JOHN A
Olympic Team: 1948
BLOOD, EDWARD J. NC
Olympic Team: 1932, 36
BODNAR, BELA A. XC
C Team: 1971-72
Olympic Team: 1976
BOHLIN, CHARLES XC
Ski Team: 1964
BOWER, JOHN NC
A Team: 1962-68
Olympic Team: 1964, 68, 76, 80

FIS Team: 1962, 66, 78
BOWES, HEIDI A
B Team: 1984-
C Team: 1979-83
BRADLEY, DAVID J. A
Olympic Team: 1940
BRADLEY, STEVE A
FIS Team: 1937
BRENNAN, JIM J
A Team: 1959-62
FIS Team: 1962
BREWER, DOROTHY A
Olympic Team: 1936
FIS Team: 1937
BRIGGS, RICHARD D. A
Ski Team: 1978
BRIGHT, ALEXANDER H. A(D)
Olympic Team: 1936
FIS Team: 1935
BRIGHT, CLARITA (HEATH) A
Olympic Team: 1936
FIS Team: 1937
BRISTOL, JOE XC
B Team: 1971-72
BRITCH, BARBARA (JAYE) XC
Olympic Team: 1972
FIS Team: 1970
BROCKWAY, BEVERLY (ANDERSON) A
A Team: 1960
Olympic Team: 1960
BROMAN, JOHN J
A Team: 1979-83
B Team: 1977-79
Olympic Team: 1980
FIS Team: 1982
BROOKS, DON J. A
A Team: 1962-67
FIS Team: 1966
BROOMHALL, WENDALL XC
Olympic Team: 1948, 52
BROWN, MARILYN (COCHRAN) A
A Team: 1968-74
C Team: 1965-68
Olympic Team: 1972
FIS Team: 1970, 74
BROWN, FRANK E. A
Olympic Team: 1960
BROWN, MIKE A
B Team: 1984-
BRUCE, CATHERINE A
B Team: 1978-79
C Team: 1976
FIS Team: 1974, 78
BRUCE, GEOFFREY S. A
A Team: 1975-77
B Team: 1978
C Team: 1973-74
Olympic Team: 1976
FIS Team: 1974, 78
BUCHIKA, ROGER XC
A Team: 1962-64
BUEK, RICHARD A(D)
Olympic Team: 1952
BURDEN, DOUGLAS A
FIS Team: 1954
BURMEISTER, GENE PAUL J
A Team: 1975-77
B Team: 1974, 76, 78
BURTON, JOHN C. XC
Olympic Team: 1952
FIS Team: 1950
BUXMAN, JOHNNY A
A Team: 1981
B Team: 1980
C Team: 1978
FIS Team: 1982
BYERLY, MATT NC
B Team: 1984-

C

CAIN, MAGDALENA "MITZI" (BOWEN) XC
A Team: 1977-78
B Team: 1976-77
FIS Team: 1978
CALDWELL, JENNIFER XC
B Team: 1979
C Team: 1976, 80
CALDWELL, JOHN XC
A Team: 1952
Olympic Team: 1952
CALDWELL, TIM XC
A Team: 1971-
B Team: 1970-71
Olympic Team: 1972, 76, 80
FIS Team: 1974, 78, 82
CAMMACK, FRANK NC
FIS Team: 1958
CAMPBELL, BUSTER NC
FIS Team: 1950
CAREY, ELIZABETH XC
B Team: 1976-79
C Team: 1979-80
CARLETON, JOHN XC
FIS Team: 1924
CARLSON, CORY A
C Team: 1979-80, 84-
CARSON, JENNY (LOCKE) A
B Team: 1969-70
C Team: 1970-71
CARTER, ADAMS A
A Team: 1937-38
FIS Team: 1937
CARTER, HANNAH (LOCKE) A
Olympic Team: 1940
FIS Team: 1937-38
CHAFFEE, RICK A
A Team: 1965-72
Olympic Team: 1968, 72
FIS Team: 1970
CHAFFEE, SUZANNE "SUZY" A
A Team: 1965-68
Olympic Team: 1968
FIS Team: 1966
CHAMBERS, ANDY A
B Team: 1984-
CHENARD, BILL NC
B Team: 1977
C Team: 1976-77
CHIVERS, HOWARD NC
Olympic Team: 1940
CHIVERS, WARREN XC
Olympic Team: 1936, 40
CLAFIN, ELEANOR (WILLIAMS) A
A Team: 1937-39
FIS Team: 1938
CLARK, HOLLY A
C Team: 1973
CLAYTON, SCOTT J
A Team: 1973-80
FIS Team: 1974
CLOUGH, JOHN A
A Team: 1966-67
COCHRAN, BARBARA ANN A
See Williams
COCHRAN, LINDY (KELLY) A
A Team: 1974-78
B Team: 1970-73
Olympic Team: 1976
FIS Team: 1974
COCHRAN, MARILYN A
See Brown
COCHRAN, ROBERT A
A Team: 1968-74
B Team: 1967
Olympic Team: 1972
FIS Team: 1970,74

CODDING, HAL   A
Olympic Team: 1940
FIS Team: 1938
COOKE, NANCY (REYNOLDS)   A
A Team: 1938-41
Olympic Team: 1940
FIS Team: 1938
COOPER, CHRISTIN   A
A Team: 1977
B Team: 1976-77
C Team: 1973
Olympic Team: 1980
FIS Team: 1978, 82
CORBIN, TOM   XC
A Team: 1968-70
B Team: 1971-75
CORCORAN, TOM   A
A Team: 1954-60
B Team: 1950-53
Olympic Team: 1956, 60
FIS Team: 1958
CORROCK, ANNE   A
C Team: 1972-74
CORROCK, KEN   A
A Team: 1969-70
B Team: 1971-72
C Team: 1968-69
CORROCK, SUSAN (HUSTED)   A
A Team: 1969-73
B Team: 1968
Olympic Team: 1972
COUGHLIN, MARTHA   A
Ski Team: 1971-72
CRAM, WENDELL   A
A Team: 1943-44
Olympic Team: 1940
CRANE, MAGGIE   A
A Team: 1977-78
B Team: 1974-77
C Team: 1975-76
CRAWFORD, GARY   NC
A Team: 1979-81
B Team: 1976-79, 82-83
Olympic Team: 1980
FIS Team: 1982
CRAWFORD, MARVIN   J
A Team: 1956
Olympic Team: 1956
FIS Team: 1954
CRESS, JOHN   NC
Olympic Team: 1960
FIS Team: 1958
CREWS, PAUL B. JR.   A
B Team: 1970-72
CROAKES, DARROCH   A
FIS Team: 1936
CROOKS, WILLIAM   A
Olympic Team: 1936
CROSS, JOHN R.   NC
Ski Team: 1960
CUNNINGHAM, BRUCE   NC
A Team: 1971-72, 74
B Team: 1969-70, 73, 75-76
FIS Team: 1974
CURRIER, DAVID   A
A Team: 1972-77
Olympic Team: 1972
FIS Team: 1974
CUTTER, CHRISTINA "KIKI"   A
A Team: 1968-70
Olympic Team: 1968
FIS Team: 1970

D

DABNEY, THOMAS   A(D)
FIS Team: 1935
DAMON, LARRY   XC
Olympic Team: 1956, 60, 64, 68

DARGAY, THOMAS   J
A Team: 1971-77
Olympic Team: 1974
DAVIS, JEFF   J
B Team: 1977-82
Olympic Team: 1980
FIS Team: 1978
DAVIS, PETER   XC
A Team: 1970-72
B Team: 1969, 73-74
FIS Team: 1970
DELFAUSSE, LEE HALL   A
A Team: 1965-67
DENDAHL, JOHN H.   XC
Olympic Team: 1960
DENNEY, JEFF   J
A Team: 1977-81
B Team: 1976, 82-83
FIS Team: 1978
DENNEY, JIM   J
A Team: 1976-80
B Team: 1974-75, 81-82
Olympic Team: 1976, 80
FIS Team: 1978
DENNEY, JON K.   A
A Team: 1980-81
B Team: 1978-79, 82-
FIS Team: 1978
DENNISON, TIM E.   J
A Team: 1968-72
DENSMORE, JASON   A
B Team: 1969-73
DEROSIER, DAVE   J
C Team: 1976-78
DEVECKA, MIKE   J
A Team: 1968-80
Olympic Team: 1968, 72, 76, 80
FIS Team: 1970, 74
DEVIN, BETSY   A
C Team: 1975, 77
DEVIN, STEVE   A
B Team: 1975-77
DEVLIN, ARTHUR   J
Olympic Team: 1948, 52, 56
FIS Team: 1950, 54
DISTIN, BILL   A
Ski Team: 1948
DODGE, BROOKS   A
A Team: 1952-56
Olympic Team: 1952, 56
FIS Team: 1950, 54
DODGE, PETER   A
B Team: 1975-76, 77-79
C Team: 1973-75
DONALDSON, FAITH   A
FIS Team: 1935
DORSEY, BECKY   A
A Team: 1977-79
B Team: 1975-77
C Team: 1974-75
FIS Team: 1978
DORRIS, MICHAEL RAY   A
B Team: 1974-76
C Team: 1973-74, 77-78
DOWNEY, JOHN MIKE   XC
A Team: 1974-78
DRAKE, KELLY E.   XC
B Team: 1973-74
C Team: 1971-73, 1974-75
DUNKLEE, EVERETT A.   XC
A Team: 1964-74
Olympic Team: 1972
FIS Team: 1970
DUNKLEE, SILAS   NC
A Team: 1950, 52
Olympic Team: 1952
FIS Team: 1950

DUNKLEE, STAN   XC
A Team: 1976-80
B Team: 1974-75
Olympic Team: 1976-80
FIS Team: 1978
DUNLAP, DALLAS (ROBERTSON)   A
B Team: 1968-71
DURRANCE, RICHARD   A
A Team: 1936
Olympic Team: 1936, 40
FIS Team: 1936
DURTSCHI, MIKE   A
B Team: 1977-78
C Team: 1977

E

EATON, GORDON   XC
A Team: 1960-65
Olympic Team: 1960, 64
FIS Team: 1962
EATON, KAREN (BUDGE)   A
A Team: 1967-72
Olympic Team: 1968, 72
FIS Team: 1970
ELLINGSON, LLOYD   NC(D)
Olympic Team: 1932
ELLIOTT, JERE L.   A
A Team: 1965-69
Olympic Team: 1968
FIS Team: 1966
ELLIOTT, JON   J
A Team: 1959-65
Olympic Team: 1964, 68, 72
FIS Team: 1962, 66, 70
ELLIOTT, MIKE   XC
A Team: 1962-72
Olympic Team: 1964, 68, 72
FIS Team: 1962, 66, 70
ENDESTAD, AUDUN   XC
B Team: 1982
ENGBERG, PATRICIA (GUTTORMSEN)
XC
A Team: 1979
B Team: 1977, 82-83
C Team: 1980-81
FIS Team: 1982
ENGEN, ALF   J
Olympic Team: 1940
ENGEN, CATHY   A
A Team: 1965-67
FIS Team: 1966
ENGEN, COREY   NC
A Team: 1940
Olympic Team: 1940
ENGER, DAVID   A
A Team: 1965-66
ERICKSON, JOHN   NC
Olympic Team: 1932
ERICKSON, WILLIAM   J
Olympic Team: 1960
FIS Team: 1958, 62

F

FARIES, DAVE   A
A Team: 1948
Olympic Team: 1948
FALK, BRUCE R.   J
A Team: 1950-52
FALK, WALT   A
A Team: 1966
B Team: 1965
FIS Team: 1966
FALSTAD, PEDAR   J
Olympic Team: 1932
FARNY, MIKE   A
B Team: 1979-81
C Team: 1977-79, 82-83

FARWELL, TED   XC
Olympic Team: 1952, 56, 60
FEARING, GEORGE   A(D)
FIS Team: 1935
FERRIES, CHARLES   A
A Team: 1960-64
Olympic Team: 1960, 64
FIS Team: 1962
FISH, IMOGENE (OPTOM)   A
Ski Team: 1952
FISHER, ABBI   A
A Team: 1975, 81-82
B Team: 1974-78, 83
Olympic Team: 1976, 80
FIS Team: 1978, 82
FISK, MARGARETTA   A
FIS Team: 1937, 38
FISK, URSULA   A
FIS Team: 1937
FLANDERS, DEBBIE   A
A Team: 1969-70
B Team: 1970-71
FLANDERS, HOLLY   A
A Team: 1979-83
B Team: 1977-79, 84
Olympic Team: 1980
FIS Team: 1982
FLECKENSTEIN, VIKI   A
A Team: 1977-80
B Team: 1974-77
Olympic Team: 1980
FIS Team: 1978
FLETCHER, PAM   A
B Team: 1984-
FORD, MARK   A
C Team: 1971-72, 75-76
FORREST, STEPHANIE   A
B Team: 1973
C Team: 1971-72
FORTNA, ROSI   A
A Team: 1967-71
Olympic Team: 1968
FRASER, DONALD W.   A
Olympic Team: 1936, 40
FIS Team: 1936
FRASER, GRETCHEN   A
Olympic Team: 1940, 48
FRASER, REBECCA (CREMER)   A
Olympic Team: 1948
FREDHIM, SVERRE   J
A Team: 1932-36
B Team: 1931
Olympic Team: 1936, 48
FIS Team: 1940
FULLER, RON   A
C Team: 1975-78

G

GALANES, JAMES B.   NC/XC
A Team: 1974
Olympic Team: 1976, 80
FIS Team: 1978, 82
GALANES, LYNN SPENCER   XC
A Team: 1975-83
B Team: 1984
Olympic Team: 1976, 80
FIS Team: 1978, 82
GALLAGER, MIKE   XC
A Team: 1961-74
Olympic Team: 1964, 68, 72
FIS Team: 1962, 66, 70, 74
GARRETT, PETER   A
Olympic Team: 1940
GIBERSON, GARY   XC
B Team: 1970-71
GILLETTE, NED   XC
A Team: 1967-69

Olympic Team: 1968
GILLIS, GENE   A
Olympic Team: 1948
GOODMAN, LEON   A
FIS Team: 1946, 50
GOODWIN, VERNE   A
Olympic Team: 1952
FIS Team: 1954
GORDER, GRAIG   A
A Team: 1973-74
B Team: 1970-73
C Team: 1968-70
FIS Team: 1974
GORSUCH, RENIE (COX)
A Team: 1960
GORSUCH, SCOTT DAVID   A
Olympic Team: 1960
FIS Team: 1958
GOYEN, JERRY   J
Olympic Team: 1964
GRAHEK, JAMES   J
A Team: 1980-81
Olympic Team: 1980
GRANT, PATRICIA   A
FIS Team: 1938
GRASMOEN, BRYNHILD   A
Olympic Team: 1948
FIS Team: 1950
GRAY, ROBERT   XC
A Team: 1962-74
Olympic Team: 1968, 72
FIS Team: 1962, 66, 70, 74
GRIFFITH, JAMES   XC(D)
FIS Team: 1950
GUSTAVSON, GEORGE   NC
Olympic Team: 1940

H

HAIK, STEVEN   A
B Team: 1977-79
HAINES, BETSY   XC
A Team: 1978
B Team: 1979-80
Olympic Team: 1980
FIS Team: 1978
HAINES, CHRISTOPHER B.   XC
A Team: 1974-76
B Team: 1970-73
Olympic Team: 1976
HAMPTON, WILMER   J(D)
FIS Team: 1950
HANDLEY, DEBI   A
Ski Team: 1974
HANNAH, JOAN   A
A Team: 1959-66
Olympic Team: 1960-64
FIS Team: 1962-66
HANNAH, SHELDEN   XC
A Team: 1940
FIS Team: 1940
HARDY, SCOTT   A
C Team: 1976-78
HARKINS, KEN   J
A Team: 1967-77
FIS Team: 1970
HARRIS, SUSAN (RYTTING)   A
Olympic Team: 1948, 52
FIS Team: 1950
HARSH, JAMES   NC
Olympic Team: 1932
HASTINGS, JEFF   J
A Team: 1981-
C Team: 1980
FIS Team: 1982
HAUGEN, ANDERS   XC/J
Olympic Team: 1924, 28

HAWKENSEN, LLOYD W.   NC
A Team: 1950
FIS Team: 1950
HELLMAN; PATRICIA   A
B Team: 1977-79
C Team: 1976-77
HENDRICKSON, RALPH J.   J
Olympic Team: 1936
HENYA, JIM   A
Ski Team: 1964
HEUGA, JIMMIE   A
A Team: 1959-68
Olympic Team: 1964, 68
FIS Team: 1962, 66
HEYER, LYNDALL   A
B Team: 1975-77
HICKS, DAVID   A
A Team: 1965-67
Olympic Team: 1964
FIS Team: 1966
HILDNER, SANDRA SHELLWORTH   A
A Team: 1964-68
Olympic Team: 1968
FIS Team: 1966
HILL, ROBERT   A
B Team: 1977-78
C Team: 1975-77
HILLMAN, HAROLD   A
A Team: 1940
Olympic Team: 1940
FIS Team: 1940
HINKLE, TWILA   XC
B Team: 1969-76
Olympic Team: 1976
HINTON, JOAN   A
FIS Team: 1940
HIRVONEN, OLAVI   XC
Ski Team: 1960
HLAVATY, JANA   XC
A Team: 1973-76
Olympic Team: 1976
FIS Team: 1974
HOECHLER, JIM "JAKE"   A
A Team: 1969-70
B Team: 1966-68
HOFFMAN, SCOTT   A
C Team: 1979-83
HOLLAND, MIKE   J
A Team: 1983
HOLMSTROM, CARL   J
A Team: 1932
Olympic Team: 1932, 36
HOSMER, TRINA   XC
A Team: 1970-74
Olympic Team: 1972
FIS Team: 1970, 74
HOUSE, JAMES   J
FIS Team: 1958
HOVDEY, PATTY (BOYDSTUN)   A
A Team: 1970-73
B Team: 1969
C Team: 1967-68
Olympic Team: 1972
HOVLAND, GEORGE   XC
A Team: 1952
Olympic Team: 1952
FIS Team: 1954
HUDSON, SALLY (NEIDLINGER)   A
Olympic Team: 1952
FIS Team: 1950
HUNTER, EDGAR (TED)   A
A Team: 1937
Olympic Team: 1936

J

JACKSON, HARRIET   A
Olympic Team: 1940

FIS Team: 1938, 40
JACKSON, WALTER   XC
FIS Team: 1958
JACOBS, TOM   XC
Olympic Team: 1952
JANSS, WILLIAM C. Sr.   A
Olympic Team: 1940
JENNINGS, BRUCE   J
A Team: 1969-72
JENNINGS, H. DEVEREAUX   A
Olympic Team: 1948
JENNINGS, MARGARET   A
Olympic Team: 1940
FIS Team: 1940
JOHANSON, SVEN S.   J(D)
Olympic Team: 1948
JOHNSON, BILL   A
B Team: 1984
JOHNSON, DON   XC(D)
Olympic Team: 1948
JOHNSON, DUANE
B Team: 1970-71
JOHNSON, ELVIN R.   XC
FIS Team: 1950
JOHNSON, JANNETTE (BURR)   A
Olympic Team: 1952
FIS Team: 1950, 54
JOHNSTONE, HANS   J
C Team: 1979-80
JONES, GREG   A
A Team: 1975-78
B Team: 1973-74
Olympic Team: 1976
FIS Team: 1974
JONES, VIKKI (WALKER)   A
A Team: 1965-68
B Team: 1964
JORGENSEN, TONI   XC
C Team: 1979-80
JOSLIN, CATHY   A
B Team: 1968-70
JOYCE, GLEN   NC
B Team: 1978-79

K

KAIER, ALCIE DAMROSCH WOLFE   A(D)
FIS Team: 1935
KASHIWA, HANK   A
A Team: 1967-72
Olympic Team: 1972   FIS Team: 1970
KAUFMANN, DEBBIE (WOLCOTT)   XC
B Team: 1971
KECK, ROBERT A.   J
A Team: 1961, 63-64
FIS Team: 1962
KEENAN, DAN   NC
A Team: 1974-76
B Team: 1973
FIS Team: 1974
KELLY, TIM   XC
A Team: 1979
B Team: 1978
C Team: 1976-77
KELLOGG, CHARLES   XC
A Team: 1968-72
B Team: 1973
Olympic Team: 1968
KEMPAINEN, TOD   XC
B Team: 1979,81
KENDALL, ROBBERT C.   NC
A Team: 1960-72
Olympic Team: 1972
FIS Team: 1970
KERN, TERRY   J
A Team: 1973-78
Olympic Team: 1976

KERR, RANDY   XC
A Team: 1975-76
B Team: 1973-75, 76-78
KIDD, WILLIAM   A
Olympic Team: 1964,68
FIS Team: 1962,70
KING, LYNN   XC
C Team: 1976
KINMONT, JILL (BOOTHE)   A
A Team: 1954-55
KIRLE, PENNY (NORTHRUP)   A
A Team: 1969-71
B Team: 1968,72
KNOWLTON, STEVE   A
Olympic Team: 1948
FIS Team: 1950
KOCH, BILL   XC
A Team: 1978
B Team: 1971-72
Olympic Team: 1976, 80
FIS Team: 1974, 78, 82
KOCH, FRITZ   XC
A Team: Team: 1970-71
C Team: 1977-78, 80
KONOPACKE, MARK   J
B Team: 1983
KORFANTA, KAREN   A
Ski Team: 1967-70
Olympic Team: 1968
KOTLAREK, GENE   J
A Team: 1958-67
Olympic Team: 1960, 64
FIS Team: 1958, 66
KRAUS, MADI (SPRINGER-MILLER)   A
Ski Team: 1952
KURLANDER, JAIME A.   A
A Team: 1977-79
B Team: 1974-76, 80
C Team: 1973-74
FIS Team: 1978

L

LAFFERTY, MICHAEL   A
A Team: 1969-74
B Team: 1967-68
Olympic Team: 1972
FIS TEAM: 1970, 74
LAMB, JOSEPH   A
A Team: 1972-74
B Team: 1971
Olympic Team: 1972
LANTZ, DAVID M.   NC
A Team: 1971-74
B Team: 1975-76
LATHRUP, STEVE   A
A Team: 1970-72
FIS Team: 1970
LAW, ELLIS (SMITH)   A
Olympic Team: 1936
FIS Team: 1936
LAWRENCE, ANDREA MEAD   A
Olympic Team: 1948, 52, 56
FIS Team: 1950
LAWRENCE, DAVID   A
Olympic Team: 1952
FIS Team: 1950
LEIN, HARRY   J(D)
Olympic Team: 1924
LETSON, EDWARD M.   MC
Olympic Team: 1960
LEVY, LYNN   A
Olympic Team: 1956
LEWIS, CHRISSY   XC
B Team: 1984
LINDLAY, ALFRED D.   XC(D)
Olympic Team: 1936

LINDLAY, GRACE C.   A
Olympic Team: 1936, 40
FIS Team: 1936, 40
LITCHFIELD, JOHN P.   J
Olympic Team: 1940
LITTLE, ROGERS III   A
A Team: 1970-72
B Team: 1967-70
LIVERMORE, ROBERT JR.   A
Olympic Team: 1936
LONG, SUE   XC
B Team: 1984-
LOWELL, JAMES A.   A
FIS Team: 1935
LUBANSKY, SCOTT   J
B Team: 1978-82
LUFKIN, JACK   XC
A Team: 1967-69
B Team: 1966
Olympic Team: 1968
LUHN, ANDY   A
B Team: 1984-
LUSSI, CRAIG M.   NC
Olympic Team: 1960
LUTICK, FRANK   A
A Team: 1969-71
B Team: 1967-69
FIS Team: 1970
LYNCH, KERRY   NC
A Team: 1978
B Team: 1977-78
Olympic Team: 1980
FIS Team: 1982

M

McALPIN, HELLEN   A
Olympic Team: 1936
FIS Team: 1935
McCOY, DAVE   A
FIS Team: 1939
McCOY, DENNIS   A
A Team: 1966-70
Olympic Team: 1968
FIS Team: 1966, 70
McDONALD, MARGO (WALTERS)   A
A Team: 1965-67
Olympic Team: 1964
McGRANE, DENNIS R.   J
B Team: 1982
C Team: 1979-891
McGRATH, LIZ   A
C Team: 1973
McKINNEY, SHEILA   A
B Team: 1973-81
C Team: 1971-72
McKINNEY, STEVE   A
B Team: 1973
C Team: 1971-72
McKINNEY, TAMARA   A
A Team: 1979
B Team: 1978
C Team: 1977-78
Olympic Team: 1980
FIS Team: 1982
McMANNUS, RICHARD "RIP"   A
A Team: 1961-65
Olympic Team: 1964
McNEALUS, JERRY   A
B Team: 1974-76
C Team: 1973
McNEIL, CHRIS   J
A Team: 1974-80
B Team: 1972-73
Olympic Team: 1976, 80
FIS Team: 1978

McNULTY, JOSEPH T.   XC
A Team: 1970-74
Olympic Team: 1972
FIS Team: 1970, 74
MACOMBER, GEORGE   A
A Team: 1947-52
Olympic Team: 1948, 52
FIS Team: 1950
MACOMBER, JOHN   A
C Team: 1974-76
MAHONEY, MARGIE   XC
A Team: 1970-72, 74-77
B Team: 1969-70
Olympic Team: 1972, 76
MAHRE, PHIL   A
A Team: 1975
B Team: 1974
Olympic Team: 1976, 80
FIS Team: 1978, 82
MAHRE, STEVE   A
A Team: 1975
B Team: 1974-75
Olympic Team: 1976, 80
FIS Team: 1978, 82
MAKI, JIM   J
A Team: 1975-77, 80
Olympic Team: 1976, 80
MAKI, RUDY   J
Olympic Team: 1956, 60
FIS Team: 1958
MALMQUIST, WALTER   J
A Team: 1976-80
B Team: 1974-75
Olympic Team: 1976, 80
FIS Team: 1978
MARICICH, MARIA   A
A Team: 1984-
B Team: 1980-83
C Team: 1979-80
MAROLT, BILL   A
A Team: 1961-68
Olympic Team: 1964
FIS Team: 1962, 66
MAROLT, MAX   A
A Team: 1953-60
Olympic Team: 1960
FIS Team: 1954, 58
MARTON, JAY   J
Olympic Team: 1964, 68
FIS Team: 1966
MARTIN, JERRY   J
A Team: 1970-76
B Team: 1968-69
Olympic Team: 1972, 76
FIS Team: 1974
MARTIN, LARRY J.   XC
A Team: 1972-76
B Team: 1970-71
Olympic Team: 1972, 76
FIS Team: 1974
MASSA, LEO E.   XC
Olympic Team: 1960
FIS Team: 1958, 62
MATIS, CLARK ARVO   XC
A Team: 1964-72
Olympic Team: 1968, 72
FIS Team: 1966, 70
MATT, TONI   A
FIS Team: 1950
MELESKI, MIKE   A
Ski Team: 1974
MELVILLE, MARVIN A.   A
Olympic Team: 1956, 60
FIS Team: 1958
MERRILL, AL   XC
FIS Team: 1950

MESERVEY, EDWARD B.   A
Olympic Team: 1940
MEYERS, LINDA (TIKALSKY)   A
A Team: 1958-65
Olympic Team: 1960, 64
FIS Team: 1958, 62
MICHAEL, DAVE   A
B Team: 1980-81
Olympic Team: 1980
MIDDLETON, KAREN   A
A Team: 1969-1970
B Team: 1970-71
MILL, ANDY RAY   A
A Team: 1974-81
B Team: 1972-73
Olympic Team: 1976, 80
FIS Team: 1974, 78
MILLER, ANDREW   XC
Olympic Team: 1956, 60
FIS Team: 1958
MILLER, JAMES G.   NC
A Team: 1966-73
Olympic Team: 1968, 72
MILLER, PAT   NC
A Team: 1970-74
B Team: 1968-70
MILLER, RALPH E.   A
Olympic Team: 1956
FIS Team: 1954
MITCHELL, DICK   A
Olympic Team: 1956
MONSON, ROLF   XC(D)
Olympic Team: 1928, 32, 36
MOONE, DAN   A
Ski Team: 1972
MORIARTY, MARVIN   XC
Olympic Team: 1956
FIS Team: 1958
MORNING, JAMES   A
A Team: 1966, 69
B Team: 1965-66
MORNING, ROBIN (GILHOLM)   A
A Team: 1965-68
Olympic Team: 1968
MOSS, LAUREN E. (LOLLY)   A
C Team: 1973-75
MOVITZ, RICHARD   A
Olympic Team: 1948
FIS Team: 1950
MUCHA, JEANNIE (ADAMSON)   A
B Team: 1971
MUMFORD, BOOMER   XC
C Team: 191973
MUMFORD, KIM (GRAY)   A
B Team: 1974-75
C Team: 1973
MURPHY, STEVE   A
C Team: 1973-74
MURRAY, SALLY DEAVER   A(D)
FIS Team: 1958
MUSOLF, JOANNE   XC
B Team: 1977-81
C Team: 1976
FIS Team: 1978

N

NAGEL, JACK
Olympic Team: 1952
NAGEL, JUDY A.   A
A Team: 1967-70
Olympic Team: 1968
FIS Team: 1970
NEBEL, DOROTHY (HOYT)   A
A Team: 1938-41
FIS Team: 1938

NELSON, CINDY   A
A Team: 1971-
B Team: 1971
C Team: 1971
Olympic Team: 1972, 76, 80
FIS Team: 1974, 78, 82
NICE, CHRIS   XC
Ski Team: 1976-77
NIELSEN, DONALD M.   XC
A Team: 1975-76, 77-81
Olympic Team: 1976, 80
FIS Team: 1978
NORBY, DAVE   A
A Team: 1967, 71
Olympic Team: 1968
FIS Team: 1966,70
NOYES, PAMELA   A
B Team: 1975
C Team: 1976

O

OAK, CINDY   A
A Team: 1982-83
B Team: 1980-81
C Team: 1978-80, 84-
OIMEN, CASPER   J
Olympic Team: 1932, 36
OLSON, CHRISTINE (DASTUR)   A
B Team: 1968-70
OLSON, SHELLY   A
Ski Team: 1974
OMAN, GUNNAR   J
Olympic Team: 1940
FIS Team: 1940
OMTVEDT, RAGNAR   XC(D)
Olympic Team: 1924
OVERBY, SIGURD   XC(D)
Olympic Team: 1924
OWEN, ALISON-SPENCER   XC
A Team: 1968-73, 78-81
Olympic Team: 1972, 80
FIS Team: 1974, 78
OWEN, SALLY   XC
B Team: 1976,77
OWEN, TRUDY (ARNOLD)   XC
A Team: 1967-71

P

PABST, FRED   A(D)
FIS Team: 1934
PABST, ROBERT E.   A(D)
FIS Team: 1934
PAGE, JIM   NC
A Team: 1962-65
Olympic Team: 1964
PAGE, PAULA   A
B Team: 1969-71
PALMER, TERRY   A
A Team: 1970-73
C Team: 1968-70
Olympic Team: 1972
PALMER, TYLER   A
A Team: 1970-72
B Team: 1968-69
Olympic Team: 1972
FIS Team: 1970
PALMER, ZANE   J
B Team: 1983-
PARSONS, RICHARD E.   XC
Olympic Team: 1932, 36
PATTERSON, BARBI   A
C Team: 1977-79
PATTERSON, PETE   A
A Team: 1976-80
B Team: 1975
C Team: 1972-74

Olympic Team: 1976, 80
FIS Team: 1978
PATTERSON, SUSIE A
A Team: 1972-79
B Team: 1970-72
Olympic Team: 1976
FIS Team: 1974, 78
PAULY, JACK E. NC
A Team: 1949-53
FIS Team: 1950
PAXSON, BETH XC
A Team: 1976-80
B Team: 1981-83
Olympic Team: 1980
FIS Team: 1978, 82
PENDLETON, MARY (WHALEN) XC
A Team: 1969-70
B Team: 1970-71
PENDLETON, SARAH A
C Team: 1975-76
PEDERSON, ERNST A
Olympic Team: 1927, 30
PERA, GEORGE M. J
FIS Team: 1950
PERKINS, DEAN XC
A Team: 1949-52
FIS Team: 1950
PERRAULT, PAUL JOE J
Olympic Team: 1948, 52
FIS Team: 1950
PERRY-SMITH, CROSBY NC
Olympic Team: 1952
FIS Team: 1950, 54
PETERSON, DOUGLAS XC
A Team: 1975-82
B Team: 1974
Olympic Team: 1976, 80
FIS Team: 1978
PETTY, KRISTEN XC
B Team: 1980-83
PETTY, RALPH A
C Team: 1973-74
PIDACKS, RALPH W. A
Olympic Team: 1952
FIS Team: 1954
PITOU, PENNY (ZIMMERMAN) A
Olympic Team: 1956, 60
FIS Team: 1958
PLACEK, JUDITH H. A
B Team: 1965-67
PORCARELLI, MIKE A
B Team: 1972
C Team: 1966-71
PORTER, TERRY XC
A Team: 1975-78
Olympic Team: 1976
POST, DODIE (GANN) A
Olympic Team: 1948
FIS Team: 1948
POULSEN, ERIC A
Olympic Team: 1972
POULSEN, LANCE V. A
A Team: 1969
B Team: 1968, 70-71
POULSEN, SANDRA A
A Team: 1970-75
B Team: 1969-70
Olympic Team: 1972
FIS Team: 1970, 74
POWELL, DOUGLAS R. A
B Team: 1978-
FIS Team: 1982
PREUSS, HEIDI A
A Team: 1977-78, 79-81
B Team: 1978-79, 82-
C Team: 1976-77
Olympic Team: 1980

PROCTOR, CHARLES J(D)
Olympic Team: 1928
PULKINEN, TAUNO XC
FIS Team: 1958
PUTNAM, LINDSAY XC
B Team: 1979-81
C Team: 1981-
PYLES, RUDD A
Ski Team: 1973

Q

QUEST, LAURIE (SMITH) A
A Team: 1968-71
B Team: 1966-68
C Team: 1965-66
QUINN, DAVE XC(D)
A Team: 1968-69

R

RABINOWITZ, JUDY (ENDESTAD) XC
A Team: 1984-
B Team: 1979-83
Olympic Team: 1980
FIS Team: 1982
RAHOI, RICHARD J
Olympic Team: 1956, 60
FIS Team: 1958
RAND, JAY JR. J
A Team: 1968-76
Olympic Team: 1968
FIS Team: 1974
RANDALL, GREG G. XC
B Team: 1981-
RANDALL, MIKE NC
B Team: 1983-
RASMUSSEN, WILBERT CHARLES J
Olympic Team: 1952
FIS Team: 1950, 58
REDDISH, JACK A
Olympic Team: 1948, 52
FIS Team: 1950
REID, ROBERT H. SR. XC
Olympic Team: 1932
FIS Team: 1932, 36
RICHTER, PAMALA RUTH XC
C Team: 1975-77
RIESCHL, STEVE NC
A Team: 1956, 64
Olympic Team: 1960
RILEY, BETSY (SNITE) A
Olympic Team: 1956,60
FIS Team: 1954,58
ROBES, PETER XC
A Team: 1969-70
ROBISON, DARRELL D. A
Olympic Team: 1952
ROCKWELL, MARTHA XC
B Team: 1969-76
Olympic Team: 1972, 76
FIS Team: 1970, 74
ROLLINS, JANE A
B Team: 1972, 74
C Team: 1971-72
ROMINE, MICHAEL W. XC
A Team: 1972
B Team: 1966-71
ROWLES, DON XC
Ski Team: 1974
RUSH, PETER A
A Team: 1966
RYAN, HARRY "REBEL" A
A Team: 1964-68
Olympic Team: 1968
RYTTING, SUSAN (HARRIS) A
Ski Team: 1948-52

S

SABICH, VLADIMIR "SPIDER" A(D)
FIS Team: 1970
SACKETT, JOHN XC
C Team: 1979-82
SATRE, MANGUS XC(D)
Olympic Team: 1936
SATRE, OTTAR XC
Olympic Team: 1936
SANSTAD, ROGER LEE XC
B Team: 1970-71
SARRINEN, LILIAN (SWANN) A
Olympic Team: 1936
FIS Team: 1935, 36
SAUBART, JEAN A
Olympic Team: 1964
FIS Team: 1962
SCEVA, PAUL H. A
FIS Team: 1937
SCHAUFFLER, JARVIS A
Olympic Team: 1940
FIS Team: 1938, 40
SHAUFFLER, F. SANDERSON A
Olympic Team: 1940
FIS Team: 1940
SCHIMELFENIG, SCOTT A
B Team: 1975-77
C Team: 1974
SCHWARZENBACH, CHRIS A
Olympic Team: 1940
FIS Team: 1938
SCHWARZENBACH, LILO A
FIS Team: 1935, 36
SCOTT, RUSTY XC
B Team: 1975
SEATON, MARY A
A Team: 1977-78
B Team: 1979
C Team: 1976
Olympic Team: 1976
SHANHOLTZER, CRAIG
FIS Team: 1970
SHAW, BILL A
B Team: 1973-74
C Team: 1972-73, 74-75
SHAW, MARILYN (McMAHON) A
Olympic Team: 1940
SHAW, NONIE (FOLEY) A
Olympic Team: 1958
SHAW, TIGER A
B Team: 1984-
C Team: 1979-81
SHEA, JAMES E. NC
A Team: 1963-65
Olympic Team: 1964
SHERWOOD, ROY R. J.
A Team: 1953
Olympic Team: 1956
SEIBERT, PETE A
FIS Team: 1950
SIEBELS, TOM XC
A Team: 1974
B Team: 1973
C Team: 1976
SIMONEAU, DAN XC
A Team: 1981-83
B Team: 1979-80, 84
C Team: 1973-78
Olympic Team: 1980
FIS Team: 1982
SIMONSON, JIM A
C Team: 1971
SIMPSON, PAT A
Ski Team: 1971

SKALING, TIM   A
A Team: 1971-72
B Team: 1970-71
C Team: 1970-71
SKARO, MARCIA   XC
A Team: 1970-73
B Team: 1969-70
SMALL, ALLAN   XC
Ski Team: 1968-69
SMITH, ETHELYNNE   A
FIS Team: 1936
SMITH, LESLIE LEETE   A
B Team: 1974-79
Olympic Team: 1976
SOLNER, MARK   J
A Team: 1980-81
B Team: 1977-78
C Team: 1979-80
SOLIE, RICH   XC
C Team: 1979-80
SORENSEN, LARRY   XC
FIS Team: 1962
SPECK, JIM   NC
B Team: 1966-69
SPENCE, GAIL   A
FIS Team: 1950
SPENCER, DAVID WILLIAN   XC
B Team: 1976-78
SPRINGER, MADI (MILLER-KRAUS)   A
A Team: 1951-52, 57-58
Olympic Team: 1952
FIS Team: 1958
ST. ANDRE, JON   J
Olympic Team: 1960
STANDTEINER, HANSI   A
B Team: 1980-82
C Team: 1978-79, 84-
STEELE, JOHN   J
Olympic Team: 1932
STEELE, RON   J
A Team: 1972-78
B Team: 1969-71
Olympic Team: 1972
FIS Team: 1974
STERLING, WHIT   A
A Team: 1972-73
B Team: 1971-72
C Team: 1970-71
Olympic Team: 1972
STEWART, COLIN C.   A
Olympic Team: 1948
STEWARD, RUTHMARIE
(RADAMACHER)   A
Ski Team: 1948
STOLZLECHNER, MILLS   J
B Team: 1983-
STRALEY, LATNER   XC
A Team: 1980-81
C Team: 1978-79, 82-83
STRALEY, MONTE W.   XC
C Team: 1976-77
STRALEY, ZANE   A
C Team: 1976-79
STREETER, LES   A
Olympic Team: 1956
STRUTZ, SHARON   XC
Ski Team: 1968-69
SUDGAARD, KIP G.   J
A Team: 1976-77
B Team: 1974-75, 78-79
C Team: 1980
Olympic Team: 1976
FIS Team: 1978
SURGENOR, DOROTHY (MODENSE)   A
Ski Team: 1956
SUSSLIN, GAYLE   A
Ski Team: 1973

SWENSON, LYLE F.   J
A Team: 1963
Olympic Team: 1964
FIS Team: 1962
SWIGERT, KEVIN   XC
A Team: 1979
B Team: 1977-78
C Team: 1976
FIS Team: 1962
SWOR, GREG   J.
A Team: 1970-72
Olympic Team: 1972
FIS Team: 1970

T
TACHE, MARK   A
B Team: 1980-82
C Team: 1978-79, 83-
TARINELLI, DEBBIE   AC
Ski Team: 1974
TAYLOR, BILLIE   A
A Team: 1974-80
C Team: 1972-73
Olympic Team: 1980
TAYLOR, MISSY   A
C Team: 1971-74
TAYLOR, RICHARD   XC
A Team: 1964
B Team: 1958-61
Olympic Team: 1964
TAYLOR, ROD   A
A Team: 1970-71
B Team: 1967-69
C Team: 1970-71
TEAGUE, CE CE   A
Ski Team: 1977
TEAGUE, JOHN   A
C Team: 1977
TEMPLE, JAMIE   A
C Team: 1976-77
THOMAS, ANNE (DONAGHY)   A
B Team: 1971-73
THOMPSON, PERRY   AJ
Ski Team: 1973
TITCOMB, ANDREW A.   A
FIS Team: 1937
TOBEY, KATIE (KOCH)   XC
B Team: 1973-77
TODD, TOBY   XC
C Team: 1971-72
TOKLE, ARTHUR   J
A Team: 1948-63
Olympic Team: 1952, 60
FIS Team: 1950, 54, 58
TOMLINSON, SANDRA B.   A
Ski Team: 1952
TORRISSEN, BIRGER   XC
Olympic Team: 1936
TOWNSEND, RALPH   XC
A Team: 1947-50
Olympic Team: 1948
FIS Team: 1950
TRAFTON, RICHARD L.   A
B Team: 1970-71
TREADWELL, BOB   XC
A Team: 1979
B Team: 1977-78, 80
C Team: 1976
FIS Team: 1978
TREMBLAY, CHARLES   NC
Ski Team: 1956
TURNER JACK   XC
B Team: 1976-77
TURNER, JANET (BAUER)   A
B Team: 1970-71, 73-74
C Team: 1970, 73

TUTT, TIANIA   A
B Team: 1978-79
C Team: 1977

U
ULLAND, RAGNAR   J
Olympic Team: 1956
ULLAND, SIGURD   J(D)
Olympic Team: 1940
UPHAM, THOMAS   A
A Team: 1965-68
B Team: 1963-64
Olympic Team: 1968

V
VALAR, PAULA (KAHN)   A
A Team: 1945-50
Olympic Team: 1948
FIS Team: 1950
VALENTINE, TAMMY   XC
A Team: 1973-76
B Team: 1970-72
VALENTINE, TRACY LYNN   XC
A Team: 1978-79
C Team: 1979-80
VINCELETTE, AL JR.   A
FIS Team: 1958, 60
VOLMRICH, JEFF   J
B Team: 1984-

W
WAKEMAN, SAMUEL   A
FIS Team: 1935
WALKER, GLADYS (WERNER)   A
Olympic Team: 1952
FIS Team: 1954, 56
WALTON, STARR (HURLEY)   A
Olympic Team: 1964
WARD, CRAIG   XC
A Team: 1978
B Team: 1976, 79-
Olympic Team: 1980
FIS Team: 1978
WARD, KATHRYN   A
Olympic Team: 1936
FIS Team: 1935-38
WASHBURN, ALBERT L.   A
Olympic Team: 1936
FIS Team: 1936
WATT, ADRIAN   J
A Team: 1965-72
Olympic Team: 1968
FIS Team: 1970
WEAVER, ROY   J
A Team: 1975-76
WEDIN, ROBERT   J
A Team: 1957-62
Olympic Team: 1960
FIS Team: 1958
WEED, TEYCK   NC
A Team: 1970-73
B Team: 1968-70
Olympic Team: 1972
FIS Team: 1970
WEGEMAN, KEITH   J(D)
Olympic Team: 1954
WEDEMAN, PAUL   NC
Olympic Team: 1952
WEIR, BETTY (BELL)   A
Olympic Team: 1952
WELLS, ED   A
Olympic Team: 1940
WERNER, LORIS E.   J
A Team: 1959-68
Olympic Team: 1968
WERNER, WALLACE (BUDDY)   A(D)
Olympic Team: 1956, 60, 64

FIS Team: 1954, 58, 62
WEST, CARYN T.   A
B Team: 1969-72
WHEELER, MARK E.   NC
B Team: 1978
WIGGLESWORTH, MARIAN (McKEAN)   A
Olympic Team: 1936, 40
FIS Team: 1936, 37, 38
WILLIAMS, BARBARA ANN (COCHRAN)
A
A Team: 1969-70
B Team: 1968
C Team: 1967
Olympic Team: 1972
FIS Team: 1970, 74
WILLIAMS, TIM   J
B Team: 1980-82
C Team: 1978-80
WILSON, EUGENE A.   J
FIS Team: 1950
WILSON, ERIC J.   A
A Team: 1978
B Team: 1976-80
C Team: 1975
WILSON, JOE PETE   XC
Olympic Team: 1960
WINDSPERGER, GREGORY   J
A Team: 1972-77
B Team: 1969-71
Olympic Team: 1976
FIS Team: 1974
WINN, ANNE   A
Ski Team: 1948
WOLCOTT, JULIE   A
Ski Team: 1971
WOODS, HENRY S.   A
FIS Team: 1937
WOODWORTH, RICHIE   A
B Team: 1974-75
WOOLSEY, ELIZABETH (BETTY)   A
A Team: 1935-41
Olympic Team: 1936, 40
FIS Team: 1935-39
WREN, GORDON L.   J
Olympic Team: 1948
FIS Team: 1950
WRIGHT, JEFF   J(D)
A Team: 1974-75
B Team: 1973
WRIGHT, ROBERT   NC
FIS Team: 1950
WYATT, KATHY (RUDOLPH)   A
Olympic Team: 1952, 56
FIS Team: 1950, 54
WYNN, ANN JEANETTE   A
Olympic Team: 1948

Y

YALE, KENT   A
C Team: 1973
YEAGER, RON   XC
A Team: 1972, 76
Ski Team: 1971
Olympic Team: 1972, 76
FIS Team: 1974

Z

ZDECHLIK, KRIS   XC
A Team: 1969-70
B Team: 1970-72
ZDECHLIK, JON CONRAD   NC
B Team: 1980-81
ZELENAKAS, DANA C.   J
A Team: 1971-73
B Team: 1969
Olympic Team: 1972

ZETTERSTROM, OLLE   XC(D)
Olympic Team: 1932
ZINCK, ERIC   A
B Team: 1978-79
C Team: 1979-80
ZUEHLKE, REED   J
A Team: 1977-78
B Team: 1981-
Olympic Team: 1980
FIS Team: 1982
ZOBERSKI, TED   J
A Team: 1936, 50
Olympic Team: 1940

ISBN 0-913927-01-5
Library of Congress Catalog Card Number: 83-82974
Printed in U.S.A.